Grieving as a Teacher's Curriculum

Bold Visions in Educational Research

VOLUME 67

The titles published in this series are listed at *brill.com/bver*

Grieving as a Teacher's Curriculum

Relevant Prose and Postscripts

By

Edward Podsiadlik III

BRILL

SENSE

LEIDEN | BOSTON

All chapters in this book have undergone peer review.

Library of Congress Cataloging-in-Publication Data

Names: Podsiadlik, Edward, III, author. | Schubert, William Henry, writer of foreword.
Title: Grieving as a teacher's curriculum : relevant prose and postscripts / by Edward Podsiadlik III ; foreword by William H. Schubert.
Description: Leiden ; Boston : Brill Sense, [2020] | Series: Bold visions in educational research, 1879-4262 ; volume 67 | Includes bibliographical references and index.
Identifiers: LCCN 2019050010 (print) | LCCN 2019050011 (ebook) | ISBN 9789004389748 (hardback) | ISBN 9789004422490 (paperback) | ISBN 9789004422506 (ebook)
Subjects: LCSH: Teachers--Psychology. | Teaching--Psychological aspects. | Grief. | Grief in literature.
Classification: LCC LB2840 .P64 2020 (print) | LCC LB2840 (ebook) | DDC 370.15/34--dc23
LC record available at https://lccn.loc.gov/2019050010
LC ebook record available at https://lccn.loc.gov/2019050011

ISSN 1879-4262
ISBN 978-90-04-42249-0 (paperback)
ISBN 978-90-04-38974-8 (hardback)
ISBN 978-90-04-42250-6 (e-book)

For my mom

All that I am, or hope to be, I owe to my angel mother.
– Abraham Lincoln

CONTENTS

FOREWORD

Edward Podsiadlik's *Grieving as a Teacher's Curriculum: Relevant Prose and Postscripts* is a book worth pondering deeply. If you are a teacher or plan to become one, I urge you read it carefully. I entreat you to let it seep into you, become part of who you are. The questions posed should be embodied as a spirit of life-long inquiry. If you teach in any capacity at all, as a parent especially or a person who seeks to influence others to compose their lives, you should peruse this book. Teacher educators, as Dr. Podsiadlik exemplifies, must move far beyond merely teaching prospective teachers to prepare lesson plans, follow standards, manage classrooms, and prepare students for simplistic tests. The good teacher, after all, helps students think deeply about who they want to be, why, and how to become such a person. Teachers must help students to live fully in the world and contribute to it. This requires studying the best understandings humans have created. Edward Podsiadlik shows how literature can contribute immensely to this process.

Like Dr. Podsiadlik's (2014) earlier book, *Anecdotes and Afterthoughts: Literature as a Teacher's Curriculum*, *Grieving as a Teacher's Curriculum* continues to caste original light on what it means to be a teacher by perceiving both literature and curriculum in deeper and more significant ways than these terms are usually treated. I have long argued that curriculum is much more than the subject matter conveyed by schools and teachers (Schubert, 1986). Curriculum is the whole of lived experience, the gestalt of all dimensions of life, the basis to enable us to continuously reflect and reconstruct our lives. As Dr. Podsiadlik compels readers to understand, this image of curriculum embraces the teacher's intellectual, emotional, social, and ethical depths. It focuses on meaning-making embodied in students' and teachers' hearts, minds, and spirits. Teachers have the duty and privilege of getting to know students as whole beings who are educated both in and out of school (Schubert, 2010).

Understanding the lives of students is a never-ending process. This is where the meaning of literature is paramount. Literature portrays the complexities, nuances, and uncertainties of life. It helps us understand that the most profound questions need to be continuously addressed, and cannot be fully answered, since each situation and every moment entangles our reflections and actions in novel and dynamic configurations. While I agree that scholarly research should include a review of the literature, I have long deemed it ironic that few research studies in education contain actual literature (e.g., novels, stories, poems, songs, plays). Both of Podsiadlik's books exemplify the relevance of literary works for educational research. In *Grieving as a Teacher's Curriculum*, he addresses the experience of grief, by constructing each chapter around a key literary work by a noteworthy author: Rabindranath Tagore, Virginia Woolf, Franz Wedekind, Steven Sater and Duncan Sheik, Pat

Conroy, Virgil, Stephen King, and Charles Dickens. These literary figures are rarely emphasized in books on teaching and curriculum.

Moreover, Dr. Podsiadlik augments insights from them by elaborating on works by other diverse literary figures, philosophers, social and cultural commentators, educational theorists, public intellectuals, and more (e.g., Maya Angelou, William Ayers, Jerome Bruner, Martin Buber, Jacques Derrida, John Dewey, Kieran Egan, Elliot Eisner, Paulo Freire, John Gray, Maxine Greene, Mark Johnson, Soren Kierkegaard, C. S. Lewis, A. A. Milne, Nel Noddings, Edgar Allen Poe, Bertrand Russell, William Shakespeare, Leo Tolstoy, and Walt Whitman). In fact, my late colleague and co-author, George Willis (1978) pioneered the idea of understanding and evaluating curricular experience through literary criticism. Over a decade later, he and I invited thirty-five scholars of curriculum and teaching to reflect on and write about how artistic and literary works have shaped their outlooks on the heart of educational inquiry (Willis & Schubert, 1991). The work of Dr. Podsiadlik extends and expands our efforts, and flows in the tradition of Maxine Greene (e.g., 1965, 1973), whose writing shows that literature can broaden and deepen one's experience through portrayals of persons not met.

Reflection on *Grieving as a Teacher's Curriculum* brings many of my educational and life experiences into bold relief. For instance, it reminds me of my eight years of teaching in elementary school, before I became a professor, and how I quickly concluded that the school district's professional development activities, no matter how good, were too few and far between. Thus, I decided I had to create my own professional development experiences, which I pursued almost every day. Much of my study focused on works of literature: fiction, poetry, essays, philosophy, and film. I searched libraries, museums, galleries, and the minds of diverse persons and groups. Later in my career, as a professor of education, I would ask both students who were preparing to teach and graduate students to identify works of literature or art that gave special meaning to their lives. Then I challenged them to explain how the work was a curriculum for them. How could an author who did not know them personally reach and teach them so powerfully?

Literature helps us continuously address what Robert Ulich (1955) called "the great mysteries and events of life: birth, death, love, tradition, society and the crowd, success and failure, salvation, and anxiety" (p. 255). Moreover, excellent literature, as Dr. Podsiadlik has selected here, addresses these mysteries and events without over-simplifying them–by maintaining their complexity. We need to understand that the glory of such study and reflection is that its meaning resides in realizing that the biggest questions–because they are unanswerable–always beget other questions, and new situations which require reconstructed ideas, interpretations and concomitant actions.

As Dr. Podsiadlik encourages readers to realize, there is a remarkable interplay between literature and life experience. Since it is so important to understand life's complexities, if one wants to teach well, it is necessary to learn from our experiences as fully as possible. Literature expands our capacity to do that, by helping us experience more of life than we can in our limited first-hand experience. Nonetheless, we can strive to learn from and about the many persons and events we meet. In teaching, we meet about thirty students per year as elementary teachers, perhaps one hundred twenty-five as middle school or secondary students, and many as college teachers. As an elementary teacher I challenged myself to discover areas of expertise embodied in each student so that they could be resources for our learning together. Ultimately, I concluded that we, as teachers, are curricula for our students–everyone we meet, for that matter. Moreover, students are not only persons we teach; they are curricula that help us grow if we pay sufficient attention (Schubert, 1986, p. 423).

I was powerfully alerted to this when I began doctoral study and had an assistantship to teach undergraduates who were preparing to be teachers. My father, then retired due to heart disease, came to visit. I asked him to reflect on his long career as an educational leader and advise me on the most important things to teach students who want to be teachers. His response surprised me, given his rather tough reputation as a coach and administrator. He told me that teachers should learn to speak the language of their students and to feel the hurt in each of them. How to do this, he inferred, was up to me. I was grateful for his advice and held on to it as an empathic challenge throughout my career. Little did I realize that my father would pass away within the year.

I had often confided with him and I experienced considerable grief at his passing; however, I was motivated to continue working hard to help educators learn the language of children, realizing that each child had a unique personal language as well as what is normally considered a formal cultural language. I am convinced that the same is true for teenagers and adults, so his advice pertains to all levels of education. I was increasingly convinced that my father's notion of language provides paths to respond to the hurt within the student, and the hurt can open doors to participate in their multiple languages. These notions of language and hurt are reciprocal or symbiotic, as is amplified through Edward Podsiadlik's call to perceive the interplay between literature and grief, language and hurt, within learners.

At first glance, Dr. Podsiadlik's selection of the topic of grief made me reflect on grief I have experienced. As I began to ponder his book, I thought of grief experienced during the illnesses and deaths of loved ones. I thought of the grief accompanying conflict and harassment in my life and those I have loved. I thought of the stresses, illnesses, and deaths of students. I expanded my view and considered grief as pervasive in any population, including a classroom. I reflected on the multiple forms of grief brought to school from the diverse lives of the students. The grief they embody is a central dimension through which they interpret everything that happens to them, including the teaching and curriculum that I orchestrate. Sometimes we know about their grief and its sources; however, more often it remains in silence. Novelist, Mary Anne Evans (George Eliot, 1888) powerfully expresses this circumstance, saying: "If we had a keen vision of all that is ordinary in human life, it would be like hearing the grass grow or the squirrel's heartbeat, and we should die of that roar which is the other side of silence" (*Middlemarch*, Chapter 22).

Ironically, the composite of grief in a classroom or school, though enormous by comparison to the grief with any individual, which doubtless seems insurmountable to that person, is minimized in comparison to the curriculum. After all, the curriculum (almost any conception of it) is what we teach to introduce students to the world. The grief that interpenetrates the world brings to my mind vast numbers of humans characterized by Frantz Fanon (1963) as the wretched of the earth. As educators we must address our grief, that of our students, and the grief of humanity. As you read this book and some of the literary works mentioned in it, I urge you to ponder deeply the questions Dr. Podsiadlik raises at the end of the chapters. Moreover, I implore you to consider the following:

- How does literature help you respond to the grief in your lives?
- What literary works have helped you consider basic curriculum questions, such as: What is worth needing, knowing, experiencing, doing, being, becoming, overcoming, sharing, contributing, wondering, imagining, and improving?
- How can you embark on a journey (curriculum) that continuously reconstructs your life?
- How can experiences of grief (from personal ones to those in the educational community, to world-wide dimensions) be transformed into inspiration for growth and contribution through education?

REFERENCES

Eliot, G. (1888). *Middlemarch*. Cleveland, OH: The Burrows Brothers, Co.
Fanon, F. (1963). *The wretched of the earth*. New York, NY: Grove Press.
Greene, M. (1965). *The public school and the private vision*. New York, NY: Random House.
Greene, M. (1973). *Teacher as stranger*. New York, NY: Wadsworth.
Podsiadlik, E. (2014). *Anecdotes and afterthoughts: Literature as a teacher's curriculum*. Rotterdam, The Netherlands: Sense Publishers.
Schubert, W. H. (1986). *Curriculum: Perspective, paradigm, and possibility*. New York, NY: Macmillan.
Schubert, W. H. (2010). Outside curricula and public pedagogy. In J. Sandlin, B. D. Schultz, & J. Burdick (Eds.), *Handbook of public pedagogy: Education and learning beyond schooling* (pp. 10–19). New York, NY: Routledge.
Ulich, R. (1955). Response to ralph harper's essay. In N. B. Henry (Ed.), *Modern philosophies of education, fifty-fourth yearbook (Part I) of the National Society for the study of education* (pp. 254–257). Chicago, IL: University of Chicago Press.
Willis, G. H. (1978). *Educational evaluation: Concepts and cases in curriculum criticism*. Berkeley, CA: McCutchan.
Willis, G. H., & Schubert, W. H. (Eds.). (1991). *Reflections from the heart of educational inquiry: Understanding curriculum and teaching through the arts*. Albany, NY: State University of New York Press.

William H. Schubert
Professor Emeritus of Curriculum and Instruction
University of Illinois at Chicago

ACKNOWLEDGMENTS

Acknowledgment and appreciation go out to John Bond, Irma Nunez, and Joyce Allen for their time, expertise, and honesty in reading and offering valuable insights and feedback. Thanks to Brent Nequin and Omar Hernandez Ku for their technological expertise in helping to format the manuscript.

The quoted material used throughout this book has been kept to a minimum rather than offered to anthologize. I used portions of diverse literature and selected quotes to illustrate points and to enhance personal reflection. Use here will not infringe on or affect the market for the original or for subsequent permissions sought from the copyright holder.

Special gratitude is extended to William H. Schubert for his thoughtful foreword and for his continued support and encouragement in my work as teacher and scholar.

CHAPTER 1

PROLOGUE

Teachers are not automatons. An educator's personal beliefs, values, concerns, and aspirations cannot be cleaved from one's professional life without impacting the quality and relevance of meaningful teaching and learning. Parker Palmer (2007) writes that teachers "must stand where personal and public meet" (p. 18) if a bridge between one's inner truths and his or her outer performance is to be forged.

This book is designed to deepen our understanding of the intricacies that constitute the depth and expanse of a teacher's work by examining this space where the personal and professional intersect. It is not intended to be a prescriptive manual or catalogue of specific pedagogical procedures. Its philosophical discourse is not meant to be a search for definitive answers. Instead, it is a quest toward a deeper understanding of the relationship between who we are as individuals and how that shapes our roles and identities as professional educators. Its ontological framework emphasizes probing more deeply beneath outer identities as teachers (and students) to the heart of our humanity.

Leo Buscaglia (1982) observed that "we are failing in schools of education because we're not helping teachers to shed the role of teachers and become human beings.… To the extent to which they recognize this, so will they be successful in the classroom" (p. 9). My hope is that readers will find this reflective journey affirming as a way to better understand teaching and learning as fundamental opportunities that speak to the core of our humanity.

More specifically, this is a journey that draws us into an arena within which we are highly vulnerable: moments of grieving. In the eulogy for his friend Max Loreau, Jacques Derrida (2001) reflects on what he calls moments of reckoning—critical times when one's public and personal lives intersect. He calls these "moments that lack cartography" (p. 98) because external markers and outer landscapes no longer apply. During periods of grief, individuals are often confronted with obstacles, fears, and uncertainties that define, reflect, and challenge their personal and professional identities. It is at these moments when we are called to more closely reflect upon and reconcile our outer lives with our inner values and beliefs.

As a teacher's curriculum—as a curriculum of life—grief has much to teach about sympathy, compassion, vulnerability, and resilience. Rabindranath Tagore (1933) warns that because an "education of sympathy is not only systematically ignored in schools, [but is also] severely repressed" (p. 142), teachers and students are "made to lose our world to find a bagful of information instead" (p. 143). Jeffrey Berman

© KONINKLIJKE BRILL NV, LEIDEN, 2020 | DOI: 10.1163/9789004422506_001

(2004) explicitly describes education as a manifestation of life. I am inspired by his idea that the cadence of teaching and learning ought to align with the flow of life itself. Just as loss is a major aspect of our humanity, so too, Berman argues, it is an important aspect of the life force inherent to education:

> We generally think of education as the acquisition of knowledge, but the gain in understanding often reminds us of the inherent losses in life and the inevitability of death. But it is not only death with which we must come to terms but also the fact that new knowledge implies the giving up or even destruction of old knowledge. Teaching may thus be viewed as a kind of mourning, a working through of grief and sorrow. (pp. 130–131)

This book validates and celebrates education's capacity to guide individuals toward finding meaning in their lives. It advocates for a change to the perception that the best measure of a school's success is found in skills-based assessment data. It endeavors to recognize the many layers of impact an education can have on people's lives beyond job preparation and increased standardized assessment scores. It aims to substantiate the role educators play in the growth and development of students as they continue learning (and *relearning*) to understand themselves and the world around them.

This urgency to relearn one's life is acutely felt during periods of grief. Despite an emphasis on content-based curricula, schools have the potential to nurture one's emotional and moral growth and development as well. Maxine Greene (1978) described the potential of meaningful reflective practice to enable individuals to "break through the cotton wool of daily life and to live more consciously" (p. 185) and to "create domains where there are new possibilities of vision and awareness" (p. 196). This qualitative journey shares her daring vision as it explores the following questions:

- How can our most vulnerable moments serve to strengthen the purpose and practice of our work as educators?
- What impact can personal grieving have on remembering, recovering, and reidentifying with one's professional mission and vision?
- In what ways can we teachers harness the power of introspection to transform our work, our lives, and the lives of our students?
- To what extent can grief help us better understand the scope and depth of the educators we are and have the potential to become?

Although, in general, educators are well-trained in distributing knowledge and information, in what ways are they adept in nurturing inner growth and development? The curriculum of grief is concerned with the challenges and aspirations individuals face as they evolve emotionally, morally, and spiritually. William H. Schubert (1986) observes that "philosophy lies at the heart of all educational endeavor" (p. 116). As these guiding questions indicate, this study is rooted within a philosophical landscape.

The issues raised and questions asked in each chapter are designed to provoke readers into reexamining the meaning and purpose of their personal and professional lives. Rather than focusing on what teachers do, this journey examines what they believe and value. It delves beneath the outer world of specialized techniques and pedagogical tools and considers the inner beliefs, values, challenges, and assumptions that inform and shape their work and their lives. This ontological framework invites readers to reflect more closely on the kinds of educators and individuals they are being and becoming.

Instead of collecting knowledge and information, this book asks readers to consider what pieces of knowledge and information are most worthwhile to living a meaningful life. In this way, dimensions of life and education merge. Hence, an axiomatic thread runs through this study that invites readers to examine the ethical dimensions of their public work as educators. Readers are challenged to reflect on the extent to which their personal and professional values and identities align.

MY PROFESSIONAL JOURNEY HERE

This book marks a return to my roots. I began my professional career in education as a middle school language arts teacher, transitioned to educational administrative positions, and am currently a field supervisor for college students in their final semesters prior to receiving teacher licensure. In each of these roles (spanning almost thirty years), I have experienced what Parker Palmer (2007) describes as an academic culture that builds "a wall between inner truth and outer performance" (p. 18). As a young teacher, I first became aware of this wall late on a Friday afternoon prior to Mother's Day weekend. Having studied sonnets together for some time, I challenged my middle school students to channel their inner Elizabeth Barrett Browning by writing an original sonnet for their mom (or someone comparable in their lives, like a grandmother, aunt, godmother, or sister). What I thought would be a lighthearted end-of-week activity soon turned into a dramatic moment for one student whose public life was about to intersect with her personal grieving.

When the student handed me her sonnet (which was, by the way, perfectly constructed), she decided to use the moment to publicly express some of the grief she had previously kept to herself. She announced that she had written the sonnet for *me*. The classroom fell silent. She went on to say that I was "more of a mother to [her] than anyone else in [her] life." I later learned that this student was grieving the loss of her mother, who had recently relocated out of state after a divorce. *How is it that I taught this student every day for so many months and never knew that she was emotionally struggling in this way?*

What followed that afternoon further surprised me. Other students began sharing similar personal feelings and experiences. Although the mandated Common Core Curriculum goal for that lesson was to create a "technically accurate" sonnet, my students and I engaged in a conversation that far exceeded the mechanical devices of a sonnet. In fact, our ensuing discourse embodied the kind of emotional intensity and

3

poignant introspection for which sonnets are famous. Despite the personal nature of the discussion, we found the courage and mutual trust to embrace our vulnerabilities as we connected with one another as human beings struggling together to better understand ourselves and the world we live in. What began as a lesson to construct sonnets became a kind of symposium that demonstrated how sonnets served as emotional outlets through which we could better understanding ourselves and each other. This was the first moment wherein I can remember experiencing the personal and professional lives of teacher and students explicitly converge.

I felt humbled. In what ways did my students see me as more than an enforcer of rules and a dispenser of information? When did they begin to perceive our classroom as a safe space within which to discuss such sensitive and personal matters? What other losses are students grieving of which I am unaware? What other kinds of personal connections might students be making to issues, concepts, ideas, and discussions raised in class? My understanding of what it meant to be a teacher began to change. I was beginning to see that the depth of my responsibilities as an educator exceeded the measurable goals set in the curriculum manuals.

After eighteen years of classroom teaching, my work shifted to an educational administration role that focused on providing professional development to school faculties. During one of these teacher workshops, I presented strategies to a group of veteran teachers: (1) to help them better connect with the needs and backgrounds of their changing student population(s); and (2) to introduce a new set of assessment protocols that the district office decided would be implemented to further hold teachers accountable for student academic progress.

It seemed straight-forward. I had not anticipated the unwelcome reception I was to receive. In retrospect, I realize that my presentation, despite its good-intentions, was metaphorically pushing the veteran teachers up against a "wall between inner truth and outer performance" (Palmer, 2007, p. 18). Without knowing it, asking educators to make fundamental changes to their teaching practices tacitly implied that what they were doing was less effective than they had come to believe.

In my enthusiasm to share new strategies and resources, I'd forgotten that teaching is more than what these individuals did for a living—*it is who they are*. Asking teachers to reconsider their beliefs on how children learn and directing them to change the practices they had developed over time was akin to questioning their identity, discounting their experience, and challenging their expertise.

Nevertheless, the world of teaching and learning *had* changed. The learning demands (including available tools and resources) were no longer what they were even ten or fifteen years previously. In effect I was asking teachers to *relearn* the realities of their professional lives. As with other kinds of loss, facing new realities, procedures, and administrative priorities (that challenged existing beliefs and habits) made them personally and emotionally vulnerable.

In my current work with senior-year college teacher candidates, I am repeatedly reminded that one's personal sense of self and his or her emerging professional identity are closely intertwined. I have come to understand that too great an emphasis on the external processes of teaching and learning (i.e., instructional strategies, content information, assessment protocols) distracts and in some ways diminishes the emotional, ethical, and spiritual dimensions of education.

The largest struggles my teacher candidates face are not with the more mechanical duties of teaching (i.e., record-keeping, lesson-planning, locating available resources). The greatest challenges lie in the students' efforts to relearn who they are and how they operate in a professional world which for them is unfamiliar on a variety of levels. Many of the hidden complexities of being an educator arise, for instance, when an individual teacher's private beliefs are challenged by administrative demands; when a teacher's personal mission and vision confront unforeseen classroom challenges; or when the outer structures of classroom life are not enough to tame the inner despair and helplessness individuals feel when living through grief.

William James (1899/2008) reflects on what he calls "a certain blindness in human beings" (p. 121) that occurs when there is too much emphasis on issues and concerns of the outer world and too little consideration of the inner beauties and challenges that all human beings possess. James warns that when we become too "stuffed with abstract conceptions, and glib with verbalities and verbosities" we risk "grow[ing] stone-cold and insensible to life's more elementary and general goods and joys" (p. 135). He feared that the more we rely exclusively on intellect, the less we would strive toward and appreciate a deeper understanding of life (p. 146). In my journey as teacher, I have come to revere what James calls education's capacity to nurture a "higher vision of an inner significance" (James, 1899/2008, p. 127).

This book is my opportunity to honor James's vision of teaching and learning as the foundation for "what makes a life significant" (p. 139) on moral, emotional, and spiritual levels. To do so, I decided to focus specifically on the experience of grief because it is during times of tragedy and loss that: (1) emotional, ethical, and spiritual hurt is most felt; (2) a person's beliefs, values, and emotions are most vulnerable; and (3) individuals (teachers and students) struggle to *relearn* their understanding of the world and their place in it. The capacity of teaching and learning to be an emotional and spiritual lifeline during these critical life moments elevates the work of educators from the commonplace to the sacred.

MY PERSONAL JOURNEY HERE

I have always regarded education as sacred in its capacity to expand an individual's understanding of life and its many complexities. After the passing of my mom eighteen months ago, that belief was tested as never before. My grief reminded me that much of my work as a teacher relies on and is indicative of who I am as a person (i.e., my beliefs and values). I felt as if my grief was summoning me to reconsider the ways I was being and becoming the educator—and the person—I aspired to be. I would discover that revisiting one's public and personal sense of mission and vision, as grief called me to do, is akin to reimagining one's personal, moral, and spiritual lives.

While grieving, I often felt that I was half the person I had been. Was I also half the teacher? I frequently urge my students (aspiring teachers in the College of Education) to reflect upon their emerging and evolving personal and professional identities. How often (and how recently) had *I* done so. Grief seemed to strike at the very intersection of my professional and personal lives. I have come to understand that regarding grief as a curriculum is less about examining one's life than *re-examining* it.

Martha Nussbaum (1986) asks "whether the act of writing about the beauty of human vulnerability is not, paradoxically, a way of rendering oneself less vulnerable" (p. xliii). I suspect that I began this book as a project to help "render myself less vulnerable" to my grief. The extent to which this is possible or ultimately even desirable is unclear to me. I will, however, revisit these considerations in the *Epilogue* (Chapter 9).

PATHWAYS OF INQUIRY AND EMERGENT THEMES

I am interested in examining the spaces where an educator's public and private identities, values, and beliefs intersect. I consider these critical places where a teacher's intrinsic hopes, fears, and aspirations are unbound from externally imposed measures and restrictions. Experiences of loss and grief are simultaneously universal and intimate. Hence, grieving is an integral part of our shared humanity, while at the same time highly personal.

Although teaching and learning touch on a common core of knowledge, its lessons and experiences can resonate on a variety of intrinsic levels. Because the nature of this exploration demands personal and emotional introspection, it requires explorative pathways that integrate the public act of teaching with the private processes of reflection. To this end, I am modeling an innovative inquiry process designed to engage readers from diverse backgrounds and life experiences.

This qualitative journey relies on an eclectic blend of methods and resources intended to allow the process of reflection to be more organic, dynamic, and emotionally authentic. Three components—educational philosophy, literature, and reflective inquiry—drive this exploration of grief as a teacher's curriculum. My undertaking is influenced by George Willis and William H. Schubert's (1991) work that utilizes the arts as a source of reflective inquiry, and Eliot Eisner's (2002) scholarship that further validates the relationship between the cognitive and the aesthetic. Although this book uses significant works of literature as lenses through which to explore grief as curriculum, the reader does not need to have read the complete novels. I share relevant excerpts from the narratives in the spirit of exploration and imagination inspired by Maxine Greene's (1965/2007) observations:

> No amount of talking about a work of art can be equivalent to a direct encounter with what it is and what it does. And no amount of description can exhaust the levels of experience each work has the capacity to touch.... Simplistic

descriptions will recede; facts will arrange themselves in new designs. Pursuing our questions, our uncertainties, we may find a kind of freedom in our explorations.... We will move backward in time at first; then we will move forward in our effort to rediscover the meanings in the past to rediscover something of ourselves. (pp. 5–6)

Teachers can turn to anecdotes, metaphors, and images embedded in literature as pedagogical tools for introspection and sense-making. F. Michael Connelly and D. Jean Clandinin (1990) write that "humans are storytelling organisms who, individually and socially, lead storied lives. The study of narrative, therefore, is the study of the ways humans experience the world" (p. 2). The stories of emotional, spiritual, and moral growth and development that accompany grief can be a critical component to forging one's future. Consequently, the life stories of teachers and students are integral to their learning experiences.

My intention, then, is to present relevant novel passages, philosophical summaries, and personal anecdotes that together create a unique mosaic of thoughts and ideas. From an epistemological perspective, literature, philosophy, and lived experiences are the means through which knowledge and understanding are gleaned. My hope is that the resulting collage of images, impressions, and perspectives will inspire meaningful introspection and provocative discourse regarding the deeply personal nature of a teacher's work.

The literary selections used throughout this book dramatize the effects grief can have on an individual's public and private lives. Although fiction, the underlying themes which the literature conveys reflect the reality that a person's grief is a fundamental part of an individual's identity. Thus, one's private pain is felt in public places, and one's professional duties are influenced by his or her personal pain.

The diversity of literature utilized and the variety of educational philosophers cited throughout this study serve to expand and deepen its examination of grief as a teacher's curriculum. Reflecting on moments of *individual mourning* leads to considerations related to *collective mourning*, including the grief felt by communities enduring conditions of poverty, bias, and street violence; and the losses endured by schools and their surrounding communities related to the increase in reported school shootings.

Alternating motifs of grief that imprisons with healing that emancipates are embedded throughout the chapters, especially as the exploration of *private grief* extends into spaces of *public grieving*. In what ways are educators challenged to "stand where personal and public meet" (Palmer, 2007, p. 18)? Exploring and reflecting on this central query is intended to deepen our understanding of the emotional and spiritual nuances of an educator's intricate public work.

By integrating literature, philosophy, and personal reflections, this book aims to weave a metaphorical tapestry of thoughts, emotions, beliefs, and ideas that cut across the personal-professional divide that too often separates inner truths from outer realities. Relevant ontological and axiomatic threads run through each of the chapters creating a thematic unity across this journey. Does the true nature of an individual's (and an educator's) existence lie behind or within his or her public appearance? To what extent does in-school curriculum align to the curriculum of one's life, especially in terms of leading individuals toward lives that are morally, spiritually, and intrinsically worthwhile? Variations and permutations of these kinds of questions arise throughout this exploration of grief as a teacher's curriculum. I believe that the scope and depth of such reflection has the capacity to expand our understanding of teaching and learning beyond intellectual concerns into spaces of emotional and ethical import.

CHAPTER INTENTIONS

This book is divided into nine chapters. Each chapter uses a specific literary text as its primary lens through which to explore the impact of grieving on an individual's identity, values, and aspirations—personally and professionally. Woven into the literary analysis are related excerpts from educational philosophers and curriculum theorists. For me, the decision to consider grief as a teacher's curriculum was repeatedly affirmed the more I explored these literary and philosophical texts. Although the themes, characters, and points of view spanned centuries, the writers' language, metaphors, beliefs, and ideas embodied a timeless essence of our shared humanity: the search for inner purpose and meaning despite an outer world that is often unpredictable, incomprehensible, and emotionally hurtful.

Emerging from the dual lenses of literature and philosophy is a series of reflective questions and considerations designed to help readers more closely examine some of the critical emotional and moral nuances that impact a teacher's life and work. Each chapter concludes with a series of "Topics for Reflection" which I hope readers will find useful for further individual and collective contemplation.

Chapter 2 begins our exploration examining the prose and poetry of Bengali scholar Rabindranath Tagore. A common theme of Tagore's writings is that the ultimate objective of education is to guide teachers and students toward a "unity of truth" (Tagore, 1933, p. 153). This unity refers to the interconnectedness of a person's intellectual, emotional, and spiritual growth and development. Specific questions explored include: To what degree are educators prepared emotionally, intellectually, and spiritually for their role as teacher? In what ways are students encouraged to make sense of their worlds on these levels?

The scholarship of Larry Cochran and Emily Claspell (1987) helps guide the exploration through Tagore's body of work using a lens of grief. Their research examines how personal manifestations of grief impact the public lives of teachers and students. On a more expansive scale, Paul Connerton's (2011) scholarship examines grief's collective impact on communities and cultures. His work broadens the scope of our journey as Connerton focuses on groups who suffer what he calls a "massive amount of unprocessed sorrow" (Connerton, 2011, p. 67) through the imposition of societal injustices (i.e., racial and ethnic bias, institutionalized segregation, slavery).

Specific real-world examples are then presented that demonstrate how these ideas relate directly to the life of classrooms. A variety of educational considerations and relevant introspective questions are offered to deepen one's understanding of how personal and collective grieving impacts learning and classroom engagement.

Chapter 3 uses Virginia Woolf's *Orlando* (1928) to look more closely at grieving as a process of relearning who and what is most worthwhile in our lives. In a metaphorical sense, the book's protagonist personifies grief itself. The novel provides pathways along which to consider the potential of teaching and learning to help students and teachers make sense of a world in which one is continuously in a process of relearning one's place in it. As Orlando grieves the passing of previously held beliefs, s/he grows in empathy. As s/he mourns the loss of values and ideas s/he previously held in blind faith, s/he learns lessons in honesty and compassion.

Woolf's novel demonstrates synergies between teaching and learning and the growth and development of one's identity, values, and beliefs. The chapter challenges readers (1) to see beyond binary choices toward a more dynamic way of understanding the world; (2) to traverse imaginative pathways that defy the restrictions of linear logic; and (3) to contemplate successful teaching and learning that is based not on the number of correct answers given, but on the depth of questions asked and explored.

Chapter 4 explores what Soren Kierkegaard (1843/1959) calls the difference between an aesthetic life (wherein one strives to escape melancholy and despair) and an ethical one (wherein one accepts and attempts to work through intrinsic hardships such as sadness and remorse). The characters of Franz Wedekind's *Spring Awakening: A Children's Tragedy* (1891/2010) are a group of high school students experiencing their rites of passage toward adulthood. They grieve the passing away of childhood beliefs and values as they begin to experience a world they no longer recognize. They are operating on an ethical level as they begin to challenge beliefs and values that they previously accepted without question, but that no longer make sense in their quickly changing lives.

Their parents and teachers, on the other hand, are operating on an aesthetic level—advocating for a more binary and linear perspective of life. From a William Jamesian perspective, the children are struggling with issues of identity and ethics (i.e., "what makes a life significant" [James, 1899/2008, p. 139]), while the adults are experiencing "a certain blindness" (p. 121) and "grow[ing] stone-cold and insensible to life's more elementary and general goods and joys" (p. 135).

The chapter explores what Nel Noddings (2005) describes as a gap between in-school curriculum and the larger curriculum of one's life. Passages from Steven Sater and Duncan Sheik's (2007) retelling of Wedekind's work further illustrate the students' struggles as they grieve the passing of the binary "right or wrong" perspective of their childhoods and enter a world that lacks clear and definitive answers. The works of Sater and Sheik (2007) and Wedekind (1891/2010) provide an emotional tableau from which to reflect more deeply on the spiritual, ethical, and emotional nuances of our work as educators.

9

The chapter builds on these concepts and eventually frames them within a contemporary setting where public grief and private mourning converge: Marjory Stoneman Douglas High School (Parkland, Florida), the site of a 2017 school shooting incident in which seventeen students were murdered. The themes of loss and the subsequent search for meaning in Sater and Sheik's (2007) *Spring Awakening* connected to the lives of this community in profound ways. The cathartic power of teaching and learning is explored as the Sater and Sheik play is used as a means for the school and its surrounding community to collectively mourn and heal.

Chapter 5 explores grief in intimately personal terms. Parker Palmer (2007) writes that "when teachers dismiss inner truth and honor only the external world.... students as well as teachers lose heart" (p. 19). Tom Wingo, the protagonist of Pat Conroy's (1986) novel *The Prince of Tides,* is a linguistic embodiment of Palmer's observation. Tom is a popular high school English teacher until the tragedies of his past can no longer be denied or suppressed. His inner grief demands to be acknowledged and felt. The ensuing emotional turmoil nearly destroys Tom's personal and professional life and work.

Tom embodies Nick Wormeli's (2018) declaration that "the way we teach is often a statement of who we are" (p. 1). *The Prince of Tides* dramatizes the intricate process of grieving and healing (and its impact on one's personal and professional identity) through two recurring motifs: *diminishment becoming remembrance* and *recovery informing reidentification.* This chapter explores these themes as they relate to similar emotional and spiritual growth inherent to meaningful teaching and learning. As a story of catharsis and healing, the novel affirms the power of introspection to transform an educator's life and work.

Virgil's *Aeneid* (Book X, 19 BCE/1981) is used in Chapter 6 to explore questions that delve more deeply into the ethical dimensions of a teacher's work: To what extent are we being and becoming the educators we have aspired to be? In what ways does our public work align with our personal values and beliefs?

The story's hero, Aeneas, is preparing to complete vital public tasks that will positively impact the lives of hundreds of thousands of people. He is unable to achieve these goals, however, until he confronts and grieves important events from his past. Aeneas's descent into the mythological ancient Roman underworld is a metaphorical device that epitomizes his journey of grief. Due to the universality of Virgil's work, Aeneas's crisis of integrity is *our* crisis; his wrangling with guilt and loss is *our wrestling*; and his grieving is *our* grieving.

Aeneas's past cannot be separated from his present. He needs to learn how to reconcile previous errors of judgment with his future role as a public figure of integrity. He cannot create a personal or public path forward until he deals with his grief, guilt, and remorse. Relevant to this, the chapter explores Paulo Freire's (2008) assertion that education has the capacity to help students and teachers *create and recreate* their relationship to the world in meaningful ways. Aeneas travels through the underworld as he examines his past in order to make sense of his present and to fortify himself for the future. Similarly, meaningful teaching and learning has the capacity to "reach back to yesterday, recognize today, and come upon tomorrow" (Freire, 2008, p. 3).

Chapter 7 challenges readers to temporarily suspend pre-conceived ideas of truth and reality. Using Stephen King's *Pet Sematary* (1983) to examine a curriculum of grief demands that educators—whose work mostly prioritizes rational knowledge, facts, and carefully assessed outcomes—consider emotions, beliefs, and values that are immeasurable and oftentimes inexplicable. Like grief itself, King's novel depicts metaphysical spaces that simultaneously defy rationality *and* reveal hidden truths. Because grief challenges one's linear understanding of the world, this chapter explores the value of what Paul Lynch (2013) calls "teaching for uncertainty" (p. 38).

The images and dialogue King uses throughout *Pet Sematary* heighten the visceral experience of grief and lay bare an individual's emotional and spiritual vulnerabilities. Whereas the *curriculum of schooling* neatly resides within a well-organized and logically devised framework, the *curriculum of life*, as Barbara Regenspan (2014) points out, speaks to unpredictable ghosts of fear and uncertainty. As this chapter gleans lessons from *Pet Sematary*'s surreal depiction of grief and mourning, it ultimately asks educators to reflect on the extent to which they are *teachers of curriculum* or *teachers of life*.

Chapter 8 uses Charles Dickens's (1867/2003) *Oliver Twist* to explore four nuances of grief: identity, vulnerability, resiliency, and grace. Oliver's experiences as a young orphan trying to make sense of his world demonstrate the intimate role grief plays in how we learn. A close examination of the novel reveals what Kay Chang (2017) calls the "parallel healing psychological process—living respectfully with vulnerability and hopefully with resiliency" (p. 4).

Four of the teacher-figures in Oliver's childhood exemplify an educator's potential to influence—and sometimes transform—the lives of students both morally and spiritually. These teacher-figures demonstrate how teachers' personal experiences and inner beliefs implicitly infuse their instruction with values and ideas that extend far beyond information, facts, and data points. The chapter examines the idea "that teaching is an intrinsically moral act" (Kottler & Zehm, 2000):

> How are children supposed to learn such moral values as treating others with respect and fairness unless they see their teachers practicing these behaviors on a daily basis? (p. 13)

In this chapter I draw on a variety of perspectives, including those of educators (Kieran Egan, Paul Tough), philosophers (Martin Buber, Nel Noddings), writers (William Styron, Andrew Solomon), poets (Emily Dickinson, William Wordsworth), moralists (Horace Mann, Clifford Mayes), spiritual thinkers (Dalai Lama Suyra, Joseph Cardinal Bernardin), playwrights (Steven Levenson, Benj Pasek, Justin Paul), and educational researchers (Geert Kelchtermans, G. D. Fenstermacher). This expansive collection of voices and viewpoints creates a composite of thoughts and ideas on which to further reflect what grief can teach us about our emerging and evolving personal and professional identities. These are the kinds of lessons that can ultimately transform teaching and learning from ordinary to sacred.

The Epilogue (Chapter 9) reflects on the themes and issues that emerged from the proceeding chapters. I describe and examine lessons learned along the way with an eye towards the future. Rather than concluding with answers and solutions, the Epilogue raises new questions inspired by the journey itself. This is appropriate in that grieving is about *relearning* who we are and *reexamining* our lives. As Mike Rose (2009) asserts, "a good education helps us make sense of the world and find our way in it" (p. 31):

> We are driven—as surely as we are driven to survive—to find meaning in our lives, to interpret what befalls us, the events that swirl around us, the people who cross our paths, the objects and rhythms of the natural world. We do this instinctively; it is essential to being human. (Rose, 2009, p. 31)

My hope is that this journey and the questions it raises will inspire increasing numbers of educators to further reflect on the synergy between schooling and living. Both are essential to our humanity in terms of exploring three basic curriculum questions: What knowledge is most worthwhile? Why is it worthwhile? How is it acquired or created (Schubert, 1986, p. 1)? These are the kinds of questions that can help guide us toward being and becoming the educators—and the individuals—we aspire to be professionally, personally, and ethically.

POETIC VOICE OF GRIEVING

Prose and Poetry, *Rabindranath Tagore*

The word grief derives from *gref* (Middle English), meaning *heavy*. It denotes the kinds of heaviness that weigh on individuals intellectually, physically, and spiritually. The weight of grieving is unique in that its emotional toil cannot be neatly untangled from intellectual mourning or spiritual upheaval. Bengali poet, educator, and philosopher Rabindranath Tagore (1861–1941) believed that we human beings have a great deal to learn from the weight of our grieving.

Tagore's writings highlight the importance of learning to embrace the heaviness of one's interconnected physical, intellectual, and spiritual demands and needs. Tagore insists that teaching and learning are sacred acts. His experimental school, Santiniketan, served as a laboratory within which to put into practice his visionary approach to education that emphasized his sweeping humanistic beliefs.

In his treatise *My School*, Tagore (1933/2004) remarks that "the highest education is one that does not merely give us information but makes our life in harmony with all existence" (p. 142). He argues passionately that "the object of education is to give man the unity of truth" (p. 153).

> But when there came the separation of the intellect from the spiritual and the physical, the school education put the entire emphasis on the intellect and on the physical side of man. We devote our sole attention to giving children information, not knowing that by this emphasis we are accentuating a break between the intellectual, the physical, and the spiritual life. (p. 154)

Tagore (1933/2004) believed that for teaching to be personally relevant and emotionally authentic, learning experiences need to move beyond extrinsic facts, narrow curricular content, and regimented skill sets. He emphasized the importance of prioritizing individuals over categories, understanding over information, and values over facts. The sacredness of teaching and learning lies in its capacity to help teachers and students wrestle with life's inconsistencies, ambiguities, and heartbreaks. It is in this spirit that Tagore's writings urge us to reconceptualize education as a means to nurture the fullest humanity of students and teachers.

This chapter uses Tagore's words as a lens through which to better understand ways in which grief, personal and collective, plays a critical role in helping individuals better understand themselves and each other. If, as Tagore (1933/2004) insists, "in our spiritual attainment gaining and giving are the same thing; as in a lamp, to light itself is the same as to impart light to others" (p. 164), then the curriculum of grief—of bearing our spiritual, physical, and intellectual heaviness—is prioritized. When viewed from these philosophical and spiritual perspectives, we truly have much to learn from our grief.

THEMES OF GRIEVING

Larry Cochran and Emily Claspell (1987) identify what they call "themes of grieving." Their research relies on extensive interviews with individuals experiencing grief associated with a variety of losses. Based on their qualitative data, Cochran and Claspell created a set of categories that frame some of the aspects of grief in ways that can help others articulate and reflect on its pedagogical aspects and potential. One of these categories is emotional disorientation. This can take a variety of forms: Normal routines may seem unfamiliar, habits of behavior and conversation become tentative, feelings of uncertainty replace confidence, and one's sense of purpose is destabilized. Tagore (1933/2004) challenges us to consider these difficult moments as opportunities for personal growth:

> We pass through dark periods of doubt and reaction. But these conflicts and waverings belong to the true aspects of reality.... I for my part believe in the principle of life, in the soul of man, more than in methods. I believe that the object of education is the freedom of the mind which can only be achieved through the path of freedom. (p. 178)

Tagore proposes that the course of an authentic curriculum does not follow a linear construction or a pre-configured path. Teachers, students, or administrators looking for a prescribed pedagogical formula will not find any in Tagore's work. He believed that lessons planned and delivered in carefully plotted day-by-day and week-by-week sequence are out-of-synch with the lived reality of teachers and students. He insisted that no "clockwork orange arrangement" could account for the "true aspects of reality" that most often "make their appearance unexpectedly" (p. 178).

Tagore emphasizes that the spiritual and philosophical dimensions of teaching and learning are as important (if not more vital) to the lives of teachers and students. Accordingly, his work is a good fit for our exploration of grief as a teacher's curriculum. Consider, for instance, the book analogy that Tagore (1933/2004) proposes:

> The introduction and the conclusion of a book have a similarity of features. In both places the complete aspect of truth is given. Only in the introduction it is simple because undeveloped, and in the conclusion it becomes simple again because perfectly developed. Truth has the middle course of its career, where it grows complex, where it hurts itself against obstacles, breaks itself back into pieces to find itself back in a fuller unity of realization. (p. 139)

Using Tagore's analogy as a model to demonstrate the organic nature of a teacher's journey, those at the beginning chapters of their careers are the novice teachers who operate with a clear (oftentimes idealized) vision of their prospective role as educators. Teachers in the middle chapters of their careers experience a variety of situations and crises that frequently contradict their often previously untested personal and professional ideals, beliefs, and values. For example, they may have been required to enforce an administrative policy that does not align with their personal beliefs; or they may need to enforce a district-wide protocol that contradicts the underlying values of their professional mission or vision.

During these times, individuals can become "suspicious as to the efficacy of their own ideals" (Tagore, 1933/2004, p. 178). They are challenged to carry the weight of their ensuing disorientation on emotional, spiritual, and/or moral levels. Tagore (1933/2004) writes, however, that these kinds of struggles are not in vain. Although there may be grief in the passing away of some beliefs and dreams, in its wake lie critical opportunities to reassess and relearn one's path forward. For teachers, these are growth opportunities that, when experienced, can help one's personal and public mission and vision mature and evolve.

Tagore's (1933/2004) analogy concludes by comparing a book's closing chapters to the latter years of a person's life (or, in the case of this exploration, the later years of a teacher's career). The characters of a novel often reach epiphanies through which they can now comprehend what previously was unclear. Similarly, teachers in the latter portion of their careers often come to understand what their younger selves could not. Their more seasoned perspectives are the result of having experienced and learned from many inner and outer crises throughout their career (and lives). Times of difficulty have seasoned and matured their youthful ideals. Although there is grief at the loss of one's more idealistic understanding of life, Tagore reminds us that there is also a kind of grace and wisdom that comes with a more authentic understanding of the depth and expanse of the many spiritual and emotional nuances that comprise one's life.

As a teacher educator, I have personally witnessed similar moments of transformation happening in the lives of the student-teachers I mentor. Teacher candidates invariably encounter disconnects between what they envision being a teacher will look and feel like versus what they experience in classrooms. The emotional stress of these disconnects weighs heavily on them. As they articulate their challenges, I listen not only as a field supervisor and as a veteran middle school teacher, but as a fellow human being. In their discourse I often hear echoes of grief from beyond the specific experiences they are relating. For example, student-teachers frequently struggle with feelings of uncertainty that emerge when their sense of stability or purpose is challenged. The world and their place in it, after all, are rapidly changing. In a larger sense, the students are grieving life's inconsistencies and ambiguities.

When inner beliefs and values conflict with external demands and pressures, a person's understanding of the world is oftentimes shaken. Tagore (1933/2004)

15

understood that no body of knowledge or tome of scientific information can resolve what he describes as the "uncompromising civil war between [one's] personality and his [or her] outer world" (p. 139). In what ways we preparing students for the inevitable emotional, intellectual, and spiritual crises they will face? When teachers and students experience personal crises that challenge their beliefs, values, and expectations, what supports or resources are available to assist them? These questions speak to the importance of considering grief as a teacher's curriculum.

Tagore advances the idea that within the emotional and spiritual depths of teaching and learning lies the potential for solace and healing. He believes that authentic spaces of teaching and learning have the potential to inspire and support individuals as they struggle to put the metaphorical pieces of their emotions, beliefs, and aspirations back together. Because patterns of grief and solace and cycles of suffering and healing are natural parts of our humanity, they are inherently relevant to the organic nature of teaching and learning.

Life's journey, of which grief is an integral part, is an educative process. Individuals are called to relearn facets of themselves and their lives. It requires *relearning* our understanding of ourselves and our place in the world. Tagore reminds us that teaching and learning constitute critical opportunities in the journey (of students and teachers) toward living worthwhile lives. If an educator's role is reduced to dispensing impersonal information and promoting adherence to rules and regulations (mostly impacting external behaviors), then opportunities for exploring and ascertaining what constitutes meaningful lives are lost.

As a philosopher, teacher, and public figure, Tagore was concerned with what he feared was the increasing dehumanization of individuals in his country and around the world. He was unapologetically candid in his criticism of schooling that ignored a student's—and a teacher's—humanity.

> Have not our books, like most of our necessities, come between us and the world? We have got into the habit of covering the windows of our minds with their pages, and plasters of book phrases have stuck into our mental skin, making it impervious of all touches of truth. A whole world of bookish truths have formed themselves into a strong citadel with rings of walls in which we have taken shelter. (pp. 172–173)

But there is nowhere to hide from grief. Although a person may try to deny or bury its existence, there exists no genuine reprieve that can shelter individuals from the emotional and spiritual experiences of grieving. Where, how, and when will children learn to make sense of their worlds? In what ways and in what spaces will they grieve? These are the kinds of questions that examine teaching and learning on emotional and spiritual levels.

And yet, Tagore (1933/2004) warns that schooling too often denies the inner lives of teachers and students. Tagore's (1933/2004) treatise, *My School*, is critical of schools that operate more as impersonal manufacturing facilities that prioritize conformity and uniformity at the expense of individuality. Almost ninety years later, his concerns remain relevant to our work and our lives as educators. Consider contemporary efforts and initiatives intended to tailor classroom instruction to fit standardized curricula and narrow assessment measures. Where in these efforts and initiatives are emotional, moral, and spiritual growth and development considered?

Tagore (1933/2004) warns that "according to school, life is perfect when it allows itself to be treated as dead" (p. 141). A curriculum disconnected from life allows itself to be neatly arranged, ordered, and measured. When students are uniformly expected to measure up to prescribed markers of achievement, the inconvenience of needing to differentiate for individual strengths and weakness is removed. Grief reminds us that we are living creatures with emotions, belief systems, and values that transcend lifeless external measurements and protocol. Our humanity cannot be rigidly prescribed from exterior demands—especially in the wake of grief.

The lives of students and teachers do not neatly adhere to predictable paths along pre-planned straight lines. If a curriculum is to be meaningful, it needs to be a living document that adapts and responds to the continuously changing and oftentimes unpredictable lives of teachers and students. Tagore (1933/2004) cautions that if education does not tend to the dynamic nature of the spiritual and emotional aspects of our humanity, we are more likely to enter unprepared into those moments of life when we are most vulnerable to sadness, loneliness, and despair. No amount of information, mathematical expertise, or other cognitive measures offer or inspire solace, compassion, or empathy.

With this in mind, consider the extent to which the emotional and spiritual lives (of teachers and students) are relevant to the teaching and learning happening in schools. To what extent are teachers and students expected to focus on intellectual endeavors while leaving critical pieces of their inner humanity (i.e., grief, loss, emotional hurt) outside on the doorstep? Tagore (1933/2004) recalls ancient Indian stories of teaching and learning (before school buildings were erected) that occurred outdoors—in people's backyards and nearby forests. He praises the practice, saying "the school was there where was the life itself" (p. 156):

There the students were brought up. Not in the academic atmosphere of scholarship and learning, or in the maimed life of monastic seclusion, but in the atmosphere of living aspiration.... This was possible because the primary object of these places was not teaching but giving shelter. (p. 156)

In what ways do our schools qualify in terms of offering this kind of atmosphere and shelter? Although school buildings may protect teachers and students from physical hardships (rain, snow, cold temperatures), in what ways do they offer emotional and/ or moral shelter? For instance, although increased security measures purport to protect students and teachers schools against the threat of armed intruders, what spaces are available wherein teachers and students can aspire toward addressing their fears and vulnerabilities rather than running from them or weaponizing themselves against them?

These questions continue to be relevant when viewed through the lens of twenty-first-century concerns. Consider, for instance, the increase of reported school shootings throughout the United States in the past twenty-five years. Teachers and students are left to grieve the loss of their faith in believing that schools are safe from such episodes of violence. Regard the heightened vulnerability of students and their families surrounded by outbursts of street violence. Or those who fear bias and discrimination against immigrants, refugees, and their families. Or individuals who suffer the victimization imposed by physical or sexual abuse. When the emotional, spiritual, and personal well-being of students, teachers, their families, and their communities are threatened, there is much to grieve.

These are some examples of crises that deteriorate an individual's sense of safety and security, and weaken otherwise hopeful spirits. Cochran and Claspell (1987) explain that during such times of emotional duress, people struggle to function in their outer lives while they inwardly suffer strong feelings of hopelessness and powerlessness in a world in which they no longer feel safe. This especially impacts children. A child's emotional unrest often expresses itself in rebellious behaviors, verbal outbursts, and episodes of anger and frustration. Students unable to function in the outer world (i.e., adhere to external demands and expectations) are often sent out of the classroom to face disciplinary consequences. Instead of receiving shelter from these emotional storms, their sense of loneliness, helplessness, and isolation is increased.

By contrast, Tagore (1933/2004) describes a school's potential to be a sanctuary. He specifically refers to the classroom as an *ashram*—a natural space that nourishes all aspects of our humanity. Tagore writes that infusing classrooms with a spirit of *ashram* means acknowledging that the "subconscious mind [of teachers and students is] more active than their conscious intelligence" (p. 168):

> Students and the teachers who have come together in this *ashram* are daily growing towards the emancipation of their minds into the consciousness of the infinite, not through any process of teaching or outer discipline, but by the help of an unseen atmosphere of aspiration that surrounds the place. (p. 168)

Education of this caliber prioritizes teaching and learning that encourage students (and teachers) to examine their lives from the inside out. Learning in an *ashram*-inspired environment centers around pertinent questions that derive from students' lives, interests, and concerns. After all, although information and facts inform our minds, it is the questions we ask that have the potential to deepen our understanding of life.

During periods of loss and grief, the urgency to have the space and time to ask relevant questions becomes more tangible. Tagore describes an *ashram's* climate as one that does the following: (1) calls for students and teachers to be "fully awake" rather than passively receiving information; (2) engages participants in an on-going search for truths rather than disseminating prescribed curriculum and external facts as truths; and (3) aligns more closely to the natural cycles of life. Like crops, plants, and flowers, we human beings experience seasons of life. We change, grow, expand, and expire like the stars and skies above.

To what extent do our classrooms share in this spirit of *ashram*? How often and in what ways are students and teachers gathered to explore, reflect on, and openly discuss the seasons and cycles of their lives? In what ways do the questions, challenges, and mysteries that concern our students serve to drive or inform instruction? What spiritual, ethical, or emotional relevance can be found in accumulating facts and data points? Of what merit is acquiring knowledge that informs our minds if it is otherwise disconnected from our lives?

More specifically, Tagore (1933/2004) reminds us that personal change, loss, and grief are not separate from the world around us; they are its integral components. He warns that when these critical life experiences are overlooked, "the greatest of educations for which we came prepared is neglected, and we are made to lose our world to find a bagful of information instead":

> We rob the child of his earth to teach him geography, of language to teach him grammar. His hunger is for the Epic, but he is supplied with chronicles of facts and dates. He was born in the human world, but is banished into the world of living gramophones. (p. 143)

SILENCES OF GRIEVING

Throughout his treatise on education, Tagore (1933/2004) uses images that contrast individual freedom and systemic bondage (i.e., emancipation of soul versus suffocation of spirit, soul freedom versus the encasement of a school, the full strength of freedom versus the narrowness of an individual's caged-up future, the path of freedom versus the bondage of dust). These images reflect Tagore's role as a national figure who spoke out against British colonial rule in India. His essays and poems advocate for education as a means to empower the politically, socially, and morally silenced voices of indigenous peoples.

Paul Connerton (2011) mourns the silences that abound throughout history and continue today. They represent entire communities of people whose languages, belief systems, writings, histories, artworks, and more have been politically, culturally, and economically stifled. When a community's suffering or despair is silenced beneath institutional structures (including educational bureaucracies), the unprocessed sorrows fester in ways that deteriorate self-esteem and diminish personal and collective freedom (Connerton, 2011, p. 67).

Tagore and Connerton believe that acknowledging, mourning, and articulating these silences are emancipatory actions. They advocate that education has the means and capacity to break these cycles of silence and that schools have the potential to be sacred spaces wherein silent sorrows can be heard rather than denied. This includes those who are grieving spiritual and emotional losses incurred from poverty, bias, abuse, injustice, and neglect. Connerton (2011) writes that when these silences are systematized, there emerges entire generations of "children [who] grew up in the ambience of the unspeakable" (p. 73):

Parents explained nothing and children asked nothing. Children feared to ask for answers to the question which they dared not ask their parents. Parents transmitted to their children only the wound, but refused them the memory. (p. 73)

Providing legitimate opportunities for individuals and communities to publicly voice their "narratives of mourning" (Connerton, 2011, p. 12) is a first step toward validation and healing. Connerton believes that classrooms can become critical "sites of celebration and remembered grief" (p. 13). I am inspired by a teacher with whom I recently worked who created such an emancipatory space in his fifth-grade classroom. The low-income, urban neighborhood surrounding the school had recently been victimized by a series of gang-related violent incidents. School policy directed teachers and students to leave neighborhood troubles outside the school and to focus on their academics instead.

Consequently, there was no official space in the school that allowed the students to grieve family, friends, and neighbors impacted by the violence. Student fears, anxieties, and uncertainties were being silenced for the sake of their academic work. In effect, the prescribed curriculum was being prioritized over the lives of the students. Although student fears and uncertainties were not to be discussed during school hours, its emotional toll showed in other ways: students grew increasingly distracted and inattentive; emotional and oftentimes hostile outbursts became more frequent; and the overall cooperative spirit of the classroom was deteriorating.

The teacher felt that his students needed to be mindful that there was much more to who they were as individuals and as a community than street violence, poverty, and an increased police presence. He grieved that the students were having a negative identity imposed on them. This teacher decided to plan and implement a literacy/social studies project that would create classroom spaces wherein the students could express and celebrate their families, values, and culture.

Although the topic, "African-Americans throughout history," was broad, the learning focus was narrow: students were asked to identify a relative or close family friend who embodied greatness. Using a personal connection as their central focus, students were invited to interview friends and family, collect relevant artifacts and memorabilia, and explore "why is this person important to me and what legacy did s/he leave behind that remains important today."

The students were encouraged to assume ownership of the project. Instead of submitting written reports, they shared their work publicly during classroom time. Even the assessment protocol was student-centered: a peer-designed rubric emphasized content over grammar and spelling; and feedback would come from the students themselves. Several of my teacher candidates and I were invited to their presentations. Although we may not have realized it at the time, we were witnessing a space of *ashram*: a sanctuary and sacred space of remembrance. The tenor of the classroom assumed an emotional and spiritual relevance that felt incredibly authentic and healing:

- One student described his grandfather who was a Tuskegee pilot during World War II. He explained how his grandmother searched the attic to retrieve her husband's

pilot jacket. The student proudly wore his grandfather's Tuskegee jacket during the presentation (and insisted on wearing it throughout the entire school day).
• Another student explained that she went home to complain about the assignment because she felt she had nothing to say. Her great-aunt spent hours searching for family photos of cousins who attended a 1964 Martin Luther King speech and a 1966 civil rights rally. This normally shy (and underperforming) student presented an eloquent and moving testimonial of her growing understanding of race in America and of her family's personal involvement in its history.
• A third student shared the story of his uncle from Mississippi whom he never even knew existed. His relative served in a platoon during the Vietnam War and was assumed killed in battle. Students in the classroom were astounded—did African American soldiers fight in the Vietnam War? They had never heard of anything like this in their history classes. At the teacher's urging, the student located and verified his uncle's name imprinted on the Vietnam War Memorial in Washington, DC.

This classroom experience embodied the spirit of *ashram*. It allowed students to actively investigate the past and publicly share histories that were emotionally pertinent to their personal and collective self-esteem. The project transformed the classroom into a space of shelter and safety from the emotional storms of fear, anxiety, and bias. It engaged students in an exploration of truths germane to their personal and collective identities.

James White (1997) observes that when people feel imprisoned by grief, they tend to role-play outer lives that they believe adhere to a "functional" life. Unfortunately, the inauthentic nature of playing a role too often fortifies and expands spaces of silence. Cochran and Claspell (1987) describe how grieving individuals often project a pretense of carrying on with routines and daily interactions despite the emptiness or despair they might be feeling inside:

> Like an actor playing a role, a person pretends in carrying on one's life, feeling both "on stage" and as if in a façade of life. People who grieve become more or less adept at role playing… While role playing helps one stay functional it is also like a trap. (p. 72)

Tagore (1913/2011) uses the analogy of a seed to more closely examine the conflicts between one's *dharma* (genuine nature and destiny) and *avidya* (pretense of a life). While the former represents freedom, the latter embodies imprisonment. "The freedom of the seed," Tagore wrote, "is in the attainment of its *dharma*, its nature and destiny of becoming a tree; it is the non-accomplishment which is its prison" (p. 160). He advises that "we must rid ourselves of the *avidya*, our ignorance, and then our mind will find its freedom in the inner idea…. Let us pass through [this ignorance] to the idea which is emancipation" (p. 159).

Tagore's images have pedagogical import for today's educators. Consider, for instance, the dangers of students hiding their *dharma*, their authentic identities, because of a perceived urgency to assimilate within a dominate culture, or perhaps from fearing societal biases. For years while teaching in a community comprised primarily of first-generation Latinx students, I was saddened by students' reticence to speak in their native Spanish. Students showed a hesitation, even a discomfort, in referring to family customs or traditions. It was as if pieces of their *dharma* were being imprisoned.

There is much to be grieved here: The identities, values and beliefs of students can become like seeds kept out of the sun. I did not want my students to feel that they ought to suppress their language, history, and customs in order to somehow fit into an image of how they thought they should look, sound, and behave. I decided that as a learning community we needed to work at eradicating this cultural, historical, and linguistic *avidya*. I researched and organized a field trip to the National Mexican Fine Arts Museum in Chicago, Illinois, in the heart of a historically Latinx community.

As an educational experience, the outing surpassed my expectations. My students and I were immersed in a space that acknowledged and celebrated a variety of authentic Mexican traditions (art, music, poetry, storytelling). The featured exhibit celebrated *Dia de Muertos* (Day of the Dead) with a variety of intricately designed *ofrendas* (private altars). Museum docents and artists traced the history of this modern Mexican holiday back hundreds of years to the sacred Aztec festival honoring the dead. Each *ofrenda* was a testimonial to personal and collective memories of loved ones. Information was given and stories shared in both English and Spanish, and the students were encouraged to reply in either language. Eventually, most of the students were proudly conversing in Spanish. They became *my* teachers as they translated for me their discussion.

In the gift shop, a variety of indigenous artwork was available, including Mexican sugar skull sculptures (a representation of the belief that death is a continuation of the life cycle), handmade *picado* banners, and recordings of authentic Mexican music (i.e., *conjunto jarocho*, mariachi, *banda*). The students seemed to "come alive" in ways I had never seen. As they explored the gift shop, they began to share more stories and experiences that validated and celebrated their cultural and linguistic identities. Their *dharma* (true nature), which had been like a seed within them that was not allowed take root and grow, now began to sprout:

> Only when the tree begins to take shape do you see its *dharma* [its innermost true nature], and then you can affirm without doubt that the seed which has been wasted and allowed to rot in the ground has been thwarted in its *dharma*, in the fulfillment of its true nature. In the history of humanity we have known the living seed in us to sprout. (Tagore, 1913/2011, p. 160)

My students and I then shared lunch at a local Mexican restaurant where they continued to open up and share experiences and stories that celebrated their identities as Mexican-Americans. The students were beginning to step away from the role-play that had previously defined their outer lives. In other words, they were learning that it was safe, acceptable, and even honorable to freely express themselves—to be themselves. The experience became an annual event that grew in attendance each year as parents, family members, and neighbors were anxious to participate.

I came to understand that this excursion and all it represented were a critical cornerstone of my instruction. It embodied what Tagore (1913/2011) describes as education's potential to empower individuals (personally and collectively). It demonstrated the transformational nature of education in its capacity to "set yourselves free from the *avidya*; know your true soul and be saved from the grasp of the self which imprisons you" (p. 160). The students were learning to move forward from the *avidya* and were beginning to express their more authentic *dharma*.

Tagore (1907a/2011) writes that authentic growth and development happens from the inside out. But there are no comparable tools to measure or account for inner transformation. These areas adhere to the intrinsic worlds of the spirit, heart, and soul. Tagore urges educators to better understand education's capacity to help individuals create personal spaces of *ashram* within themselves:

> There is a difference between the outside world and the human world. The human world does not inform us of what is black and white and what is large and small. It tells us of what is dear and vile, what is beautiful and ugly, and what is good and bad in different ways. This human world has always flowed in our hearts. This stream is old and ever new. Through newer senses and newer perceptions, this age-old flow always assumes new forms. But how do we locate ourselves in this flow? (p. 156)

The September 11, 2001, terrorist attack that destroyed the Twin Towers in New York City and took the lives of thousands of people sent waves of fear, grief, uncertainty, and helplessness throughout the nation, the world—and my classroom. I was a middle school social studies teacher. On the day of the attack and for months afterward, Tagore's (1907a/2011) question echoed in my mind. As a person, a citizen, and a teacher, I struggled with how my students and I would make sense of an outer world that was suddenly unfamiliar, unpredictable, and frightening.

Reminiscent of Tagore's (1907a/2011) words, it felt as if "the world [became] another world in our mind" (p. 155). Our national identity and personal security were shattered. There was a great deal of grieving to be done. Sweeping feelings of loss, powerlessness, anger, and apprehension formed an existential blanket that shrouded us in *avidya*. How would we find ourselves in this darkness?

No matter how I attempted to explain events in a dispassionate, information-based manner, I understood clearly the anxiety, helplessness, and fear that simmered beneath. Since my college days I had always been inspired by the image of a teacher carrying a lamp of knowledge into the classroom. But now I became frustrated that despite my best efforts, I was unable to lead my students out of the darkness of the *avidya*.

In retrospect, I understand that I was misapplying the lamp of knowledge metaphor. As teacher, I needed to be more than the carrier of the lighted lamp; I needed to *be* the light, or at least the nurturer of the light:

The lamp contains its oil, which it holds securely in its close grasp and guards from the least loss…. But when lighted it finds its meaning at once; its relation with all things far and near is established, and it freely sacrifices its fund of oil to feed the flame. Such a lamp is our self. So long as it hoards its possessions it keeps itself dark, its conduct contradicts its true purpose. (Tagore, 1913, p. 161)

Although sharing information per newspapers and media outlets may have spoken to my students on a cognitive level, it did nothing to alleviate the *avidya* of their emotional, spiritual, and moral fears. The work of mourning could not be done exclusively on an intellectual level. Trying to provide answers when none existed was like trying to light a lantern without any oil in it. Facts and information would not free my students (or me) from our grief; only solace and compassion could.

I needed to find a path forward. I decided that each day we would dedicate time to reflect on a single visual image (i.e., photograph, artwork). Sometimes it was a picture direct from the day's newspaper, at other times it was an archived photograph (i.e., from the Holocaust or the Japanese World War II internment camps); one day it might be a work of sacred Islamic art, another day an ancient Hindi sculpture. The artwork brought its own kind of light into the classroom within which we could safely reflect on spiritual, emotional, and ethical issues. We no longer were searching for answers that could not be found due to the tumultuousness of the time. Instead, we were freed to share thoughts, feelings, and impressions that reflected how these events impacted our lives. Maggi Savin-Baden and Katherine Wimpenny (2014) observe that using art as inquiry "prompts students to question and critique rather than focus on attaining a "right" answer" (p. 4):

Arts-inquiring pedagogy focuses on higher order thinking in the context of exploring challenges and issues. It is often used to describe a form of learning where the students decide on their own questions and queries. (p. 6)

Instead of imposing information on the students, I allowed the art to create an environment wherein students (and I) were free to explore, interpret, ask questions, make connections, analyze, and—perhaps most importantly—express our feelings and impressions. By shining a light on visual artifacts and encouraging students to respond to the works, art became the teacher. Tagore (1913/2004) writes that "when [the lantern] finds illumination it forgets itself in a moment, holds the light high; and shares it with everything it has" (p. 161). The visual artifacts (i.e., photographs, paintings, sculptures) became the points of light needed to help disperse the emotional darkness of the *avidya*. I learned that "the lamp [or the teacher] must give up its oil to the light and thus set free the purpose it has been hoarding. This is emancipation" (p. 161).

Despite the emotional distress that followed the post-September 11 tragedy, or rather *because* of the distress, I believe that my understanding of what it means to be a teacher of *ashram* blossomed closer to what Tagore (1933/2004) describes:

[An environment where students and teachers] are daily growing towards the emancipation of their minds into the consciousness of the infinite, not through any process of teaching or outer discipline, but by the help of an unseen atmosphere of aspiration that surrounds the place. (p. 168)

The aspiration of bringing light to personal *avidya* affirms the transformative potential of teaching and learning. It evokes an educator's capacity to ultimately illuminate the spirit, heart, and soul of students.

VOICES OF GRIEVING

In 1913, Tagore received a Nobel Prize in Literature "because of his profoundly sensitive, fresh and beautiful verse, by which, with consummate skill, he has made his poetic thought, expressed in his own English words, a part of the literature of the West" (nobelprize. org). He soon became known as *viswa-kabi* (universal poet). His mystical and meditative poems demonstrate his efforts to "describe the indescribable" and express "the inexpressible" (Tagore, 1907a/2011, p. 157). As a curriculum for educators—and for all human beings—his poems describe matters critical to humanity's spirit, heart, and soul:

Dark nights of sorrow have come to my door / Again and again. / Its only weapons I saw—pain's distorted grimace and Fear's hideousness— / Its intention—to delude one in the darkness. ("Dark Nights of Sorrow," lines 1–5, Tagore, 1941/2011, p. 308)

Consider students (and/or teachers) experiencing such "dark nights of sorrow" as they grieve personal loss or emotional suffering. To what extent do we as teachers see, acknowledge, or understand such grieving and its impact on learning?

If it were only a question of grieving / Of glistening eyes and tears being shed, / Of pale lips, and a sad face— / You'd see the pain in me easily, / You'd read my thoughts instantly… But what if you don't understand me… / who could ever the whole comprehend? ("Unfathomable," lines 37–41, 47, 51, Tagore, 1893c/2011, pp. 236–237)

Tagore's poems teach that suppressing or denying grief and its emotional partners (i.e., pain, loneliness, sadness, anger) means ignoring major pieces of one's humanity. Otherwise indescribable hurts forage for expression, validation, and solace within his verse:

Clouds rumble; rain pours down incessantly. / I sit all alone on the shore, uncertainly…. No room on that small boat—no room at all! / My golden harvest was enough to make it full. / On this rainy day, as clouds all over me swirl / On the desolate riverbank I lie down forlorn— / All I had with that golden boat is gone! ("The Golden Boat," lines 1–2, 26–30, Tagore, 1893a/2011, pp. 228–229)

Is there any accounting for how grieving impacts learning or classroom engagement? To what extent do lesson plans continue on a linear trajectory without any concern being given to the inner needs and curiosities of the learners? In what ways do educators search for their students in terms of where they reside emotionally or spiritually? How often do classrooms embody an emotional and spiritual climate that resembles in tone the desolate riverbanks or forlorn shores Tagore describes?

Where is the humanity of our classroom life? What is the benefit of rising assessment scores at the expense of becoming emotionally isolated? What is the profit of increasing content knowledge while personal and collective values are disregarded in the process? Of information accumulated but empathy lost? Of meeting external goals and academic benchmarks but losing ourselves?

In addition to considering the individuality of students, it is equally important to respect the humanity of educators. How often do students see the reality or authenticity that lies beneath a teacher's professional façade? If students only perceive robot-like teachers dispensing information and directives and all that teachers see are students as receptacles for information, then what is education other than a disbursement and regurgitation of facts and figures? The transactional nature of this kind of exchange greatly reduces the potential for authentic relationships, discourse, and interactions. It increases the likelihood that we are headed toward the kinds of emotional desolation imagined in Tagore's poetry.

Tagore (1940/2011) expresses faith in humanity's resiliency. He wrote that a person's inner spirit is perpetually on a journey toward fulfillment. Even when life's course becomes marked by tragedy or grief, anger, loneliness, and desperation do not need to be stops of final destination.

The soul is the night's train / Setting forth.... / Flickering in the faint light, / It speeds past / Unknowable and unfamiliar stops / For some invisible destination. A pilgrim on a distant voyage, / in the mute night— / Where it will end / I can't comprehend. ("The Night Train," lines 1–2, 9–16, p. 303)

Imagine teachers and students as fellow travelers on this night train. Tagore believed that education has the potential to guide us toward pathways of sympathy and sunlight. These opportunities are squandered, however, when teaching and learning focus too narrowly on the intellect without recognizing and tending to emotional and spiritual growth and development. Tagore (1933/2004) wrote "we find that this education of sympathy is not only systematically ignored in schools, but it is severely repressed" (p. 142). He warns that if children had even a glimmer of understanding that their enthusiasm to learn and grow would soon be surrendered to the protocol and precepts of boards of education, they would think twice before starting out.

Tagore's words provide a critical lens through which to reflect on my teacher candidates anxious to begin their careers. Like the young children Tagore describes who are excited to begin their school journeys (anxious to learn and grow), senior student-teachers usually begin with enthusiasm and great aspirations. But they soon face an assortment of written licensure exams, bureaucratic protocol, and teaching demands that emphasize content over creativity and assessment scores over student engagement. Paraphrasing Tagore, I find that they are made to lose their passion for teaching to find a bagful of bureaucracy, uniform regulations, and pedagogical information instead. Had they known this, would they have thought twice before pursuing careers as educators?

Nevertheless, Tagore's poetic images also sew hope. He traces movements from loneliness to spaces of empathy and from places of anger or desperation to life-affirming perceptions and senses. Grief is not a destination but a critical piece of humanity's journey. Embedded throughout the journey are lessons of empathy, hope, and new beginnings.

This movement through grief is the explicit topic explored in "I Won't Let You Go!" (Tagore, 1893b/2011). Similar to his "Night Train" poem, the notion of a journey is central to this work that imagines a carriage transporting readers through an individual's inner experience of grief. As the narrator begins his journey, he grieves the loss of loved ones:

> The farther I go the more clearly I hear / Those poignant words "Won't let you go!" / From world's end to the blue dome of the sky / Echoes the eternal cry: "Won't let you go!" / Everything cries, "I won't let you go!" / Mother Earth too cries out to the tiny grass / it hugs on its bosom, "I won't let you go!" / Someone trying to snatch from darkness the flame of a dying lamp exclaims / A hundred times, "I won't let you go!" (Tagore, 1893b/2011, "I Won't Let You Go!," lines 99–108, p. 234)

These lines are reminiscent of Tagore's (1913/2011) lamp analogy. The lamp's flame represents a person's inner light that is threatened by the heaviness of grief. A period of *avidya* pervades as the narrator journeys through difficult times. The next portion of the (1893b/2011) poem conveys the depth of the narrator's grieving. The lines are at once universal and personal:

> Though sad-faced and in tears, / Its pride shattered at every step, / love refuses to accept defeat and cries out / In desperation "Won't let you go!" Defeated each time it blurts out, / "Can the one I love stay away? / Can anything in the universe compare in strength or be as boundless as my desire?" / And even as it proclaims proudly, / "Won't let you go!" the one it treasures is blown away instantly, like dust / Wafted by the arid wayward breeze. And then tears stream down its eyes. Like a tree / Uprooted, it collapses headfirst, humiliated. / And yet Love insists, "God keeps his Word." ("I Won't Let You Go!," lines 130–144, p. 235)

Tagore (1893b/2011) expresses the idea that external possessions, devices, or information cannot release *ashram* (light) into one's personal darkness. This is an intrinsic journey. It has more to do with a person's values, beliefs, and feelings than with the physical world. It is in this spirit that Tagore continues to use images of nature rather than scientific data points:

And so Love, / Undying, though weighed down by Death, / Pervades the universe, solemn-faced, / Full of fears, forever in a flutter and tears. / A weary hopefulness covers the world / Like a gray fog…. / Responding, / Listless Earth sits down in a paddy field / By the river's side, loosening her tresses / Flinging a golden scarf across her bosom that gleams in the golden sun. ("I Won't Let You Go!," lines 149–154, 164–168, pp. 235–236).

He describes hope as weary, but not destroyed. Gray fog is depicted less as a symbol of despair than as a blanket of hopefulness. The sun and scarf, both golden, are reminiscent of Tagore's (1933/2004) many references to light as a symbol of spiritual attainment. The image of "giving and gaining" is also relevant to the teacher-student relationship. At what point does a teacher's "giving" stop and his or her "gaining" begin? When does a student's "gaining" end and his or her "giving" begin? To what extent are they mutually reliant? These questions support Tagore's (1933/2004) later description of education as an endeavor wherein "children grow in their spirit along with their own teachers' spiritual growth" (p. 156).

In "The Fountain's Awakening," Tagore (1883/2011) further ponders how the light of hope and faith can emerge out of the darkness of one's mourning. The narrator describes an experience of emotional reawakening as he moves from the darkness of grief to the light of morning wherein "his heart suddenly stirs again" (p. 223). This awakening is not procured with information or some calculated set of external data because it is a transformation not of mind but of heart:

I'll stream down compassion / I'll smash this stony prison / Overflowing my banks I'll flood the world. Spreading passionately my song of deliverance / Letting my hair flow, gathering all fallen flowers, / And spreading rainbow-colored wings, I'll pour out my heart till the sun's rays start smiling. (Tagore, 1883/2011, "The Fountain's Awakening," lines 25–31, pp. 223–224)

The narrator is moving beyond the confining limits of his schooling to a space where his understanding of himself and his world is expanding and deepening. Similarly, Tagore (1933/2004) writes that in school he often felt "groaning under the suffocation of a nightmare" as if the "soul of my country that seemed to be struggling for its breath through me" (p. 158). He later reflects upon his own experience of inner awakening:

Thus when I turned back from the struggle to achieve results, from the ambition of doing benefits to others, and came to my innermost need, when I felt that living one's own life in truth is living the life of the world, then the unquiet atmosphere of the outward struggle cleared up and the power of the spontaneous creation found its way through the center of all things. (Tagore, 1933/2004, pp. 162–163)

Tagore's experiences as a student moved from the mundane to the sacred when he learned to prioritize creativity over explanation (Tagore, 1907b/2011, p. 154).

He reflected that "this world is more precious to the imaginative individual than the outside world.... The mind helps this world become more suitable for access into people's hearts" (pp. 155).

An educator's use of imagination and creativity is a testament to emotions and values which in many ways defy the restrictions and limitations that words impose. John Dewey (1934) wrote that creative arts have the unique capacity to simultaneously express, explore, and validate conditions of humanity in ways that science and the physical world cannot (p. 11). Douglas J. Simpson, Michael J. B. Jackson, and Judy C. Aycock (2005) expound on Dewey's thinking in ways that recall Tagore's words:

> Teachers as artists are engaged in activities that are designed to accomplish what they were previously incapable of doing and doing such for themselves and others.... Both the process and product of these activities must be life encouraging, enabling, enhancing, and enriching if they are genuinely artistic. (pp. 24–25)

Imagine the insights that could be attained when Dewey's notion of the teacher as artist is viewed through Tagore's language and images. I propose considering the following excerpt from *The Significance of Literature* (Tagore, 1907a/2011) through a Deweyan lens of education. To help accomplish this, I have exchanged Tagore's use of the word *author* with *teacher* and his use of *literature* with *education*. Hence, the significance of *education*:

> The human heart seeks to shape and express itself in [education]. This process has no end and is remarkably diverse. [Teachers] are mere instruments of this eternal struggle of humanity.... That song of the self, that creative impulse reverberating in tune with divine creation, is [education]. Inspired by the breath of the universe, the heart, like a reed, sings; [education] seeks to capture that tune. [Education] is not exclusively for the individual, nor is it for the [teacher or student] alone. [Education] is divine utterance. (p. 158)

In their research on how grief impacts people's lives, Cochran and Claspell (1987) describe how individuals of diverse ages, backgrounds, and cultures struggle in their search for a new way of understanding themselves and their place in a world without the loved one(s) for whom they grieve (p. 79). It is a journey of self rediscovery that emanates from within an individual's heart. Grief reminds us that some of the greatest questions humans beings can ask and some of the most important answers they seek will not be found in books, laboratories, or the Internet. Formal curricular disciplines, while pragmatic, do not inherently illuminate the intrinsic nature of a person's emotional, spiritual, and moral identity.

During periods of grief, there is a heightened urgency to question and explore deeper realities that underlie the experiences of the outer world. When sadness and despair threaten one's hopes, values, and beliefs, all the information and knowledge we've been schooled in are rendered meaningless unless they can help us imagine a path

29

forward and create a life that honors the past and aspires to the future. Grief reminds us that in many ways we are the artists of our lives. Within imagination and creativity lies our capacity to transform our work and our lives. We are called to imagine a life beyond grief. We are challenged to create pathways of hope and renewal.

Teachers and students are perpetually involved in the authorship of their own life stories. Fundamental to these experiences are the emotional and moral nuances embedded within them. Despite this, Kieran Egan (1986) points out that most models of teaching and learning prioritize the rational and cognitive while devaluing human emotions, values, and intentions (p. 29). In order for academic content to become emotionally and spiritually relevant, he advocates "for stories and against skill" (p. 113). Storytelling, Egan writes, has traditionally helped "shape the world's meanings for us" (p. 113). It follows then that stories can be powerful teaching tools to guide and instruct individuals as they compose the stories of their own lives. One way or another, grief is eventually a part of everyone's story and storytelling can be a powerful tool in understanding how grief influences the totality of a person's life.

An author's use of imagination and creativity is a testament to the emotions, beliefs, and values that in many ways defy the restrictions and limitations imposed by labels and cognitive categories. The remaining chapters specifically use works of fiction as the primary lens through which to better examine the complexities of grief and its impact on an individual's personal and professional identity. The literary texts validate imagination over information and affirm the affective power of creativity over facts. The characters, metaphors, and themes forge an introspective path toward what Dewey (1934) describes as "the deeper reality of the world in which we live our ordinary experiences" (p. 202).

TOPICS FOR REFLECTION

1. What is your reaction to Tagore's vision of classroom as an *ashram* (or sanctuary)? What qualities of *ashram* would you most like to see in your classroom or school? Pretend that you woke up one morning with magic powers. What kinds of things would you then use your magic wand to conjure up within your classroom or school to create your imagined *ashram*?

2. Where do you stand on Tagore's (1933/2004) notions that the purpose of education is to give individuals an understanding of the "unity of truth" (p. 153) and to create a path toward a "freedom of mind" (p. 158)? Can you reflect on experiences you have had (as a teacher or a student) that touch on these ideals?

3. To what extent are teachers so focused on what and how they are teaching that the "why's" of teaching get overlooked? How relevant is this question to your daily work as an educator? Is such a consideration rare or ordinary between you and your peers or administrators? If the question were raised at a professional development session, how do you think it would be received? What kinds of issued or criticisms do you suspect individuals would voice?

4. Have you ever imagined your career as a kind of *personal and professional journey*? How might this perspective alter your outlook and daily routines? Imagine three lists of words that respectively describe your journey's past, present, and future. What on the list surprises you, disappoints you, inspires you, or perhaps enlightens you?

5. In what ways were you prepared emotionally, intellectually, and spiritually for being a teacher? How might you have been better prepared for the early chapters of your career? What resources would have been useful to sustain you during the middle chapters of your career?

6. How often have you felt more like a teaching machine, robotically following protocol and dispersing information, than a flesh-and-blood individual interacting with your students? To what extent does your response to this question align with your teaching philosophy? In what ways does your response address the expectations you once held as a person pursuing education as a career?

7. Reflect on lessons, activities, or specific classroom moments that you feel truly help your students learn to make sense of their world? Or that helped you make further sense of *your* world? How might educational systems, curriculum planners, or local school administrators support or nurture these kinds of meaning-making moments?

8. Have you or someone you know been personally impacted by gun violence or school shootings? How reasonable—or humane—is it to expect teachers to separate their sympathy, compassion, and grief from their interactions and discourse with students?

   How realistic—or developmentally appropriate—is it to expect students to set aside their grief, fear, and anger long enough to learn new pieces of information that they will be responsible for per written assessments? What kinds of resources or supports might help schools address the emotional and social impact of these issues and concerns?

9. To what extent are the social outcries of children (and their families) silenced? How might educational systems address these kinds of concerns in meaningful ways?

10. In your experience, in what ways and to what extent have teachers seen, acknowledged, or tried to address the grieving of students? What is your understanding of how personal and/or collective grieving impacts learning or classroom engagement? How can lesson plans, despite their linear trajectory, take into account the intrinsic aspects of the learner? In what ways might teachers locate students emotionally and spiritually?

11. To what extent or how often do you think students see beyond your teacher façade to the "real you" beneath? Are there times when perhaps all they see is

some kind of "teaching machine"? Brainstorm the pros and cons of heightening the humanity of a teacher's work and identity. What would this look, sound, and feel like—for you and for your students?

12. Consider Tagore's (1933/2004) words:

> If [young children] had any idea that they were about to open their eyes to the sunlight, only to find themselves in the hands of the education department till they should lose their freshness of mind and keenness of sense, they would think twice before venturing upon their career. (pp. 150–151)

Where in this image might veteran teachers see themselves? What are the kinds of circumstances that could increase the likelihood of educators losing "their freshness of mind and keeness of sense"? Brainstorm resources that could help prevent this from happening.

How many students during their early and middle school years experience injury to their "freshness of mind and keenness of sense"? How might this prevented?

13. Have you ever wondered in what ways you have emotionally or morally influenced the lives of your students? How have your students impacted *you*? Try to recall moments or experiences in which students have gifted you with insights and/or provacative thoughts that have remained with you long after the students have moved on.

14. How do you feel about John Dewey's notion of "teachers as artists"? How important are creativity, imagination, ingenuity, and resourcefulness to your work?

Suppose that beings from another planet have observed your school in order to understand what a typical teacher on Earth looked, acted, and sounded like. What might they see or hear that would lead them to conclude that teachers are artists? What are some of the other conclusions they might infer (i.e., teachers as military generals, as zoo keepers, as magicians, as miracle workers)?

15. Imagine you have been transported to an alternate universe and find yourself as a defendant in a courtroom. Consider the following charges:

An "education of sympathy is not only systematically ignored in schools, it is severely repressed" (Tagore, 1933/2004, p. 124). You are being charged with suppressing an "education of sympathy." How do you plead? What evidence will you offer in your defense?

"We are made to lose our world to find a bagful of information instead" (Tagore, 1933/2004, p. 143). You are charged with overloading students' minds with "bagsful of information."

"We have got into the habit of covering the windows of our minds with their [textbook] pages, and plasters of book phrases have stuck into our mental skin, making it impervious of all direct touches of truth" (Tagore, 1933/2004, p. 173). You are being charged with the following acts of deliberate and willful vandalism: (1) covering up the windows of children's minds with an over-abundance of information and (2) plastering over students' emotions with so many layers of "mental skin" that students have become dangerously "impervious of all direct touches of truth."

How do you plead? If the penalties for being found guilty were severe, to what extent would you continue to defend your mission and vision of teaching?

ILLUSIONS, TRUTHS, AND TEARS

Orlando, *Virginia Woolf*

Grieving as a teacher's curriculum is not an expected topic in a teacher preparation program; nor, I suppose, is it an anticipated item on a school's professional development schedule. Similarly, John Dewey's (1934) idea of teachers as artists is generally not, I imagine, regarded as an educational priority by most boards of education. Instead, teacher training mainly focuses on strategies and materials designed to help students procure mastery of specific and measurable cognitive skills. As Tagore (1933/2004) warned, however, if we "devote our sole attention to giving children information… we are accentuating a break between the intellectual, the physical, and the spiritual life" (p. 154).

Considering the personal, emotional, and ethical dimensions of teaching and learning, Eliot Eisner (1979) identifies what he calls the four senses of the art of teaching: infusing teaching with grace and beauty; enhancing a lesson's qualitative tone, climate, and tempo; relying on organic, spontaneous, and authentic contingencies; and deferring to creative, innovative, and original thinking (pp. 154–155). These descriptors focus on teaching as an art versus a dissemination of content information. The criteria Eisner lays out depends less on prescribed lessons and measureable outcomes than on shared experiences and reflection.

The current organizational structures of education in the United States largely rely on standardized and grade/age level designations. The scope and sequence of content are neatly laid out in an orderly linear and sequential manner. Consequently, the intellectual life of a classroom is regimented according to these externally-imposed structures. By contrast, the emotional, spiritual, and ethical lives of students are unlikely to be orderly, linear, or easily categorized.

Virginia Woolf's (1928) novel *Orlando* explores human experiences that defy categorization and standardization. The novel describes the central character's journey of grief. Orlando struggles to engage in an outer life wherein his inner beliefs, values, and perceptions are evolving beyond what can be rationalized or explained with external data alone. He learns that understanding one's inner life requires imagination, original thinking, and authentic experiences.

This chapter uses *Orlando* as a means to reflect on a teacher's (and students') inner growth and development. As elementary and high school teaching becomes increasingly focused on cognitive/intellectual information and tasks, to what extent will issues of the heart, spirit, and soul be ignored, denied, or suppressed?

© KONINKLIJKE BRILL NV, LEIDEN, 2020 | DOI: 10.1163/9789004422506_003

Orlando's journey of grief leads to an understanding that "where the Mind is biggest, the Heart, the Senses, Magnanimity, Charity, Tolerance, Kindliness, and the rest of them scarcely have room to breathe" (Woolf, 1928, p. 213). Despite the quality and quantity of knowledge he possessed, Orlando's lack of spiritual awareness and emotional understanding became like the absence of oxygen—he was suffocating.

Without considering the intrinsic aspects of our personal and professional lives, teachers and students are similarly vulnerable to personal suffocation. Examining *Orlando* (1928) informs our understanding of pedagogical practice that reaches beyond intellectual aspirations. It reveals ways in which teaching and learning have the capacity to not only build cognitive intelligence but to nourish deeper insight into realities embedded within an individual's heart, spirit, and soul. In this way, Woolf's novel demonstrates ways in which teachers can evolve from being disseminators of information to nurturers of life.

ILLUSION OF TIME AND SPACE

A shifting of "the whole boundary and circumference of a living person." (Woolf, 1928, p. 73)

Throughout *Orlando,* Woolf (1928) demonstrates that a person's inner life cannot be understood or explained per external measurements or standardized expectations. She explains that "time, unfortunately, though it makes animals and vegetables bloom and fade with amazing punctuality has no such simple effect upon the mind of man" (p. 98):

The mind of man, moreover, works with equal strangeness upon the body of time. An hour, once it lodges in the queer element of the human spirit, may be stretched to fifty or a hundred times its clock length; on the other hand, an hour may be accurately represented on the timepiece of the mind by one second. This extraordinary discrepancy between time on the clock and time in the mind is less known than it should be and deserves fuller investigation. (p. 98)

In their professional lives, even teachers are categorized within linear demarcations (i.e., years of experience, number of degrees earned, tenure tracks, length of resume). External classifications are used to designate an individual's place along an anticipated continuum of professional expertise (i.e., veteran versus novice, master-teacher versus provisionary, probationary versus tenured). Woolf (1928) reminds us that although these sorts of numerically-driven categories account for a variety of external criteria, they are unreliable in capturing internal growth and development.

By the second chapter of *Orlando,* the narrator reports that Orlando has endured seven calendar days of grieving. Woolf (1928) points out, however, that seven days of measured time in our outer, physical world could represent months and/or years of one's inner life:

In such thinking (or by whatever name it should be called) he spent months and years of his life. It would be no exaggeration to say that he would go out after breakfast a man of thirty and come home to dinner a man of fifty-five at least. Some weeks added a century to his age, others no more than seconds at most. (p. 99)

Consider the third grader who leaves school a student of eight. Perhaps that evening her sibling is the victim of a gang shooting, the kind of random act of violence frequently reported in daily news reports. Despite her chronological age, she is likely to be returning to class the next day as an intrinsically grieving fifty-five-year-old. Imagine the emotional disconnect when her teacher tries cognitively relating to an eight-year-old while just beneath the student's physical surface is an emotional torrent of grief and fear as if she had emotionally aged overnight with the speed of what Woolf calls a "gnat-winged fly" (Woolf, 1928, p. 99).

Orlando demonstrates the importance of learning to see beyond external measurements and facades. Imagine a middle schooler who is dismissed from class Friday ostensibly a student of fourteen. Perhaps he is living with a terminally ill parent whose condition deteriorates over the weekend. Despite his outward appearance, he may be returning to school on Monday morning a grieving seventy-year-old trapped underneath his early adolescent appearance.

Of the hundreds of middle school students I have taught and the many teachers I have worked with, I can assert with the wisdom of hindsight that I have had occasion to interact with many individuals whose physical years did not align to their emotional age. For example, I recall a grieving *twelve/forty-year-old* student who lost both parents over the course of two years—one by accident, the other due to terminal illness; an emotionally distraught *thirteen/fifty-year-old* boy whose sister was struck by an industrial vehicle while crossing the street to the public library (while he paused to speak with a friend); and a *thirty-five/ten-year-old* veteran teacher who decided to set up makeshift shrines throughout his room honoring his recently deceased father.

This kind of existential landscape Woolf proposes removes the validity of Time and Space as reliable measures. Glancing at class portraits, I wonder how often people see the layers of inner realities that lie beneath the one-dimensional veneer of photographed faces. Reflecting on the many students and peers I have interacted with over the years, I wonder how much grief and suffering went unnoticed. Oh, dear. How many students might have benefited from my acknowledging and responding to their struggles to find solace and to relearn their place in the world?

All we are told of Orlando's early life is that words and relationships "without meaning were as wine to him" (Woolf, 1928, p. 57). The nature of the life-changing tragedy he suffers is ambiguous. The narrator reveals only that after a "disastrous winter which saw the frost, the flood, the deaths of many thousands" came "the complete downfall of Orlando's hopes" (p. 65):

Orlando retired to his great house in the country and there lived in complete solitude. One June morning he failed to rise at his usual hour, and when his groom went to call him he was found fast asleep. Nor could he be awakened. He lay as if in a trance, without perceptible breathing… he did not wake, take food, or show any sign of life for seven whole days. (p. 66)

Orlando is suffering in spirit and soul. Concerns regularly associated with daily living are suspended within grief's emotional stronghold. Medical efforts to help him heal are ineffective. After all, while remedies address his physical symptoms, they ignore the inner maladies of his anguish:

The doctors were hardly wiser then than they are now, and after prescribing rest and exercise, starvation and nourishment, society and solitude, that he should lie in bed all day and ride forty miles between lunch and dinner, together with the usual sedatives and irritants, diversified, as the fancy took them… they left him to himself. (p. 67)

Orlando is experiencing what Thomas Attig (1996) calls "the poignancy of disruption of life entailed by loss and on the daunting challenges persons address as they cope" (p. 7). After having spent more than twenty years teaching, writing, and researching grief and bereavement, Attig has come to understand grieving as a centrally important human experience that challenges individuals to relearn how to behave and think in an outer world that has become unfamiliar. Living with grief involves reeducating oneself on the beliefs and values that shape his or her reality (pp. viii–ix).

In despair, Orlando is left alone to relearn his personal identity within an outer world he longer recognizes. While grieving, he experiences acute loneliness and isolation:

"I am alone," said Orlando, aloud since there was no one to hear. That silence is more profound after noise still wants the confirmation of science…. [His] loneliness is apparent. (Woolf, 1928, p. 184)

Through her prose, author Virginia Woolf lays bare the inner landscape of Orlando's grief. An individual's spiritual and emotional loneliness, however, often goes unnoticed to the outer world. Imagine a classroom filled with students busily engaged in an assortment of learning activities. How would a teacher know if one of the students were emotionally suffering on the inside? How important would it be to know? These kinds of considerations speak to the potential of the teacher-student relationship as something much more than impersonal transactions of information or scripted discourse focused on academic skills. Nevertheless, except for concerns related to cognitive benchmarks and classroom management, how many students, like Orlando, are left to themselves?

Similar concerns affect teachers as well. Can you imagine a classroom filled with students in which the teacher standing at the center of the activity is nonetheless silently feeling emotionally isolated? He or she may have returned to the classroom looking like the same thirty-five-year-old who was standing there yesterday.

Internally, however, the teacher may be experiencing the depths of fear and anger with the helplessness of a grieving five-year-old child.

Grief can do these things. Although there are no fast answers or simple solutions, consider the capacity of teaching and learning to foster communities wherein students and teachers collectively work to better understand themselves and each other. In addition to learning to read the words printed on paper (or displayed on an electronic tablet or computer screen), imagine taking the time to learn to read each other. Instead of classroom instruction that prioritizes dispensing and receiving information, to what extent can you conceive of educational practice committed to Eisner's (1979) vision of teaching and learning that values and even prioritizes grace, beauty, and intuition (pp. 154–155)?

There existed no such community of support to which Orlando could turn. The narrator reports that Orlando "worn out by the extremity of his suffering, died for a week, and then come back to life again" (Woolf, 1928, p. 67):

> But if sleep it was, of what nature, we can scarcely refrain from asking, are such sleeps as these?... Are we so made that we have to take death in small doses daily or we could not go on with the business of living? And then what strange powers are these that penetrate our most secret ways and change our most treasured possessions without our willing it? (p. 67)

Woolf's referencing events that "seem likely to cripple life forever" and that are destined to become our "most galling memories" (p. 67) may at first appear overly melodramatic for a discussion of classroom life. And yet, on Tuesday, April 20, 1999, at a high school in Columbine, Colorado, Woolf's surreal images became all too real. Early afternoon news outlets reported an incident that immediately "penetrated our most treasured possession without our willing it" (Woolf, 1928, p. 67). In the high school, an active but unidentified gunman was on targeting students, staff, and faculty. The safety, security, and sanctity of the school were being violated in real time in an almost surreal event that "seem[ed] likely to cripple life forever" (Woolf, 1928, p. 67).

At 2 p.m. that afternoon, near the end of the instructional day, instructors in my school (myself included) received a brief, ambiguous, and disturbing memo from administrators that news outlets were reporting a serious occurrence at a high school in Colorado. Without any other details, we teachers were directed to expedite all end-of-day classroom activities and dismiss students in as timely a fashion as safety allowed. All after-school activities and sports were canceled. School grounds were to be cleared as quickly as possible. Faculty was directed to leave immediately afterward. This occurred before the era of smart phones and instant personal electronic communication. Hence, my middle school students and I had no idea what was happening.

Over the next few hours, widespread news reports confirmed that two teens at a Colorado high school embarked on a shooting rampage. Thirteen people were killed and more than twenty others wounded before the shooters took their own lives. Teenage witnesses recounted scenes—"the most galling memories"—(Woolf, 1928, p. 67) of bullets, blood, gunfire, and panic throughout the school, including the hallways, cafeteria, library, gymnasium, and parking lot. For the students, their families, faculty, and the surrounding community, life would never be the same.

The boundaries of grief and loss exceeded geographic boundaries. An entire nation (U.S.A.) mourned the deaths and the passing away of its previously-held (and unquestioned) belief that schools were safe spaces. Issues concerning gun control, mental health, local security protocol, and bullying swiftly erupted into public consciousness and conversation. Returning to my classroom the next day was like entering an entirely new space. In an instant, the world had abruptly changed. The import and gravity of these events could not be left on the doorstep of the school. It was as if fears of uncertainty were emitting "a luster, an incandescence" of "the ugliest and basest" kind (Woolf, 1928, p. 67).

How would students, teachers, families, and communities learn new ways of living in the aftermath of this tragedy? I can attest to feeling a tangible sense of fear, uncertainty, and confusion in the classroom (among students and faculty) in the months following the Columbine High School tragedy. I remember planning lessons focused on current events with ample time allotted for questions and discussion. It was during these discourse sessions that students and I acknowledged our sense of helplessness and vulnerability.

This experience of collective grieving also taught me the value of honoring classroom silences. My students and I would found solace just being together and sharing space as human beings trying to grieve and support one another. Attig (1996) warns that children are especially vulnerable to the impact of grieving:

> Unprecedented feelings frighten some and leave them at a loss as to what to do or say.... Loss often disrupts or undermines the development of self-confidence, self-esteem, and identity. Some feel helpless and need to learn that they have choices in response to choiceless events.... Children lack models for, and need guidance and support in finding, appropriate things to do in the mourning period and in putting together new life patterns. (p. 91)

News reports and public officials externalized the tragedy by turning to legislative issues (i.e., gun control, mental health). School administrators directed teachers and students to resume normal instruction and activities while reassuring parents that security protocol would be closely examined. But as a teacher during these days, I can attest that these public gestures did not address the individual and collective fear and uncertainty that now permeated the lives of students, faculty, community, and families. Although the efforts attempted to provide external comfort and reassurance, they did nothing to heal the emotional and spiritual wounds incurred by the tragedy.

Despite calls to "return to normal," educators, students, and entire communities had awakened to a new world in which so much of what had been taken for granted was now in doubt. Although outer routines and external protocols of school life resumed, they could not hide or dispel the fear and uncertainty that existed beneath.

Similarly, after Orlando arises from the slumber of his grief, it is not his physical needs (i.e., being hungry or thirsty) that concern him. He awakes instead with acute awareness of inner needs—those of his spirit and soul:

> What the future might bring, Heaven only knew. Change was incessant, and change perhaps would never cease. High battlements of thought; habits that had seemed durable as stone went down like shadows at the touch of another mind and left a naked sky and fresh stars twinkling in it.... And in this new power of bearing an argument in mind and continuing it with someone who was not there to contradict she showed again the development of her soul. (Woolf, 1928, p. 176)

Orlando demonstrates that "relearning the world is a multifaceted transitional process" (Attig, 1996, p. 107). Grieving teaches that although a person's life might look the same on the outside, its inner landscape often tells a different story:

> As we grieve, we appropriate new understandings of the world and ourselves within it. We also become different in the light of the loss as we assume a new orientation to the world. (Attig, 1996, p. 107)

Orlando comes to realize that the safety and security he previously felt were in many ways only the appearances of safety and security. External comforts and reassurances did not help ease his inner suffering. His former existence had been disrupted by the nightmarish dream-like landscape of his grief. Woolf portrays this as a confrontation between phantoms of external reality versus the authentic spirit of intrinsic truth. Orlando's despair is expressed through a cacophony of existential trumpeters demanding, "Truth, come out from your horrid den" (Woolf, 1928, p. 136):

> We are, therefore, now left entirely alone in the room with the sleeping Orlando and the trumpeters. The Trumpeters, ranging themselves side by side in order, blow one terrific blast:—"THE TRUTH!" at which Orlando woke. (p. 137)

Orlando awakens to an understanding that there are alternative pathways through which to understand one's world besides the physical paths of the five senses. He boldly proclaims that "illusions are to the soul what atmosphere is to the earth" (Woolf, 1928, p. 203). He acknowledges that his illusions (comprised of thought, impression, feeling, and intuition), although not facts in the traditional scientific sense, are truths nevertheless:

> Roll up that tender air and the plant dies, the color fades. The earth we walk on is a parched cinder.... It is marl we tread and fiery cobbles scorch our feet. By the truth we are undone. Life is a dream. 'Tis the waking that kills us. He who robs us of our dreams [our illusions] robs us of our life. (p. 203)

To what extent are the deepest parts of our humanity buried beneath similar veils of reality? To what extent can we ascertain what is truth amid an accumulation of information, facts, and figures? During Orlando's journey of grief, he has a prophetic dream of three mysterious sisters who remove the veil of the outer world to reveal emotional and spiritual realities beneath:

> With gestures of grief and lamentation the three sisters [purity, chastity, and modesty] now join hands and dance slowly, tossing their veils and singing as they go: "Truth, come not out from your horrid den. Hide deeper, fearful Truth. For you flaunt in the brutal gaze of the sun things that were better unknown and undone; you unveil the shameful; the dark you make clear." (Woolf, 1928, p. 136)

These three sisters embody the depths of one's humanity. Because their truths (immeasurable and unseen) are separate from the outer world, they are often overlooked. Instead, external constructs (routines, profit and loss spreadsheets, etc.) help structure and organize our lives. When tragedy or loss occurs, however, the journey of grief leads us to these three sisters. They open the metaphorical (and metaphysical) doors to the emotional and spiritual layers of inner realities normally hidden beneath the order and method of our outer existence.

The three sisters are spiritual entities that defy our linear understanding of space and time. No X-ray or MRI technology will detect them. After all, there are no tools of measurement or scientific gauges to account for matters of the heart or soul: "the poet's then is the highest office of all. His words reach where others fall short" (Woolf, 1928, p. 173). These sisters are of a poetic nature. Of a poet's ability to articulate an understanding of humanity's inner life, recall this Woolf excerpt:

> Here is someone who does not do the thing for the sake of doing; nor looks for looking's sake; here is someone who believes in neither sheep-skin nor basket; but sees something else. (Woolf, 1928, p. 146)

The rational outer world is composed of facts and information that help us understand external realities. But our inner lives are not governed or explained by the same criteria or means. The three sisters embody an inner world that lies beyond the constraints of rational or scientific laws. Of this world, "thoughts are divine" (Woolf, 1928, p. 173) and, as Orlando learns, "one can believe entirely, perhaps, in what one cannot see" (Woolf, p. 198).

Whereas facts and information are externally generated from the natural world, an individual's beliefs and values are generated from within. Physical laws (i.e., gravity, photosynthesis, electromagnetism) do not apply to emotional and spiritual truths. *Orlando* suggests a tier of pedagogical possibilities that emerge from the inside out. Public events (i.e., school shootings, terrorist attacks) and private ones (i.e., death of a loved one, passing away of beliefs previously taken for granted) often leave individuals searching for emotional comfort and spiritual solace which science cannot provide.

Emotional and spiritual truths lie deep within our humanity and therefore cannot be detected beneath the lens of a microscope. These are the truths that the three sisters summon: "Truth, come... out from your horrid den.... The dark you make clear" (Woolf, 1928, p. 136). Woolf tells us that "the development of [Orlando's] soul" (p. 176) depended on his "tearing down high battlements of though and habits that had seemed durable as stone" (p. 176). Orlando's grief is teaching him that in order to understand what is most worthwhile in his life, he needs to search *within himself.*

This question of "what is worthwhile" carries with it critical educational import. Accordingly, William H. Schubert (1986) proposes it as a fundamental curriculum question. He asks educators to look beyond the surface of their work toward the values, beliefs, aspirations, and challenges that lie at its core:

> What knowledge is most worthwhile? Why is it worthwhile? How is it acquired or created? These are three of the most basic curriculum questions. They are the "bottom line" of all activities commonly associated with educational theory and practice. All of the educational research, all of the debate by school district committees, all of the financial planning... and all of the activities engaged in by students are for naught if they are not infused with these fundamental questions. Without direct consideration of *what* is worthwhile to know and its correlates of *why* and *how*, the foregoing activities are devoid of meaning, purpose, and direction. (p. 1)

EXTERNAL FACTS, INTRINSIC TRUTHS

Nothing is any longer one thing. (Woolf, 1928, p. 305)

Orlando's grief, which initially turned his "rhapsody to sluggishness," eventually opened within him "something intricate and many-chambered, which one must take a torch to explore" (Woolf, 1928, p. 175). Woolf compares grief's sluggishness to being carried away on a "little boat climbing through the white arch of a thousand deaths" (p. 322). Despite the emotional and spiritual gravity evoked by these images (or perhaps because of them), Orlando observes, "I am about to understand" (p. 322). He is coming to realize that there is more to reality than what his eyes report.

As Orlando now focuses on his emotions and inner grief, he becomes less restricted by confinements of outwardly imposed labels and classifications. The more deeply grief is embraced, the more external measures and outer appearances go by the way of "the white arch of a thousand deaths" (Woolf, 1928, p. 322). Orlando is learning that physical facts do not always align with internal truths. He begins to question external facts and scientifically-imposed categorizations to which he had previously given little or no thought.

Acknowledging life's ambiguities includes questioning the uncertainties of gender as narrowly defined by binary constructs. As he begins to see that "nothing [including gender] is any longer one thing" (Woolf, 1928, p. 305), Orlando considers the dual realities of gender: "His form combined in one the strength of a man and a woman's grace" (p. 138). From this point in the narrative, Woolf (1928) primarily refers to Orlando as female. Moving forward, I will use the first-person pronoun *s/he* to refer to both genders at the same time.

Daniel Chandler (2002) uses a Saussurean model of linguistics to argue that the language we use to classify and order our world "does not 'reflect' reality but rather *constructs* it. [Hence] we can use language to say what isn't in the world, as well as what is" (p. 28). Following this thinking in terms of the arbitrariness of external labels, Woolf (1928) writes that "in every human being a vacillation from one sex to the other takes place":

> Often it is only the clothes that keep the male or female likeness, while underneath the sex is the very opposite of what it is above. Of the complications and confusions which thus result everyone has had experience. (p. 189)

Woolf is ahead of her time. The idea that gender defies simple classification is now receiving the larger public's attention. For example, eighty-six years after *Orlando* was published, Ritch Savin-Williams (2017) interviewed hundreds of young men and identified a wide spectrum of gender self-identification that ranged from male to mostly male to slightly male. He poses the question: "Given that *mostly straight* is the fastest growing sexual orientation identity today, who knows how many sexually and romantically fluid young men there are?" (Savin-Williams, 2017, p. 205).

Questioning one's previously unchallenged understanding of his or her identity, of which gender is a significant component, is part of what Attig (1996) calls grief's "multi-faceted transitional process" (p. 107). He asserts that "relearning the world is not a matter of *learning information about the world* but *learning how to be and act in the world*" (p. 107):

> As we relearn, we adjust emotional and other psychological responses and postures. We transform habits, motivations, and behaviors. We find new ways to meet biological needs. We reshape our interactions and connections with others. And we change understandings and interpretations and alter spiritual perspectives. Relearning is thus holistic. Our grieving is organic, and we experience it organically. (p. 108)

Left to her grief, Orlando's "visible world is obscured for a time" (Woolf, 1928, p. 323). S/he is free to examine the thoughts "at the back of her brain (which is the part furthest from sight)" which "dwell in darkness so deep that what they are we scarcely know. She now looked down into this pool or sea in which everything is reflected" (p. 323). Orlando's previous understanding of life, which relied solely on the outer physical world, now dramatically expands:

> In Orlando's eyes—the thing one is looking at becomes, not itself, but another Thing, which is bigger and much more important and yet remains the same thing. If one looks at the Serpentine in this state of mind, the waves soon become just as big as the waves on the Atlantic; the toy boats become indistinguishable from ocean liners. (Woolf, 1928, p. 286)

Here again Woolf (1928) challenges readers to look beyond externally-imposed classifications of time and space. For instance, at one point, Orlando "turned back to the first page [of her journal] and read the date, 1586, written in her own boyish hand. She had been working on it for close on three hundred years now" (p. 236). As with Orlando's ambiguous gender, Woolf declares that Orlando "need neither fight her age, nor submit to it; she was of it, yet remained herself" (p. 266). Woolf comments that "it is an open question in what sense Orlando can be said to have existed at the present moment" (p. 307).

Whereas categories and tools for measuring time are precise and irrefutable per the external world, Woolf (1928) asks readers to consider "this extraordinary discrepancy between time on the clock and time in the mind" (p. 98). Orlando is discovering that the laws of the physical world may not align to the wisdom of her heart. S/he is beginning to ascertain that there is more to truth than can be understood by our physical senses alone. In other words, s/he is learning to see and feel with her heart.

Woolf describes Orlando's lifestyle prior to her emotional breakdown as one marked by wealth and privilege. Orlando's reality was informed and defined by her possessions (including fine china and linen, houses, menservants, exotic carpets, horses, items of gold and silver). Once she experiences deep grief, however, the material articles offer Orlando no solace. After s/he boldly calls for truth to "come out from your horrid den" (p. 136), s/he begins for the first time in her life to see reality beneath the gilded surfaces.

The opulence of Orlando's home had become "haunted every day and night by phantoms of the foulest kind" (Woolf, 1928, p. 118). Beneath the luxurious veneer of her linens, for instance, s/he now saw the hands of the poor and underprivileged child laborers who produced them. S/he now saw beneath the shiny gold and silver surfaces of her jewelry and grieved for the indigenous peoples from whose raided lands the items were stolen.

Orlando felt as though s/he had previously been suffering from a kind of disease that caused an inner blindness. S/he explained that "it was the fatal nature of this disease to substitute a phantom for reality" (Woolf, 1928, p. 74). Outward opulence had so captivated Orlando that s/he mistook its veneer for reality. The wealth and extravagance that had surrounded her privileged life was a kind of veil that, like a phantom, became a drape that rendered the inner truths and realities that lay beneath it invisible. Now "her eyes [were] bright as lamps" (p. 268):

> Everything was partly something else, and each gained an odd moving power from this union of itself and something not itself so that with this mixture of truth and falsehood her mind became like a forest in which things moved; lights and shadows changed, and one thing became another. (p. 323)

Orlando is learning that much of what s/he had assumed to be truths in her life were merely illusions of truth. S/he compares the deception to having been cast beneath a spell of enchantment:

The truth would seem to be—if we dare use such a word in such a connection—that all these groups of people lie under an enchantment. The hostess is our modern Sibyl. She is a witch who lays her guests under a spell. In this house they think themselves happy; in that witty; in a third profound. It is all illusion... but as it is notorious that illusions are shattered by conflict with reality, so no real happiness, no real wit, no real profundity are tolerated where the illusion prevails. (Woolf, 1928, pp. 199–200)

With her inner eye, the mythological Sibyl sees what others do not. Her visions reveal inner realities and truths that normally reside beneath external facts and beliefs. According to ancient Greek mythology, Sibyl was an oracle (*orare*, to speak) who, when enveloped within a magic sleep, would repeat mystic words of prophesy revealed by Mother Earth (D'Aulaire, 1962, p. 42). The Sibyl's words defied the realities of the outer world and, consequently, frightened her visitors. She spoke of apocalyptic images and cryptic symbols (Dibbley, 1993) that stripped away the surface layers of the physical that people relied on to feel secure and safe in their lives. Woolf (1928) observes that many individuals would sooner live under a spell of enchantment where they could "think themselves happy" (Woolf, 1928, p. 199) than "believe entirely in what one cannot see" (p. 198).

Attig (1996) observes that most individuals "live life, for the most part, straightforwardly, not self reflectively" (p. 106). The same can be said about Orlando—until grief interrupted her life. Attig continues that "bereavement challenges us to relearn virtually all elements of our worlds as we experience them... Losses transform the world as we experience it, sometimes pervasively. Coming to terms with the changes requires that we relearn the world" (p. 106). Orlando once believed that the outer beauties displayed throughout her home helped give her life meaning. She is now understanding that despite the shine and sparkle of the gold and silver surfaces, they were, in truth, not intrinsically worthwhile:

Vainly, it seemed, he had furnished his house with silver and hung the walls with arras.... Thus realizing that his home was uninhabitable, and that steps must be taken to end the matter instantly, [he left]. (Woolf, 1928, p. 118)

Orlando is reassessing and relearning what makes her life genuinely worthwhile. What's worth thinking? What's worth knowing? What's worth considering? These questions recall Schubert's (1986) curriculum questions: What knowledge is most worthwhile? Why is it worthwhile? At what point should an educator's emphasis on *student learning* also include considerations of *relearning*? The pedagogical aspects of relearning how students (and teachers) see themselves and how they understand the world around them are critical to what Attig (1996) describes as "establishing a new integrity in our pattern of caring involvement" (p. 107).

To what extent do educators distinguish between learning information about the world versus reflecting on their understanding of themselves and their world? In other words, in what ways are we teaching "straightforwardly, not self-reflectively"

(Attig, 1996, p. 106). Schools are efficient at measuring a teacher's proficiency at teaching facts, figures, and information (the basis of most curricular expectations). Orlando speaks to a different criteria: In what ways are schools uncovering veils of illusion and leading students to discover and reflect on some of the ambiguities and/or contradictions that lie beneath? How often in the name of education are we "substituting phantoms for reality" (Woolf, 1928, p. 74)?

In schools, many of these phantoms reside in the categories imposed by educational bureaucracies. Labels are commonly used to denote differences in learning styles, lifestyles, socio-economic status, beliefs, values, race, languages, and more. What happens emotionally and morally when these labels (and the messages of otherness or inferiority they imply) get mistaken for truths? Eliot D. Landau and colleagues (1976) write that "each label, often libelous, sears to the self-concept. The learner approaches the task of learning armed with everything that has happened to him in his family and in the world that has nurtured him. He learns what he has lived" (p. 96).

If teachers cannot see beneath the veil of external markers and measurements, students may never realize their true capabilities and talents. The same issues apply to educators as well. How many teachers have the potential to inspire countless students but are held back because their self-confidence is buried beneath layers of self-doubt? Teachers and students are left to grieve this loss of self-esteem and mourn the more authentic lives they may have had if only others had seen the truths they carried within.

For example, as Orlando begins to see beneath one-dimensional labels created by the outer world, she asks herself whether "the poet has a butcher's face and the butcher a poet's" (Woolf, 1928, pp. 77–78). Imagine how the illusion of a "butcher's identity" (created by outward appearances) might eventually erode a person's aspirations to become a poet. In any given classroom, which students have the soul of a poet hidden beneath what others may have labeled the face of, say, a troublemaker or a gang-banger? If a teacher never sees and nurtures the student's inner poet, s/he may reinforce (and the student may resign him/herself to) an illusion of what life will be rather than what it could—or should—be.

Consider how many students suffer low self-esteem because of cruel labels placed on them by bullies or even by those in positions of authority. How many students are categorized from an early age based on assessment scores? How many students are treated differently because of language or skin color? Sadly, this list could continue for a long time. There is much to grieve here.

In addition, there is a cumulative effect over time. Once outer labels and categories are normalized, they become systematized by the larger society. Instead of *individuals* being hidden under a veil, *entire groups* of people become imprisoned beneath an outer shell that denies their inner truth. Throughout history there have been efforts by entire societies to silence others based on biases against people of color, of certain religions, ethnicities, gender, social and economic classes, and more. Orlando pondered that "at one and the same time therefore, society is everything and society is nothing. Society is the most powerful concoction in the world and society has no existence whatsoever" (Woolf, 1928, p. 194):

> This mysterious composition which we call society, is nothing absolutely good or bad in itself, but has a spirit in it, volatile but potent, which either makes you drunk when you think it, as Orlando thought it, delightful, or gives you a headache when you think it, as Orlando thought it, repulsive. (p. 196)

Ninety years after Woolf recorded these thoughts, their import, sadly, still resonates. Consider, for instance, the current trend of street violence in neighborhoods throughout the city of Chicago, Illinois. In what newspapers called "Chicago's weekend from hell," sixty-two people were injured and twelve killed (ranging in age from eleven to sixty-two) during two days (August 5–6, 2018) of gun violence (Leone et al., 2018, p. 1). The *Chicago Tribune* described this tragedy as part of an ongoing trend specifically affecting low-income communities of color:

> In 2015, there were 485 homicides in Chicago. A year later, the number of victims skyrocketed to 764.... Much of the city's gunfire victimizes residents of struggling neighborhoods: Five South and West side communities with 9 percent of Chicago's population accounted for nearly half the city's increase in 2016 homicides. African-American men ages 15–34 made up more than half of the city's homicide victims in 2015 and 2016 while accounting for just 4 percent of the city's population. (Leone et al., 2018, p. 14)

What collective truths about ourselves as a society are lurking beneath this veil of statistical data? For communities living under these conditions, societal biases are simultaneously everything and nothing. Based on daily news reports and statistical data, society is made to feel that it knows everything. But little is known of the authentic values and aspirations of these communities. Little is known of their sustained grief.

Law enforcement and local government officials have attempted to remedy the immediate external problems through additional policing and increased penal threats including extended incarceration. But the underlying social, emotional, and ethical concerns remain. Imagine the spiritual impact all this has on residents individually and collectively. How will the children from these communities learn to see the world around them? What lessons are they receiving about themselves and their place in the world? What are they being taught (intentionally or otherwise)? To what extent can educators see the depth of personal and collective grieving that lies beneath the statistical data and formal statements issued by officials?

TEARS

Is this what people call life? (Woolf, 1928, p. 195)

After being secluded within her grief for some time, Orlando eventually returns to the outside world. S/he re-joins former acquaintances and sets out to usher in the new (nineteenth) century atop a recently constructed high-rise structure with a bird's-eye view of a "new London." Buildings, businesses, and entire neighborhoods that existed for generations have been removed in the name of progress. While her acquaintances admire the glitter and glamour of the renovated city, Orlando observes "all was dark; all was doubt; all was confusion [as] the Eighteenth century was over [and] the Nineteenth century had begun" (Woolf, 1928, p. 226). S/he understands that beyond the illusions of wealth and progress are phantoms of the past:

> She remembered the city, if such one could call it, lay crowded, a mere huddle and conglomeration of houses… a black shadow at the corner where the wine shop used to stand was as likely as not, the corpse of a murdered man. She could remember the cries of many a one wounded in such night brawlings… troops of ruffians, men and women, unspeakably interlaced, lurched down the streets, trolling out wild songs with jewels flashing in their ears, knives gleaming in their fists. (p. 224)

Although Orlando is surrounded by lively music and gay festivities, s/he grieves the personal hardships and collective injustices that undergird this outer illusion of celebration and progress. For Orlando, the suffering of the exploited poor, working classes, and impoverished immigrants could no longer be hidden beneath a veneer of bright lights and glamour. S/he now feels an emotional affinity with those whose homes, work sites, churches, and more have been forcibly removed in the name of progress.

Orlando's inner journey of grief has deepened her sense of empathy. S/he understands that other people's tragedies are *her* tragedies as well. Their concerns and grievances are no longer separate from Orlando, but a part of her:

> For she had a great variety of selves to call upon, far more than we have been able to find room for, since a biography is considered complete if it merely accounts for six or seven selves, whereas a person may well have as many as a thousand. (p. 309)

Unlike her friends who remain mesmerized by the outer majesty and luster of the newly constructed London skyline, Orlando sympathizes with the many "selves of which [it is] built upon, one on top of another, as plates are piled on a waiter's hand" (Woolf, 1928, p. 308). Booming structures do not vanquish the traces of heartless exploitation that remain beneath the opulent veil of wealth and privilege. Hence, "tears came to [Orlando's] eyes" (p. 165).

Orlando and her acquaintances admire the newly-constructed St. Paul's Cathedral ("Bravo! Bravo!" p. 222). Orlando ponders that her "belief in magic returns" (p. 300). The magic s/he speaks of is that of a disappearing act: entire neighborhoods (schools, homes, stores, and places of worship) have vanished—as if by magic. Orlando grieves for the inhabitants who were forcibly displaced. For Orlando, the past can no longer be buried and forgotten.

In the past twenty years, a similar trend has re-occurred in many urban communities throughout the United States. When neighborhoods struggling with issues including widespread poverty, violence, street gangs, and illegal drug trafficking are deemed unsafe and beyond repair, what is commonly referred to as a regentrification process begins. Current residents are forced to relocate. Their homes, churches, businesses, and schools left behind are demolished. New mid-to-upper priced housing and businesses are built in its place. Expensive upscale developments rise where low-income public housing once stood.

Areas which were home to disenfranchised communities of poverty, are rebuilt as beacons for up-and-coming college-educated young professionals. As with Orlando's friends, society's collective "belief in magic returns" (Woolf, 1928, p. 300). After all, the poverty and crime seem to have miraculously disappeared. But just as Orlando observed, "the harpies are not so easily banished as all that" (p. 118). The exterior renovation of these areas does not erase the underlying issues of poverty, racism, and unemployment. Those issues are relocated. They are now what is commonly referred to as "someone's else's problem."

When people see the shiny, expensive new developments where low-income public housing once stood, how many grieve for the families who have been removed to make room for "progress"? How many feel the fear and anger of the families whose homes were demolished and replaced with expensive housing which they can no longer afford? These questions evoke what Connerton (2011) describes as an intersection of history and mourning:

> And then there are more routine forms of suffering… to which others, the poor and the defeated, are especially exposed: experiences of deprivation, of exploitation, of degradation, of oppression. Sufferings of this type might be exemplified by the losses endured under apartheid, or by the enforced migration suffered by political refugees, or by the chronic unemployment to which particular social classes are exposed. (p. 16)

Connerton (2011) calls out the societal forgetfulness that often takes place afterwards. A collective amnesia emerges when more empowered members of a society decide to let go of the past and move on with a clear conscience, unburdened by difficult memories or emotional connections. Those less privileged, however, are left behind to grieve. They are rendered powerless as their identities and histories are wiped away with the imposition of a newly created reality. It is as if their past has been disposed of without apology.

In her former life, Orlando and her peers belonged to the more empowered group due to their wealth and social standing. They dismissed other people's hardships as something they were grateful to have avoided by virtue of their ancestry. They felt no sense of responsibility toward others and rationalized that it had not been their fault that the social and economic systems had been designed to disadvantage other groups of people. After all, they were not to blame for societal systems that were constructed to privilege their race and social standing over others.

And yet Orlando noticed that "slowly there had opened within her something intricate and many-chambered, which one must take a torch to explore" (Woolf,

1928, p. 175). Her newly awoken empathy was like a lamp that lit up the darkness that lived beneath the shiny surfaces of the outer world. Within this darkness lie the unspoken (and/or forgotten) losses and griefs on which so-called progress had been built. Orlando, now having an empathic torch of enlightenment with which to explore these areas of darkness, evokes the earlier image of the prophetic three sisters who proclaimed that truth "come out of its horrid den" (p. 136).

Grief taught Orlando to see the world as more than one-dimensional. S/he has begun to view life from "a great variety of selves" (Woolf, 1928, p. 309) and perspectives unrestricted by physical limitations. Time and place have become irrelevant. Orlando's life is no longer measured by hours and years. Past, present, and future have become one. Whether time was "under the influence of the elephant-footed deity" or "of the gnat-winged fly" (p. 99), we are not told. It is the infinite life of her spirit and soul that now informs how s/he understands the world. In this way, Orlando becomes a multi-dimensional representation of our inner life. S/he embodies our human potential to observe past linear markings and to see beyond binary limitations imposed by the outer world:

> "Nothing is any longer one thing. I take up a handbag and I think of an old bumboat woman frozen in the ice. Someone lights a pink candle and I see a girl in Russian trousers. When I step out of doors—as I do now," here she stepped on to the pavement of Oxford Street, "what is it that I taste? Little herbs? I hear goat bells. I see mountains. Turkey? India? Persia?" Her eyes fill with tears. (p. 305)

As her soul "expanded with her eyeballs" (Woolf, 1928, p. 143), Orlando developed a deepened sense of sympathy with and empathy for the larger world. Hence, her tears: at the magnificent St. Paul's Cathedral, "tears came to her eyes" (p. 165); at the London celebration of the New Century, "her eyes fill with tears" (p. 305); outside Westminster Abbey, s/he "burst into a passion of tears" (p. 151); and when setting off for an excursion into the London countryside, s/he prepares "to get into her motor car with her eyes full of tears and visions of Persian mountains" (p. 305). Woolf does not specify whether Orlando's tears are the kind that run down one's face or if they are tears of her "innermost eye" (p. 295). They are a little bit of both, I suspect.

As Orlando admires the outer majesty of Westminster Abbey and the House of Parliament, s/he wonders whether they are not more imposing than the pyramids of Egypt. At this thought, s/he is transported back several months. At the height (or depth) of her grieving, Orlando left London and spent weeks in the countryside living among a group of traveling gypsies. Initially, Orlando bragged that s/he had been born into a royal English household with 365 bedrooms that had belonged to her/his family for 500 years. S/he added that her ancestors included earls and dukes. The gypsy leader responded that "none of them would think the worse of her for that" (Woolf, 1928, p. 147).

Orlando remembers being "seized with a shame that she had never felt before" (Woolf, 1928, p. 147) as s/he realized that the gypsy's ancestors reached back not hundreds but thousands of years to the time of the Pyramids. They were, in fact, the very laborers who constructed the monuments:

> Looked at from the gypsy point of view, a Duke, Orlando understood, was nothing but a profiteer or robber who snatched land and money from people who rated these things of little worth…. [She realized then that] it is not love of truth, but desire to prevail that sets quarter against quarter and makes parish desire the downfall of parish. (pp. 148–149)

In this moment Orlando has an epiphany: s/he realizes that s/he was not the single hero of her own story. S/he understands that s/he had been deceived by the illusions of reality: "the deception roused her scorn; the truth roused her pity" (p. 217). Orlando's singular existence has become pluralized. Her understanding of the world expanded exponentially:

> These selves of which we are built up, one on top of another, as plates are piled on a waiter's hand, have attachments elsewhere… call them what you will (and for many of these things there is no name)…. for everybody can multiply from his own experience the different terms which his different selves have made with him—and some are too wildly ridiculous to be mentioned in print at all. (Woolf, 1928, p. 309)

Orlando's journey through grief transforms the way s/he understands herself and the world around her. Her journey recalls several tenets from Tagore's writing including (1) that "we have come to this world to accept it, not merely to know it" (Tagore, 1933/2004, p. 124); (2) that "we may become powerful by knowledge, but we retain fullness by sympathy" (Tagore, 1933/2004, p. 124); and (3) that through grief "the world becomes another in our mind" (Tagore, 1907a/2011, p. 155).

Orlando's grief teaches her that the vast narrative of humankind (of which grief is a major component) is much larger than our individual selves. Hence, in the sweeping story of humanity, Orlando is sometimes the hero, sometimes the villain; sometimes the brute, sometimes the victim; sometimes the teacher, sometimes the student; sometimes the bullying man, sometimes the alluring woman; sometimes the wealthy aristocrat, sometimes the repressive oligarch:

> For if there are (at a venture) seventy-six different times all ticking in the mind at once, how many different people are there not—Heaven help us—all having lodging at one time or another in the human spirit? Some say two thousand and fifty-two. (Woolf, 1928, p. 308)

Because Orlando is beginning to understand herself and the world around her "though the eyes of [her] soul" (Tagore, 1933/2004, p. 162), "nothing is any longer one thing" (p. 305). Using Tagore's words, her eyes now "suffuse the outside world differently" enabling Orlando to "individualize external reality" through empathy and compassion (Tagore, 1907a/2011, pp. 155). And so Orlando weeps tears of sympathy, not despair; and of empathy, not hopelessness. Although s/he has moved on from her grieving, s/he has not forgotten its lessons. They resonate in the ways s/he has become sensitive to the inner ambiguities, contradictions, and complexities that exist beneath the veil of daily life.

Just as Orlando's understanding of life evolved into "something intricate and many-chambered" (Woolf, 1928, p. 295), the depth and integrity of an educator's work rely on similar "intricate and many-chambered" layers of compassion and empathy. For example, consider the growing trend in the United States to label students with numbers that indicate their math and literacy proficiency. Imagine the short and long-term impact resulting from this practice (no matter how well-intentioned it may be) of reducing student identities to a quantitative scores.

Orlando reminds us that external quantifiers and classifications are less the reality of an educator's work as they are illusions of reality. Who will see beyond the surface to the "intricate and many-chambered" impact of those assessment score numbers being imposed upon a student's emerging self-identity and self-esteem? By relying too much on cognitive growth and development, and not paying enough attention to the emotional, ethical, and spiritual potential of our work, to what extent are teachers substituting "phantoms for reality" (Woolf, 1928, p. 74)? Orlando challenges us to imagine the capacity of education to engage learners in a "multi-faceted transitional process [of]relearning the world" (Attig, 1996, p. 107). Orlando reflected that "I am growing up... I am losing some illusions" (p. 174). Maybe it is time we educators did the same.

TOPICS FOR REFLECTION

1. Make a list of what you consider relevant topics of the "curriculum of school." Then create a list of topics you believe are critical to the "curriculum of life." To what extent do the "curriculum of school" and the "curriculum of life" intersect? Based on your lists and reflections, how closely does the "curriculum of school" align to the lives of your students?

2. It has just been announced that curriculum theorist William H. Schubert will be the guest speaker at your school's professional development session. The event will focus on his three key curriculum questions: What knowledge is most worthwhile? Why is it worthwhile? How is it acquired or created? What questions would you like Professor Schubert to answer? What challenges might you propose to him?

3. Of the students you have taught, can you recall those who had the curiosity of a Leonardo da Vinci, the imagination of a J. K. Rowling, the innovative spirit of a Henry Ford, or the eloquence of a Toni Morrison? In what ways did your work as a teacher specifically nurture these learners, feed their curiosity, and/or further ignite their passions?

4. During an average week, approximately how much of your instruction focuses on students conforming to routines and expectations and/or achieving standardized assessment scores? For the same week, how much of your instruction ascertains, validates, and addresses individualized interests, needs, and concerns? What is the ratio between building conformity to a standardized norm versus nurturing a student's unique capabilities and interests? Does this ratio surprise you? As an indicator of your work as a teacher, is this a ratio you are proud of?

5. "For she had a great variety of selves to call upon, far more than we have been able to find room for, since a biography is considered complete if it merely accounts for six or seven selves, whereas a person may well have as many as a thousand" (Woolf, 1928, p. 309).

   Reflecting on this quote from *Orlando*, what various inner selves do you rely upon within a single day of teaching? Consider those you have known, personally and professionally, whose spirits are enacted through you on any given day. Then turn your attention to a single student. How many "selves" might he or she demonstrate on any given day? In what ways does this concept of multiple selves complicate (in both positive and challenging ways) the art of teaching?

6. Consider the hundreds of thousands of children grieving histories of poverty, injustice, and racial/ethnic/gender bias. How important is it that teachers understand, acknowledge, validate, and respond to the growth and development of students' personal and emotional lives and spirits? Can you imagine what this kind of instruction would look and sound like?

7. In your heart of hearts, to what extent do you believe that teachers have the potential (and the capacity) to help their students make sense of a world that is continuously changing? Outside of school, what lessons are they learning about themselves and their place in the world? In what ways does the school curriculum (intentionally or not) reinforce these understandings?

8. On a scale of 1–10, how realistic is it for teachers to consider the emerging and evolving emotional and moral lives of students, given all their other duties and responsibilities? Considering the extent to which this kind of development is nurtured, what is gained and/or lost?

9. In 2015, there were 485 homicides in Chicago. A year later, that number skyrocketed to 764. Many of the victims reside in economically struggling neighborhoods of color. In 2016, five south and westside communities (almost ten percent of Chicago's population) accounted for nearly half the city's increase in homicides. African-American men ages fifteen to thirty-four comprised more than half of the city's homicide victims in 2015 and 2016, while accounting for just four percent of the city's population (Leone et al., 2018). What truths about ourselves as a society do you suspect are lurking beneath this data? In what ways do these truths influence a teacher's work?

10. Brainstorm with your peers what you believe are the top-five underlying social, emotional, and ethical concerns most relevant to your learning community. What kinds of collaborative lessons, units, projects, or events can you plan that might begin to address these concerns and challenges?

11. What would happen if each teacher in your school were responsible for identifying books, activities, projects, and/or assessments that would more respectfully represent "a great variety of selves"? Brainstorm with a peer the kinds of resources this might include. How would this kind of initiative likely be perceived by the faculty? Would it have a unifying or divisive effect? Would the benefits for students outweigh the agitation and pushback it might cause?

What would a more empathic curriculum look like? Spend some time researching teaching tools and resources that you believe would nurture empathy toward the individual and collective needs of those disadvantaged by histories of deprivation. Consider activities designed to raise awareness of societal injustices and prejudices. How would this kind of initiative likely be perceived by the faculty? Would it have a unifying or divisive effect? Would the benefits for students outweigh the agitation and pushback it might cause?

12. In what ways can teachers and students relearn ways of being and understanding who they are? What kinds of resources and/or projects can help teachers and students reflect more deeply on their place in a world that is continuously changing and evolving?

13. At one point, Orlando invokes the spirit of the ancient Greek mythological character Sibyl who sees what others do not. Although she shares her visions of the future, only those who "believe entirely in what one cannot see" (Woolf, 1928, p. 198) fully understand her prophesies. Pretend that you are temporarily transformed into a twenty-first-century Sibyl. You are invited to speak to a group of aspiring teachers shortly before they set out on their professional careers. What kinds of "visions" might you share in terms of the challenges they are likely to face as educators? In the tradition of the Sibyl (who spoke cryptically) imagine what you might share that would require your audience to "believe entirely in what they cannot see"?

14. The increasingly growing emphasis on learner productivity and reliance on quantitative outcomes all but ignores the spiritual, moral, and emotional lives of students and teachers. To what extent has the image of teachers as artists (Dewey, 1934; Eisner, 1979) been replaced by the conception of teachers as data analysts or task managers? What is gained by this trend? What is lost?

15. Paul Connerton (2011) calls attention to circumstances of collective grieving that create a unique intersection of history and mourning. He calls our attention to "experiences of deprivation, of exploitation, of degradation, of oppression" (p. 16).

In what ways do these concerns resonate within your work as an educator? To what extent do moral concerns or issues of social justice influence your work?

16. How often do textbook narratives mention the "phantoms of the foulest kind" that lurk within the pages of history? In what ways do curriculum designers represent the many cultures, languages, values, and histories of our world? Consider books, activities, and programs that can expand the inclusiveness of your curriculum.

17. Thomas Attig (1996) calls grief a "multi-faceted transitional process" (p. 107). He asserts that "relearning the world is not a matter of *learning information about the world* but *learning how to be and act in the world*" (p. 107). The former Attig calls "straight-forward" teaching; the latter he describes as "self-reflective" teaching (p. 106). Which of these terms do you feel most describes your vision and mission for teaching and learning? Which best describes your day-to-work classroom work?

Pretend you have a double-scale device to measure how much of your work as a teacher focuses on information versus, as Attig says, "learning how to be and act in the world." What activities, discussions, or plans would you list for each side of the scale? Once the scales are filled, which side do you predict will outweigh the other? How do you feel about this as a professional teacher? As a human being? As a member of your faculty? As an individual?

CHAPTER 4

THE BITCH OF LIVING

Spring Awakening: A Children's Tragedy, *Franz Wedekind*;
Spring Awakening, *Steven Sater and Duncan Sheik*

In *Orlando*, the protagonist emerges from his journey of grief with a deepened sense of compassion toward others. If everyone who has experienced grief had similar spiritual awakenings, surely our world would be a much more selfless and benevolent place. However, even Woolf (1928) observes that Orlando persevered through his grief because s/he "was of a strong constitution and the disease never broke him as it has broken many of his peers" (p. 75). Nevertheless, although Orlando re-enters daily life and perseveres with a hopeful spirit, her thoughts and feelings are now tinged with a lingering sadness.

What kind of awakening is this that opens one's eyes and heart to such sadness and leaves behind a residue of melancholy? If, through the process of grieving, our souls "expand with our eyeballs" (Woolf, 1928, p. 143), is it fair that our view of the world will forever be tinged with a sensitivity that brings tears to our eyes (p. 165)? Are people "of strong constitution" destined to survive the heartaches of grieving only to be "rewarded" with an increased awareness and sensitivity to the heartaches of living?

The image of *awakening* sounds optimistic and life-affirming. There are many hopeful awakenings that spring to mind: new days, new possibilities, new dreams. Springtime itself embodies the hopeful spirit of life renewed. But awakening to "phantoms of the foulest kind" (Woolf, 1928, p. 118) seems cruel. In the late-nineteenth-century drama *Spring Awakening: A Children's Tragedy*, Frank Wedekind (1891/2010) explores this counter-intuitive notion of a spring awakening defined by grief.

Wedekind's work dramatizes the lives of Melchior Gabor and his friends as they awaken from their childhood to the world of young adulthood. As they transition into adults, they barely recognize themselves physically, emotionally, or morally. Their pre-conceived notions of the world and their place in it—views passed on to them by their parents and teachers—are challenged.

Unlike stories of caterpillars morphing into butterflies or ugly ducklings transforming into lovely swans, Wedekind's narrative explores the inner turmoil of characters who feel as if they have no control over (or clear understanding of) the sweeping changes they are experiencing. They feel alone to grieve the loss of childhood ideals that no longer apply to their lives and to mourn the passing of previously unquestioned (and unchallenged) beliefs and values. Much like Orlando, Wedekind's characters despair that "change was incessant, and change perhaps would never cease" (Woolf, 1928, p. 176). They, too, are grieving values and beliefs that "had seemed durable as stone" but suddenly are torn "down like shadows at the touch of another mind" (p. 176).

One hundred fifteen years after the publication of Wedekind's *Spring Awakening*, Steven Sater and Duncan Sheik's (2007) reimagining of the work evolved into a popular theatre production. Like the original text, Sater and Sheik's drama is an indictment of society—specifically, of schools—that fails to honestly and ethically prepare individuals for the emotional and spiritual challenges they will face as they journey into adulthood. As Melchior and his friends struggle to make sense of a world that is no longer familiar, they grapple with personal challenges and ethical provocations veiled beneath what they previously regarded as clear and certain truths.

This chapter uses Wedekind's (1891/2010) and Sater and Sheik's (2007) *Spring Awakening* texts to explore the role grief plays in the lives of individuals passing from one stage of life to another. *Spring Awakening* has a strikingly different tone than the texts used in the previous chapters. Whereas Tagore (1933/2004) described difficult emotional times as "dark periods of doubt and reaction," Sater and Sheik's (2007) characters more bluntly refer to them as "the bitch of living" (p. 25). While Woolf (1928) describes Orlando's spiritual struggles as "a disillusionment so complete" (p. 203), the *Spring Awakening* characters label their woes as simply "another day of utter shit" (Sater & Sheik, 2007, pp. 54–55). Although the tone and language of the characters are dissimilar, the core struggles remain the same: grieving what has passed and finding a path forward.

GRIEF AS A RITE OF PASSAGE

Based on their studies of grief, Larry Cochran and Emily Claspell (1987) reflect that "in broad outline and in specific detail, the story of grief corresponds to rites of passage" (p. 125):

> The aim of a rite of passage is not just a change in being, but a revelation of the sacred. Grief is not just a change in being, but strongly spiritual in tone. One discovers that life is precious and adopts traditionally spiritual values or ways of seeing things…. Grieving people come to sense that they have been singled out for the experience, that it has a purpose. Both initiates and grieving persons are caught in a situation beyond control and gradually restore control through adopting higher meanings. (p. 125)

Whether passing from season to season (as when the bright, warm days of spring turn into the cold, dark, and long days of winter), from childhood to adulthood (through the changes and uncertainties of adolescence), or from grief to acceptance (the journey of mourning), periods of transformation heighten an individual's sense of vulnerability.

Cochran and Claspell (1987) note that life-changing inner journeys increase a person's isolation, emotional sensitivity, and personal suffering (p. 75). Although a kind of symbolic dying often occurs during these times of emotional turmoil, there also exists the more hopeful potential of discovering higher values and meanings.

These themes are explored through the characters in *Spring Awakening*. Melchior and his friends struggle with the variety of changes they are experiencing physically and emotionally. It is as if the rules and beliefs they have been taught no longer apply or make sense as the characters' understanding of themselves and their worlds keeps shifting. They are left feeling confused, frightened, and angry:

> Just the bitch of living, / as someone you can't stand… / It's the bitch of living / with nothing going on… It's the bitch of living, / and sensing God is dead. / It's the bitch of living / and trying to get ahead. / It's the bitch of living / just getting out of bed. / It's the bitch of living / and getting what you get. / Just the bitch of living / and knowing this is it. God, is this it? This can't be it. / Oh God, what a bitch! (Sater & Sheik, 2007, pp. 24–25)

Hidden beneath these exclamations and protestations lie their fears, uncertainties, and self-doubts. Thomas Attig (1996) observes that "some of us simply are better prepared than others for the psychological and emotional challenges" (p. 85) of adapting to major life changes:

> As we reach or exceed our emotional limits, the onslaught may overwhelm us…. Emotional fragility, unusual sensitivity, weak self-confidence, low self-esteem, unstable identity, or pre-existing psychological or emotional conditions such as separation anxiety, depression or mental illness complicate our grieving. (p. 85)

As their veils of anger and protestation are lifted, the inner struggles of the three major characters (Melchior, Wendla, and Moritz) are slowly revealed:

Melchior Gabor

As a child, Melchior did well in school by passively accepting everything he was taught without question. As an emerging adult, however, he is discovering that the curriculum no longer aligns in a meaningful way with his evolving understanding of the world. Melchior is beginning to question the "wisdom" of information that he is required to memorize. He is learning to no longer blindly accept it as truth:

> All that's known / in History, in Science, / overthrown at school, at home, / by blind men. You doubt them, / and soon they bark and hound you / till everything you say is just another bad about you. All they say / is "Trust in What is Written." / Wars are made, / and somehow that is wisdom. Thought is suspect… and nothing is okay unless it's scripted in their Bible. (Sater & Sheik, 2007, pp. 21)

Wendla Bergman

Wendla has a crush on her childhood friend Melchior (forgive the adolescent drama), but does not understand what she is experiencing physically. Although she begs her mother to explain the awakening of her sexuality, her mother refuses ("I would love to keep you just the way you are" [Wedekind, 1891/2010, p. 3]). Of her emerging physical desires for Melchior, Wendla is left feeling guilt, confusion, and shame ("Mother, is it sinful to think such things?," p. 4):

> Wake me in time to be lonely and sad. / And who can say what we are?... / This is the season for dreaming.... / And now our bodies are the guilty ones.... Night won't breathe / Oh how we / fall in silence from the sky.... Window by window, / you try and look into / this brave new you that you are.... Wake me in time to be out in the cold... and now our bodies are the guilty ones. (Sater & Sheik, 2007, pp. 64–65)

Moritz Stiefel

Moritz, Melchior's friend, is of a more sensitive and anxious temperament. Of his changing body, he insists that he "can't remember ever wanting to feel such excitement. Why couldn't I just be left in peace?" (Wedekind, 1891/2010, p. 9). His newly-awakened sexual desires are undermined by his strict moral upbringing. Because he believes that how he feels is sinful or immoral, his self-esteem falters as his anxiety increases:

> You wanna laugh. It's too absurd. / You start to ask. Can't hear a word. / You're gonna crash and burn.... You start to cave. You start to cry. / You try to run. Nowhere to hide. / You want to crumble up, and close that door. / Just fuck it—right? Enough. That's it. / You'll still go on. Well, for a bit. / Another day of utter shit. (Sater & Sheik, 2007, pp. 54–55)

The anger Moritz and his friends profess publicly (it's "just the bitch of living / asking 'What went wrong?'" [Sater & Sheik, 2007, p. 24]) is a veil that helps silence their private fears and inner struggles. But as the urgency of their outbursts and discourse indicates, Melchior, Wendla, and Moritz are nonetheless reaching out for guidance and compassion. Their parents and teachers, however, respond with mistruths ("the stork paid a visit last night and brought [your sister] a little boy" [Wedekind, 1891/2010, p. 30]); clichés ("things are never as bleak as they seem" [p. 31]); impersonal generalizations ("we all face crises of one kind or another at some point in our lives and we must try to overcome them" [p. 39]); and shallow platitudes ("do what you think according to your conscience" [p. 39]).

In school, lessons do not stray from a narrow curriculum (that focuses on a catechism of facts) and rigorous preparation for end-of-semester exams. The curriculum of the school does not align with the curriculum of the students' lives. Melchior pushes back. His words reflect the expanding gulf between the needs of students and the content of their education.

> But I know / there's so much more to find— / just in looking / through myself, and not at them. Still, I know / to trust my own true mind, / And to say: there's a way through this…. I'm calling / to know the world's true yearning— / the hunger that a child feels for / everything they're shown. (Sater & Sheik, 2007, p. 22)

These impassioned words evoke Cochran and Claspell's (1987) concept that "both initiates and grieving persons are caught in a situation beyond control" (p. 125). Melchior and his friends cannot control the outer demands placed on them by parents and teachers. They are frustrated by having to spend their time focused on a rigid school curriculum that they feel prevents them from learning, discussing, and better understanding those things that are most impactful to their lives.

The in-school curriculum has become a distraction. The students feel that it has become disconnected from the genuine concerns and needs inherent to the curriculum of their lives. John Dewey (1938) believed that learning needs to start with the experiences and interests of students. He asserted that teachers need to understand "what is actually going on in the minds of those who are learning" (p. 39). For Melchior and his friends, it is only when they move away from the routine (and oftentimes rote) demands of their homework that they are free to explore authentic issues relevant to their lives.

During one homework session, the conversation among Melchior, Moritz, and their friends illustrates the growing disconnect between the prescribed curriculum ("trusting what is written" [Sater & Sheik, 2007, p. 21]) versus independent critical thinking and self-reflection ("[finding] a way through this" [p. 22]). The chart below contrasts these two strands of thinking as articulated in the student discourse.

Curriculum of school: Homework-focused voices	Curriculum of life: Inner thoughts and reflections
Have you done your homework, Melchior? (Wedekind, 1891/2010, p. 4)	You can't think of anything without homework getting in the way. (Wedekind, 1981/2010, p. 5)
Central America! Louis the Fifteenth! Sixty verses of Homer! Seven equations… bloody homework! (p. 5)	I was just thinking about [the futility of homework] the other day. It must be deeply rooted in human nature. (p. 6)
Why do we go to school? To sit exams? So we can fail? (p. 5)	[I'm sailing] on the narrow strait between Scylla and Charybdis—between the rocks of religious delusion and the whirlpool of superstition. (p. 6)

Curriculum of school: Homework-focused voices	Curriculum of life: Inner thoughts and reflections
… if only the Latin composition didn't have to be turned in tomorrow! (p. 5)	A human being's sense of shame is just a product of his education. (p. 6)
I'd rather be a cart-horse than a schoolboy. (p. 5)	Have you ever wondered how we actually arrived in this madhouse? (p. 9)
I've been through the Shorter Encyclopedia from A to Z! Words—nothing but words! (p. 10)	Oh, this terrible feeling of shame! What use is an encyclopedia that doesn't answer life's number one question? (p. 10)

These snippets of discourse demonstrate the dichotomy between school-focused worries and life-centered priorities. They highlight the mechanical nature of a rigid curriculum versus the more organic processes of reflection and critical thinking. The left-side column evokes images of a curriculum that feeds students information, leaving them feeling like unthinking cart-horses (Wedekind, 1891/2010, p. 5). The right-side column suggests learning that is rooted in emotional, moral, and spiritual concerns.

The disparity between the columns recalls Tagore's (1931/2004) warnings that an "education of sympathy is not only systematically ignored in schools, it is severely repressed" (p. 142) and that "we are made to lose our world to find a bagful of information instead" (p. 143). Nel Noddings (2005) expounds on this disconnect between the in-school curriculum versus the larger curriculum of one's life:

> As human beings, we care what happens to us. We wonder whether there is life after death, whether there is a deity who cares about us, whether we are loved by those we love, whether we belong anywhere; we wonder what we will become, who we are, how much control we have over our own fate. For adolescents these are among the most pressing questions: Who am I? What kind of person will I be? Who will love me? How do others see me? Yet schools spend more time on the quadratic formula than on any of these existential questions. (p. 20)

Existential inquiry speaks to a curriculum that helps students (and teachers) explore ideas, beliefs, and values in terms of living more purposeful and meaningful lives. G. M. Malik and Rukhsana Akhter (2013) write that "existentialism is a *way of existing wherein we inquire into our existence*":

> Our Being is at issue and so we inquire into the things that have a deep and personal meaning for us! In the pursuit to understand our lives in connection with others, we begin to recognize common themes emerging such as the meaning and import of freedom, responsibility, death, suffering, guilt, and the place of authentic values in human life. (p. 87)

Moritz Stiefel embodies many of these themes. He agonizes over his emerging sexuality. He fears physical and emotional changes that he does not fully understand.

His beliefs and values have been shaped by a narrow litany of moral and religious dogma that he is unable to reconcile with his emerging physical, and spiritual maturity. Subsequently, he suffers guilt and shame, believing that his thoughts and urges are sinful:

> If you only knew what I've been through… more than guilt—*mortal terror!*… I thought I was incurable. That I was suffering from some incurable disease… These last three weeks have been my Garden of Gethsemane. (Wedekind, 1891/2010, p. 9)

It is as if Moritz's sense of comfort and security in the world is dissipating right before his eyes. His inner suffering evokes a despair of Gethsemane-like proportions that is not limited to adolescent angst. For example, while grieving the death of his wife, author C. S. Lewis is described as "a man emotionally naked in his own Gethsemane" (Gresham, 1994, p. xxvi). In his grief memoirs, Lewis (1961/1996) writes that he struggles as one who "won't accept the fact that there is nothing we can do with suffering except to suffer it" (p. 33):

> Who still thinks there is some device (if only he could find it) which will make pain not to be pain. It doesn't matter whether you grip the arms of the dentist's chair or let your hands die in your lap. The drill drills on. And grief still feels like fear. (p. 33)

Lewis perseveres through his grief. Similar to *Orlando*, he "was of a strong constitution and the disease never broke him as it has broken many of his peers" (Woolf, 1928, p. 75). On the other hand, Moritz is not of a similarly "strong constitution." In an effort to reassure him, Melchior researches the biology behind the physical changes he and his friends are experiencing and writes a short missive (with illustrations) describing and explaining issues of anatomy. The information only increases Moritz's fears and anxieties:

> There's nowhere to hide from these bones, from my mind. / It's broken inside—I'm a man and a child. / I'm at home with a ghost, who got left in the cold, / I'm knocked out of peace, with no keys to my soul. / And the whispers of fear, the chill up the spine, / will steal away too, with a flick of the light. (Sater & Sheik, 2007, p. 55)

When Moritz eventually reaches out to a trusted adult, he is told to "hold [his] head high…. We all face crises of one kind or another at some point in our lives and we must try to overcome them" (Wedekind, 1891/2010, p. 39). The advice does not acknowledge, address, or soothe Moritz's emotional and spiritual suffering. Although Moritz is assured that "things are never as bleak as they seem" (p. 39), the "phantoms of the foulest kind" (Woolf, 1928, p. 118) in his heart and mind disagree. Without guidance or support ("If only there was someone here now whom I could embrace and tell everything" [Wedekind, 1891/2010, p. 40]), Moritz feels increasingly disconnected and emotionally isolated:

I don't fit in. Let them battle it out amongst themselves. I'll step outside and close the door behind me. I'm fed up with being pushed around—I didn't ask to be born, and I don't owe God anything.... I am going to the altar like the Etruscan youth in the legend, whose sacrifice brought his brothers prosperity in the years to come. This world gave me the cold shoulder. On the other side I can see friendly, sympathetic faces. (Wedekind, 1891/2010, pp. 40–41)

The undisputed catechism of information that came to define the curriculum of school offered Moritz no spiritual solace or emotional path forward. It became so disconnected from his inner life, it is as if all Moritz heard from his teachers was a monotonous (and meaningless) "blaa blaa blaa blaa blaa blaa blaa blaa / blaa blaa blaa blaa blaa / blaa blaa..." (Sater & Sheik, 2007, p. 76). The imposition of facts and figures fails to educate or guide Moritz either emotionally or morally.

Martin Buber (1937/1957) reflects that when the structures which give meaning to our lives begin to collapse, we experience an existential homelessness (p. 137). Moritz describes his growing despair in similar terms: "A moment ago I could see the reeds and a line on the horizon. Now it's dark. Now I shan't go home" (Wedekind, p. 45). He is feeling what Arthur T. Jersild (1955) describes as an emptiness within the self (p. 76). Although Moritz has a physical home and family, he remarks that "it's not my home. Not anymore. / Not like [it] so was before" (Sater & Sheik, 2007, p. 53). Jersild (1955) writes that this "state of being homeless is an inner state: the person is not at home with himself. He is, in many ways, an aimless one, a weary wanderer, who can find no rest and no rock on which to build" (p. 77).

Moritz's education was defined by binary choices (i.e., right or wrong, correct or incorrect, good or bad). He was never taught to consider that between the two polemics there exists a wide spectrum of considerations, possibilities, and choices. He never learned to make room for deliberation or evolving truths. Consequently, Moritz believes that he has only two choices moving forward: a happy life or a sad one. He rejects sadness and simultaneously feels that happiness is outside his reach. Feeling that there are no other options, Moritz is left without choices and hence, without hope:

Cause, you know, I don't do sadness—not even a little bit. / Just don't need it in my life—don't want any part of it. / I don't do sadness. Hey, I've done my time. / Lookin' back on it all—man, it blows my mind. / I don't do sadness. So been there. / Don't do sadness. Just don't care. (Sater & Sheik, 2007, p. 66)

Overwhelmed with grief and unable to see any alternatives, "Moritz cocks the hammer of his gun. Sets the gun in his mouth. Blackout" (Sater & Sheik, 2007, p. 70).

THERE'S NO FUN IN FUNERAL

Moritz's death weighs heavily on Melchior. Cochran and Claspell (1987) describe that for some people grief initiates a process of inner transformation in which "one discovers that life is precious and [seeks to ascertain] spiritual values or ways of seeing things" (p. 125). Melchior embodies Herman Feifel's (1959) observation that "in gaining an awareness of death, we sharpen and intensify our awareness of life" (p. 123).

Contrasting this, notable existential thinkers (i.e., Heidegger, Camus, Kierkegaard) observe that many individuals exist on a level of awareness so shallow that for all practical purposes they are sleepwalking through life's experiences, including grief. These conflicting responses to grief (accepting versus ignoring it) are evidenced at Moritz's funeral in the expanse between the headmaster's public words and Melchior's private thoughts:

HEADMASTER: The suicide epidemic that is currently raging through educational communities, defying all efforts of the educator to fetter the educable to the educative state and contain a contagion that makes the educator obsolete by making the educable defunct, and thus by definition, ineducable. (Wedekind, 1891/2010, p. 46)

MELCHIOR: Those you've known, / and lost, still walk beside you. All alone, / their song still seems to find you. / They call you, / as if you knew their longing. / They whistle through the lonely wind, / the long blue shadows falling.... All alone, but still I hear their yearning. (Sater & Sheik, 2007, p. 90)

These responses are indicative of what Soren Kierkegaard (1843/1959) describes as living an aesthetic life versus an ethical one (*Either/Or*). The headmaster represents the aesthete who strives to escape melancholy and despair by turning his attention to distractions. Kierkegaard warns that too great a focus on the aesthetic can result in amorality or immorality. By limiting one's perspective and words to personal or temporal concerns, the aesthetic individual hopes to avoid personal responsibility, guilt, or remorse. The headmaster externalizes dread with the hope of separating from it.

Melchior approaches what Kierkegaard called an ethical life that James Goho (2014) describes as "a synthesis of body and spirit, of temporal and eternal, of necessity and freedom" (p. 101). Melchior's words reflect an emerging freedom from the constraints of bureaucratic or dogmatic perspectives. They indicate his psychological and emotional journey into new modes of being that extend into ethical and spiritual spheres.

Returning to Kierkegaard's (1843/1959) categories, consider the headmaster's aesthetic perspective versus Melchior's ethical one. Which of these is best suited for the work of teaching and learning: the teacher who avoids acknowledging the emotional complexities of grief or one who decides to enter spaces of empathy and mourning? Is it enough for educators to protect themselves and their reputation (a la the headmaster), even as it diminishes their compassion or extends an emotional gulf between teacher and learner?

To what extent do bureaucratic or administrative constraints limit an educator's personal or ethical freedom? To what degree is it simply easier, more convenient, or—quite frankly—more self-serving to distract ourselves from any sense of guilt or personal accountability in the crises and challenges our students and their families face?

These are the kinds of introspective questions a person living in an ethical mode contemplates. Kierkegaard (1844/1957) described this as reflective practice grounded in an understanding that there are truths and values that exist beyond immediate gratification. The ethical mode is a journey past the innocence (or ignorance) of one-dimensional and linear perspectives. It involves accepting contradictions inherent to our human condition (i.e., the coexistence of pleasure and guilt, joy and sadness, profit and remorse). It has the potential to welcome individuals to spaces of compassion and empathy:

> Only when the compassionate person is so related by his compassion to the sufferer that in the strictest sense he comprehends that it is his own cause which is here in question, only when he knows how to identify himself in such a way with the sufferer that when he is fighting for an explanation he is fighting for himself, renouncing all thoughtlessness, softness, and cowardice, only then does compassion acquire significance. (Kierkegaard, 1844/1957, p. 107)

At Moritz's funeral, Melchior's thoughts and words embody his emerging compassion and empathy. Rather than suppressing or denying the intensity of his emotions, he embraces them. By contrast, the headmaster, teachers, and other mourners at the funeral are trapped in Kierkegaard's aesthetic stage. Their reflections externalize or avoid any authentic sense of sadness or remorse. To squelch personal guilt or collective responsibility, compassion is replaced with blame and shallow defensiveness. Wedekind's (1891/2010) and Sater and Sheik's (2010) texts contrast the stark differences between the ethical and the aesthetic:

Ethical mode: Melchior (Sater & Sheik, 2007) Embracing grief's complexities	Aesthetic mode: Other mourners (Wedekind, 1891/2010) Avoiding emotional landscapes
You fold his hands, and smooth his tie. / You gently lift his chin—Were you really so blind, / and unkind to him? (p. 71)	[Teacher]: How could a child act so vindictively against its own parents? (p. 52)
All the things he never did are left behind. / All the things his mama wished he'd bear in mind; And all his dad ever hoped he'd know. / The talks you never had, The Saturdays you never spent, / All the "grown-up" places you never went. (p. 71)	[Headmaster]: Suicide is the gravest imaginable crime against the moral order and therefore simultaneous proof of the existence of that order, since the malefactor, by sparing the moral order the burden of passing judgment, confirms the validity of the moral order. (p. 52)
And all of the crying you wouldn't understand, / You just let him cry—"Make a man out of him." (p. 71)	[Pastor]: For those who love God all things are for the best. (p. 52)

Ethical mode: Melchior (Sater & Sheik, 2007) Embracing grief's complexities	Aesthetic mode: Other mourners (Wedekind, 1891/2010) Avoiding emotional landscapes
A shadow passed. / A shadow passed, / Yearning, yearning for the fool it called a home. (p. 71)	[Teacher]: In all honesty, he would probably have failed next year.... And even if he hadn't, he would almost certainly have failed next year. (p. 53)
All things he ever lived / are left behind. / All the fears that ever flickered through his mind; / All the sadness that he'd come to own. (p. 72)	[Schoolmate]: He still owes me five marks. We had a wager. He bet me he would pass at the end of the year. (p. 54)
Can't help the itch to touch, to kiss, / to hold him once again. / Now, to close his eyes, never open them? (p. 71)	[Schoolmate]: If he'd learnt his Greek Literary History, he wouldn't have had to hang himself. (p. 54)
All the things he ever wished / are left behind; / All the things his mama / did to make him mind; / And how his dad / had hoped he'd grow. (p. 71)	[Moritz's father]: He was no son of mine. I never liked him, even as a baby. (p. 53)

Being emotionally responsive to others requires courage. Individuals need to first face their inner selves. Herein lies the import of introspection and self-understanding. Although Moritz had been overwhelmed by anxiety and guilt, no one empathized. Arthur T. Jersild (1955) observed that individuals cannot engage in this depth of empathy unless they "draw upon their own capacity for feeling" (p. 133). Despite Melchior's grief and remorse, the other mourners seem incapable of connecting with him on an emotional level. Compassion, Jersild (1955) writes, demands courage:

> One must be able to accept the impact of any emotion—love or hate, joy, fear, or grief—tolerate it and harbor it long enough and with sufficient absorption to accept its meaning and to enter into a fellowship of feeling with the one who is moved by the emotion. This is the heroic feature of compassion in its fullest development. (p. 125)

At Moritz's funeral, the headmaster does not humanize Moritz enough to even say his name, only referring to him as "the malefactor" (Wedekind, 1891/2010, p. 52). Instead of speaking in terms of sympathy and addressing the community's grief, he passes judgment on Moritz's decision to take his own life and calls it "the gravest crime against the moral order" (p. 52). He fails to acknowledge any personal significance in Moritz's suffering. Jersild (1955) writes that unless an educator can recognize in another his or her own experiences with hurt, "he is not actually realizing his potentialities as a teacher" (p. 132).

Instead of empathizing with Moritz's despair, his teachers judge him: "How could a child act so vindictively against its own parents?" (Wedekind, 1891/2010, p. 52). Rather than seeing their own inner vulnerabilities reflected in this tragedy, the teachers remain focused on external matters: "In all honesty, he would probably have failed next year" (p. 53). Although Melchior is searching for solace, his teachers and headmaster offer none. Grief teaches that there is "personal significance in connection with everything we seek to learn and everything that is taught" (Jersild, 1955, p. 136):

> What is there in the lessons we teach, the exercises we assign, the books we read, the experiences we enter into, and in all our undertakings, that can help us find ourselves and, through us, help others in their search? (p. 136)

The headmaster and teachers focus on preserving the reputation of the school and protecting their own self-interests over engaging in efforts to heal their community's collective grief. They fear that others might begin asking why they had not intervened on Moritz's behalf. They worry that financial donors will begin to question the school's commitment to the safety and well-being of its students. Prioritizing their own reputations and self-interests, school authorities and faculty decide to avoid potential public recrimination (and personal guilt) by holding Melchior responsible for Moritz's suicide.

The missive Melchior had previously prepared for Moritz (wherein he explained the physiology of sexuality) is discovered. It is used as evidence of Melchior's corrupt influence. Blaming Melchior for Moritz's suicide distracts from the school accepting any accountability. The headmaster publicly chastises what he characterizes as Melchior's low moral character, and the school board votes to expel Melchior from school:

> You have as little respect for the dignity of your assembled masters as you have for the sacred gifts of modesty and decorum that betoken man's acquiescence in the divine moral order! It [Melchior's letter] is an agglutination of obscenities, a manual of abominations.... Be silent! I declare this investigation closed and call upon our secretary to terminate the protocol. —Scoot! Take him away! (Wedekind, 1891/2010, p. 51)

It is significant that most of the headmaster's sentences in this excerpt end with exclamation points—the words neither expect nor invite a response. There are several emotional and ethical ironies in his announcement: (1) the headmaster speaks of a "divine moral order" even as the decision to expel Melchior is far from ethically-motivated; (2) he insists on preserving "modesty and decorum" even as the decision knowingly ignores the suffering that simmers beneath the veneer of said decorum; and (3) although he publicly rallies against what he calls "obscenities and abominations" the headmaster's rationale and decision to unfairly punish Melchior to protect his own reputation are themselves a moral abomination.

Terrence E. Deal and Peggy Deal Redman (2009) observe that too great an emphasis on external pressures and public image "overlooks the essential core of teaching, the inner world of the teacher" (p. 59):

> The narrowing of accountability to a restricted range of calculable outcomes eats away at the noble, definitive purpose of the profession.... Reform prods an authentic teacher into an existential quandary: Do I teach the way my heart and soul tell me is right, or do I buckle under pressure?... Caving in to forces that go against one's genuine personal grain undermines the moral sway of a true teacher. (p. 61)

Kierkegaard (1844/1957) wrote that to stop aspiring toward higher moral grounds is akin to denying ourselves and each other higher levels of compassion. He notes that "striving toward the divine in the midst of so many earthly distractions and demands requires moral courage" (p. 85). Consider the nuances of courage and compassion (or lack thereof) that permeate the discourse between Melchior Gabor's parents as they deliberate their son's expulsion from school:

> MRS. GABOR: I thank God even now for showing me the way to instill in my child an honest character and a noble imagination. What has he done that is so dreadful? It is not his fault that he has been hounded out of school.... You claim to understand the principles involved better than I do, and perhaps theoretically you do, and perhaps, theoretically, you are right. But I will never allow my only son to be destroyed for the sake of a principle!

> MR. GABOR: The matter is no longer in our hands, Anna. This was a risk we took as parents. Some will stumble on the march and some fall by the wayside.... A boy who can write what Melchior wrote [Melchior's private letter to Moritz] has been corrupted at the core. The very marrow is diseased.... It documents with terrifying clarity a conscious intention, a natural propensity, a tendency to immorality for immorality's sake. It exhibits a degree of spiritual corruption that as a jurist I would call "moral insanity." Whether anything can be done about his condition is not for me to say. But if we want to preserve a glimmer of hope, and keep our consciences clear as parents, then we must act swiftly and with determination.

> MRS. GABOR: You have to be a man to be so blinded by doctrine that you cannot see what is staring you in the face.... This is incredible. It's beyond belief! What has he written in this essay? Isn't it the clearest proof of his silliness, his harmless boyish innocence that he can write such things at all?— You would have to be totally ignorant of human nature, you would have to be some desiccated bureaucrat or pedant to find in it traces of moral corruption. (Wedekind, 1891/2010, pp. 56–57)

Mr. Gabor speaks of morality and conscience in broad terms without any discernable consideration of Melchior's grief. His words do not suggest compassion for his son's predicament or his subsequent emotional pain. Nor do they indicate any sense of parental responsibility (or affection) to protect and/or comfort Melchior. Like the Headmaster, Mr. Gabor appears trapped in Kierkegaard's aesthetic stage of thinking in that he seems more concerned with how others will perceive (and judge) him as a parent than he is about his son's crisis. By focusing on squelching any responsibility he may have in the matter, compassion is replaced with further blame and shallow defensiveness.

Mrs. Gabor, on the other hand, communicates from a place of inner compassion rather than outer convention. Instead of referring to rules and bureaucracy, she speaks to "honest character and a noble imagination." With emotional and ethical earnestness, Mrs. Gabor questions the validity of ideals when challenged by real-world situations ("to be so blinded by doctrine that you cannot see what is staring you in the face"). She calls out the dangers of "desiccated bureaucrats or pedants" who assert moral high ground while acting "totally ignorant of human nature." Within Kierkegaard's (1845/2000) ethical mode of being, Mrs. Gabor embodies what he describes as "teacher of earnestness":

> As soon as someone opens the door to uncertainty, the teacher is there, the teacher who will at some time come to give a test and examine the pupil: whether he has wanted to use his instruction or not. And this testing by death… is equally difficult for all… because it is the test of earnestness. (pp. 252–253)

The Oxford English Dictionary lists heartfelt, sincere, thoughtful, and profound as synonyms for earnestness. These inner qualities nourish Mrs. Gabor's empathy and compassion for her son. Tragedies are moments of uncertainty that touch on critical issues of our human experience (i.e., life and death, suffering and healing, growth and loss). They teach us about the innate need to comfort others and to be comforted. Mrs. Gabor demonstrates the moral courage to care with an earnestness unencumbered by fears of outside judgment or external measures of propriety. Nel Noddings (2005) challenges teachers (and administrators) to similarly have the courage to show compassion:

> The best grief counseling should come from teachers who know and care deeply for their students. They are the people who should comfort, counsel, and express their common grief. In contemporary schools, teachers and students do not know each other well enough to develop relations of care and trust…. Students and teachers need each other. Students need competent adults to care; teachers need students to respond to their caring. (p. 69)

To what extent do educators qualify as teachers of earnestness (Kierkegaard, 1845/2000)? In what ways are care and trust prioritized within the life of a classroom? As a society, do we aspire to have teachers whose instruction is primarily rooted in bureaucratic protocol or personal/collective conscience? What are the consequences of teaching (and living) without a heartfelt connection with others' suffering? These questions are not easily addressed. They require honest and heartfelt introspection.

Nevertheless, the path toward a better understanding of ourselves and the world around us is not paved with answers—but with increasingly poignant and heartfelt questions. Cochran and Claspell (1987) note that "grief is one long series of questions" (p. 78):

> The experience calls into question faith, fairness, death, meaning, relationship, and so on, endlessly. Grief makes metaphysicians of us all…. Just as people question from the heart, they search from the heart, and this search does not necessarily end. It can transform life into a kind of journey… no longer merely a means, searching is part of what it is to live. (pp. 78–79)

PURPLE SUMMER

Melchior has much to grieve. The death of his best friend and his ignoble expulsion from school leave Melchior feeling frightened, angry, and confused. His sense of aloneness and isolation intensifies after he is sent to an out-of-town school where his father believes Melchior will receive "iron discipline, principles, and moral constraints to which he must learn to conform" (Wedekind, 1891/2010, p. 59).

After some time, hidden within the darkness of the night, Melchior returns to visit Moritz's grave. Here he will face "ghosts in the moonlight" and confront further "heartache without end" (Sater & Sheik, 2007, pp. 81–82). Because the scene also serves to dramatize Melchior's inner journey, Wedekind (1891/2010) uses supernatural images:

> The wind is whistling on every headstone in a different key. A symphony of pain. The wreaths are rotting and dangle in shreds—a forest of scarecrows guarding each grave. The willows groan and grope at the epitaphs. (p. 69)

Sater and Sheik (2007) further imagine what these songs of grief sound like. The imagination and creativity are critical at this point because the whisperings are not of the outer world. They are the voices of Melchior's inner grief. Thus, they are not intended for his ears but for his heart. In other words, Melchior has learned to listen with his inner being:

> Whispering… hear the ghosts in the moonlight. / Sorrow doing a new dance / through their bones, through their skin. / Listening— / to the souls in the fool's night, / fumbling mutely with their rude hands… / and there's heartache without end. (Sater & Sheik, pp. 81–82)

Melchior recognizes Wendla's voice echoed within the whispers. Although they loved each other, Melchior had not heard from Wendla since being banished from home and school. He did not know that Wendla was pregnant with his child. Her mother insisted she have a medical procedure to eliminate the unborn baby. Tragically, Wendla died during the abortion. Moritz now turns to face her tombstone:

HERE RESTS IN GOD WENDLA BERGMAN
BORN 5TH MAY 1878 DIED OF ANAEMIA OCTOBER 1892
(Wedekind, 1891/2010, p. 69)

Melchior immediately suffers guilt ("I killed her. I murdered her" [p. 69]), powerlessness ("I wasn't prepared for this. Why her? Why not me? I'm the guilty one" [p. 69]), and hopelessness ("the inscrutable ways of Providence" [p. 69]). The scene becomes surreal; it exceeds the scientific boundaries of our physical world. Melchior now resides in the emotional and spiritual landscape of his inner reality. He is standing not only before Moritz's and Wendla's tombstones, but among their spirits. Moritz is the first to beckon:

MORITZ: Shake hands. You won't regret it. And you won't find it so easy another time. I came up especially (p. 70).… We can do anything. We can smile at the young who mistake their frustrations for idealism, and the old who bear so much heartbreak in dignified silence.… It's a wonderful feeling, Melchior. It's sublime. All you have to do is give me your little finger. By the time you get such a favorable opportunity again, your hair may have turned white with grief. Then why do you hesitate?

MELCHIOR: If I do this, Moritz, I do it out of self-disgust. I'm an outcast. The hope that gave me courage is here, buried in a nearby grave. I've become unfit for honest human emotions, and I see nothing standing between me—and degradation. (Wedekind, 1891/2010, p. 71)

This interaction demonstrates Kierkegaard's (1846/1960) belief that "existence is a synthesis of the infinite and the finite, and the existing individual is both finite and infinite" (p. 350). Although finite in the physical sense, humanity's capacity for creativity and imagination is infinite. It is within this imaginative, dream-like space that Melchior confronts his ethical and personal crises. The spirit of Moritz now embodies Melchior's despair. In life, Moritz could not imagine the co-existence of suffering and hope because he had learned to understand the world only in binary terms. And so he now encourages Melchior to end his life rather than continuing to suffer.

Melchior, however, is beginning to understand that life has many nuances which cannot be reduced to binary *either/or* choices. Unlike Moritz, Melchior is coming to terms with the understanding that unexplainable and oftentimes unimaginable contradictions (i.e., grief *and* happiness, regret *and* satisfaction, suffering *and* hope) co-exist. At this point, an enigmatic figure identified only as a Masked Man appears:

MELCHIOR: Will you please tell me who you are?
THE MASKED MAN: Your first task will be to trust me.
MELCHIOR: But who are you? I can't put my trust in someone I don't know.
MASKED MAN: You will only get to know me by trusting me first.

MORITZ: My morality was the death of me. I blew my brains out to spare my parents. "Honor thy father and thy mother that thy days may be long upon the earth." The Good Book got it horribly wrong in my case. (Wedekind, 1891/2010, pp. 72–74)

These interactions are spiritual experiences that defy spatial, linear, and temporal boundaries. And yet, the poetic discourse embodies the genuine striving of Melchior's spirit. The scene is a manifestation of his emerging understanding and acceptance of life's complexities. Although none of this makes sense according to the outer rational world, Melchior finds moral strength by *imagining* his spiritual path forward:

MASKED MAN: We shouldn't lose our dignity. You were asking about morality. Morality, in my view, is the real product of two imaginary entities. The imaginary entities are called *Duty* and *Free Will*. The product is called *Morality* and its existence is undeniable... In the end everyone gets his due: for you, [Moritz], the comforting knowledge of having nothing; for you [Melchior], the agonizing uncertainty of everything to come. (Wedekind, 1891/2010, p. 74)

Melchior seeks solace that cannot be found through any of the paths of knowledge he has been schooled in. He is learning to trust in himself; and to ascertain the moral integrity that resides within his heart. By facing the spirits of Moritz and the Masked Man (which I suggest are manifestations of Melchior himself), he fortifies himself to take what Kierkegaard scholar Michael Watts (2003) calls a "leap into absurdity":

Kierkegaard wants us to realize that, ultimately, we can rationally understand neither the world we live in nor our true nature or purpose in life. As a consequence, we dissipate our energy and squander our lives in a variety of meaningless ways.... We have two choices: to remain forever in a life of complete ignorance and uncertainty about what we ought to believe or how we should live, or alternately we can choose to take the "leap into absurdity," in other words, a "leap of faith." (pp. 95–96)

Melchior's leaps of maturity and faith represent his willingness to accept a secular world filled with limitations and contradictions. He arrives at the space Kierkegaard (1846/1960) describes wherein "the existing individual is both finite and infinite" (p. 350): living in the finite world, but aspiring to beliefs, values, and ideas that abound in the infinite, oftentimes elusive, expanse of our larger existential existence. Melchior has stopped searching for quick fixes or definitive actions to assuage his grief. He now ponders life's questions with an awareness that answers are elusive and simple binary perspectives are futile.

Melchior is no longer trapped by grief because he has stopped searching for definitive answer or cures (neither of which exist). Having learned to embrace grief's range of emotions rather than trying to deny, suppress, or ignore them, Melchior is no longer emotionally distracted or spiritually paralyzed by his heavy sadness. He is beginning to accept that his suffering and grief are more expansive than himself alone. His feelings of isolation are also diminishing as he realizes that his grief and sadness actually further connect him with the larger body and spirit of humanity.

Of course, Wedekind is not the first or only writer to explore spiritual realities using creativity and imagination. William Shakespeare's (1598/1988b) *A Midsummer Night's Dream* is a classic example of a dream-like world that extends the borders of rationality into a spiritual or supernatural landscape. Like *Spring Awakening*, it ultimately informs not only our minds—but our hearts as well. G. K. Chesterton (1971) commented on the play's use of imagination to distinguish between our outer life (the "life of waking") and our inner one (the "life of the vision"):

> We cannot have *A Midsummer Night's Dream* if our one object in life is to keep ourselves awake with the black coffee of criticism. The whole question which is balanced, and balanced nobly and fairly, in *A Midsummer Night's Dream*, is whether the life of waking, or the life of the vision, is the real life, the *sine qua non* of man. (p. 104)

Melchior's experience in the graveyard (*Spring Awakening*'s final scene) is his personal midsummer night's dream. Both *A Midsummer Night's Dream* and *Spring Awakening* explore issues that transcend space and time: the former deals in the complications of love and relationships, while the latter ruminates on loss and the potential for consolation. They are works of imagination that search for understanding, not answers, and for solace, rather than solutions.

As artistic expressions of spiritual introspection, growth and development, *A Midsummer Night's Dream* and *Spring Awakening* (like grief itself) simultaneously defy rationality and speak to larger, more esoteric truths. They adhere to Virginia Woolf's (1928) idea that "one can only believe entirely, perhaps, in what one cannot see" (p. 198). The chart below lists relevant excerpts from these works that demonstrate what Jerome Bruner (2004) calls a "dual landscape of reality": a landscape of action, which entails the many tasks that comprise our lives; and a landscape of consciousness, that involves a person's inner world (p. 698):

Melchior's leap of faith	*A Midsummer Night's Dream* *(Shakespeare, 1598/1988b)*
We're beyond earthly matters, good and bad. Each of us is a world unto himself. (Wedekind, 1891/2010, p. 70)	How now, spirit! Whither wander you? (Act 2, Scene 2)
Those you've pained / may carry that still with them. / All the same, / they whisper: "All forgiven." / Still, your heart says: / The shadows bring the star light, / and everything you've ever been is still there in the dark night. (Sater & Sheik, 2007, p. 90)	The course of true love never did run smooth. (Act 1, Scene 1) Love looks not with the eyes, but with the mind. (Act 1, Scene 1)

Melchior's leap of faith	A Midsummer Night's Dream (Shakespeare, 1598/1988b)
Those you've known / and lost, still walk behind you. / All alone, they linger till they find you. / Without them, / the world grows dark around you. / And nothing is the same until you know that they have found you. (Sater & Sheik, 2007, p. 89)	I have had a most rare vision. I have had a dream, past the wit of man to say what dream it was. (Act 4, Scene 1)
Still you know / there's so much more to find / another dream, another love you'll hold. / Still you know to trust your own true mind / on your way— you are not alone. (Sater & Sheik, 2007, p. 91)	Are you sure that we are awake? It seems to me that yet we sleep, we dream. (Act 4, Scene 1)
Now they'll walk on my arm through the distant night, / and I won't let them stray from my heart. / Through the wind, through the dark, / through the winter light, / I will read all their dreams to the stars. (Sater & Sheik, p. 91)	It is not night when I do see your face, Therefore I think I am not in the night; Nor doth this wood lack worlds of company. Then how can it be said I am alone. For you in my respect are all the world. (Act 2, Scene 1)
I'll walk now with them. I'll call on their names. / I'll see their thoughts are known. / Not gone.... They walk with my heart—I'll never let them go. (Sater & Sheik, 2007, p. 92)	Be as thou wast wont to be. See as thou wast wont to see. (Act 4, Scene 1)
And heaven waits, / so close it seems... and all shall know the wonder / of purple summer.... A song of what's to follow— / the glory of the spring. (Sater & Sheik, 2007, p. 93)	The best in this kind are but shadows and the worst are no worse if imagination amend them. (Act 5, Scene 1)

The dream-like quality of the passages renders them no less emotionally authentic. They demonstrate Virginia Woolf's (1928) observation that "life is a dream. 'Tis waking that kills us. He who robs us of our dreams robs us of our life" (p. 203). Melchior's inner monologue gives voice to the emotional epiphanies he experiences. These are moments of transformation ("I have had a most rare vision" [Shakespeare, 1598/1988b, Act 4, Scene 1]) to which creativity and imagination give expression ("and all shall know the wonder of purple summer" [Sater & Sheik, 2007, p. 93]).

Tagore (1933/2004) warned that most schools "devote our sole attention to giving children information... accentuating a break between the intellectual, the physical, and the spiritual life" (p. 154). While the former two categories define what we know and do, the latter is what shapes who we *are*. Creativity and imagination have the potential to bridge the intellectual and the spiritual. Noddings (2005) writes that educators "need a scheme that speaks to the existential heart of life" (p. 47):

The spiritual aspect of self gets almost no attention in today's public schools. Most young people have a host of questions that could be discussed without violating the establishment clause: Is there life after death? Is there a god who cares for me? Am I connected to anything beyond the phenomenal world? Are there spirits with whom I can commune? Will such communion enhance my life? (p. 9)

These sorts of questions are critical as students and teachers search for meaningful ways to understand themselves and their worlds. William H. Schubert (1986) calls this "curriculum as experience" (p. 30), wherein individuals reflect on what they have learned in terms of how it relates to their lives, experiences, beliefs, and values. He describes this as "an attempt to grasp what is learned rather than to take for granted that the planned intents are in fact learned" (p. 30):

Experiences are created as learners reflect on the processes in which they engage. Curriculum is meaning experienced by students, not facts to be memorized or behaviors to be demonstrated.... They are fashioned as teachers and learners interact amid a milieu and with subject matter that gives substance to learning. (p. 30)

Sadly, events on February 14, 2017, at Marjory Stoneman Douglas High School in West Boca Raton, Florida, created such a milieu wherein the social, emotional, and spiritual relevance of *Spring Awakening* aligned directly to the lived experiences of the community. In the weeks prior to this event, the nearby Barclay Performing Arts Youth Theatre decided to produce *Spring Awakening* for its annual drama showcase. Many of the teenage performers attended nearby Stoneman Douglas High School.

Just hours before a scheduled rehearsal on Valentine's Day, a security threat sent the school into lockdown mode. By the time the imminent danger was declared over, an armed assailant had killed seventeen students. Although this was the first violent event of magnitude to impact this local community, the trend of school shootings in the United States had been growing on a national level.

Between 1999 and 2005 alone there were approximately twenty-two incidents of school violence reported and an estimated sixteen deaths in the United States alone (Los Angeles Times Staff, 2017). State and national discourse turned to proposed solutions (i.e., gun control legislation, strengthened school security, mandated school armed-intruder drills, teachers armed with live ammunition).

After the incident, there were vociferous calls for stronger school safety measures and for national legislation to further restrict the availability of weapons. There were even wide-spread calls for classroom teachers to carry concealed weapons during instructional hours. Nevertheless, no amount of safety measures, gun legislation, or armed teachers would address the depth and expanse of the personal and collective grief, especially for the students, their families and the surrounding community of Stoneman Douglas High School.

In a *Topic Magazine* article (Butler, 2018), Steven Sater commented that "the cumulative weight of our failure to address gun violence—to look at the cost our children bear so that we might maintain the polite order of our world—will bring *Spring Awakening* to relevance again and again" (p. 15). He observed in another interview that "we're failing to listen to what's going on in the hearts of our children; we're still not hearing" (Truesdell, 2018).

Student survivors, parents, and members of the West Boca Raton community decided to move forward with plans for the *Spring Awakening* youth performance. The play's themes of loss and tragedy and its depiction of characters searching for meaning in a suddenly unfamiliar world resonated closely to the realities this community faced. Although the production could not change the past, it would create a space for their personal and collective grief to be expressed and shared.

The show premiered May 2, 2017, just eleven weeks after the shooting incident. In a video-documentary of the event, student performer Sawyer Garrity described how she and her peers channeled their grief into the production:

[The show] does open wounds that you are trying to heal. I don't think it made it harder. If anything, it helped.... Art, music, and drama can help people going through something as traumatic as what happened on February 14th. We needed this show more than ever. (Costantini & Foster, 2018)

The play's director, Christine Barclay, commented in the documentary that the graveyard scene in which Melchior mourns Moritz and Wendla was a pivotal one through which the Florida students mourned their murdered classmates. She noted that they required no direction for the scene as "they instinctually understood the emotions all too well. It is hard to watch them give up their innocence" (Costantini & Foster, 2018).

In the final scene, the cast performed Sater and Sheik's (2007) *Song of Purple Summer*. The Stoneman Douglass High School community (students, parents, teachers, and friends) joined in. They sang together and thus mourned together. It was an expression of their shared suffering and grieving:

Listen to what's in the heart of a child, / A song so big in one so small. / Soon you will hear where beauty lies. / You'll hear and you'll recall... The sadness, the doubt, all the loss, the grief, / Will belong to some play from the past; / As the child leads the way to a dream, a belief, / A time of hope through the land... A summer's day, / A mother sings / A song of purple summer / Through the heart of everything... And all shall know the wonder— / I will sing the song / Of purple summer... all shall know the wonder. (pp. 92–93)

The *Spring Awakening* performance became a public act of collective grieving and healing. It demonstrates Kierkegaard's (1846[1960]) belief that "art operates to deepen and to raise to great clarity that sense of an enveloping undefined whole that accompanies every human experience. This whole is then felt as an expansion of ourselves" (p. 350). John Dewey (1934) believed that art and imagination carry us "into a world beyond this world which is nevertheless the deeper reality of the world in which we live our ordinary experiences" (p. 202). He maintained that with the arts "we are carried out beyond ourselves to find ourselves" (p. 202).

Imagine the cathartic power of teaching and learning and its potential to move students and teachers to spaces of greater empathy and compassion. What role does creativity and imagination play in our work as teachers? When and in what ways do teachers and students have the chance to create, explore, reflect on, and express their own songs of purple summer? R. W. Boos (2008) articulates the value of this kind of existential thinking in the classroom:

> As existential educators we must consider subjective experiences most valuable.... [Our students] are saying, take off your masks; be real and authentic. Students have removed the masks given to them by others and are searching for authentic teachers and adults. To be truly effective as teachers today we must have succeeded in good measure in achieving this authenticity. (p. 117)

Malik and Akhter (2013) assert that when students are encouraged to reflect on the curriculum and how it connects to their lives, then "not only is knowledge being created, but it is interdependent on a self-constructed sense of identity and awareness":

> Existential pedagogy illuminates the core of teaching and learning as personal pursuits to find meaning, define identities, and live authentically freely. Existential pedagogy applies to learners of all ages in all learning environments. (p. 90)

TOPICS FOR REFLECTION

1. Consider these two types of teachers described through a Kierkegaard lens:
   Teacher A: the aesthetic teacher who focuses on the intellectual aspects of the curriculum;

   Teacher B: the ethical teacher who uses instructional time to explore emotional, moral, and /or spiritual considerations and discourse.

   If Teacher A and Teacher B applied for a position at your school, whom would you recommend hiring and why? What conflicts might you foresee among faculty members who support the aesthetic philosophy versus those who endorse the ethical?

   Which of these two categories would have best described you as a novice teacher? As a veteran teacher, which of the categories most aligns to your current practice? If there has there been a shift over time, what do you think accounts for that happening?

2. On a scale of 1 to 10 (1 being very little and 10 to a great extent), how would you rank the importance of the arts as a means to decrease the gap between the intellectual demands of the curriculum and the emotional needs of students?

Now consider what role creativity plays in your planning and implementation of lessons. How often and in what ways are your students engaged in exploring the curriculum in imaginative ways? What role do the fine and creative arts play in your mission and vision? How closely does the reality of their use match your beliefs?

3. Imagine Melchior was one of your students and that he asked to speak with you after class. He shares with you that the work he and his friends are asked to do in school make them feel like unthinking "cart-horses" (Wedekind, 1891/2010, p. 5). How would you respond?

What if, in reply to your answer, Melchior asks whether "a human being's sense of shame is just a product of his education" (Wedekind, 1891/2010, p. 6)? What do you imagine might be motivating Melchior (if he were one of your students) to feel this way? What do you think he is trying to say? In what ways might you respond to him? What actions or changes in your instruction might you consider in terms of Melchior's concerns?

4. Pretend that you have applied for a highly sought-after position as a curriculum specialist for your school district. You are called in for an interview with the Superintendent who has a reputation for asking challenging questions. You want to make a good impression and understand that you need to convey authenticity in your reply. During the interview, the Superintendent asks three questions inspired by Arthur T. Jersild's (1955) scholarship. How would you respond?

   a. What resources does an educator need in order to "actually realize his potentialities as a teacher" (Jersild, 1955, p. 132)?

   b. What is there in the lessons we teach, the exercises we assign, the books we read, the experiences we enter into, and in all our undertakings that can help us [teachers] find ourselves" (p. 136)?

   c. How can a teacher's selection of readings, assignments and resources help students in their personal quests to "find themselves"?

5. Congratulations! You have been nominated for a teacher recognition award in the name of legendary progressive educator John Dewey. Reflect on your body of work. Describe activities, experiences, projects, and aspirations you feel most adhere to these Deweyan principles: (1) that learning starts with the experiences and interests of the students; (2) that art and imagination are important tools for leading students to a deeper understanding of themselves; and (3) that education is a process of living rather than a *preparation* for living (Dewey, 1898. p. 87).

6. Imagine you happen to overhear a group of students mocking a teacher by playfully chanting "blaa blaa blaa blaa blaa blaa blaa blaa blaa blaa blaa blaa blaa blaa" (Sater & Sheik, 2007, p. 27). Could the teacher to whom they are referring possibly be you? How you might respond? To what extent would you dismiss their joking as meaningless playfulness? Would you ignore the incident as without merit? Would you reprimand the students for disrespecting a teacher? Or would you use the moment to reflect on your own practice?

7. A new criteria has been added to the teacher performance rating system. In addition to overall efficiency and effectiveness, teachers will now be evaluated in a third category: earnestness. The qualifying behaviors of being a "teacher of earnestness" (Kierkegaard, 1845/2000, p. 252) are listed as sincerity, thoughtfulness, and compassion. Is this criteria fair, appropriate, and/or feasible? If this were the policy, what self-assessment scores would you give yourself? What kinds of artifacts or supporting data might you provide?

8. Imagine that the school administration has issued a new performance assessment criteria requiring teachers to perform all their many duties and responsibilities from a space that more clearly demonstrates compassion and empathy. Consider what changes might need to be enacted. What sorts of practices or beliefs would need to be modified or eliminated? Debate this hypothetical mandate with a peer.

9. Consider these pieces of dialogue. How much of *Spring Awakening*'s discourse resonates in some way with your personal or professional identity (currently or in the past, and for better or for worse)?

MELCHIOR GABOR: It's the bitch of living / just getting out of bed. / It's the bitch of living / and getting what you get. (Sater & Sheik, 2007, p. 24)

WENDLA BERGMAN: Wake me in time to be lonely and sad. / And who can say what we are?... / This is the season for dreaming. (pp. 64–65)

MORITZ STEIFEL: You wanna laugh. It's too absurd. / You start to ask. Can't hear a word. / You're gonna crash and burn.... You start to cave. You start to cry. / You try to run. Nowhere to hide. (pp. 54–55)

In what ways can you empathize with the emotions and beliefs that the discourse conveys and implies?

WHERE PARALLEL LIVES MEET

The Prince of Tides, *Pat Conroy*

The narrative of an individual's life inevitably will contain events that will disrupt his or her sense of emotional security and stability. Suffering and grief can weigh on his or her personal and professional life and cast an existential shadow over the present and future. Todd May (2017) writes that "the more important the past is in its contribution to one's sense of life, the larger the shadow is likely to loom" (p. 52). Its impact can sometimes be palpable—what previously inspired or motivated an individual can lose its meaning; a person's sense of tranquility can turn into a kind perpetual restlessness; and even relationships with loved ones can start to no longer feel right.

Through his studies of loss and suffering, May (2017) asserts "the role of the past as at once granting or withdrawing meaning through its contribution to the shape of one's [life] trajectory" (p. 45). Hence, "the affirmation of one's past is required because of its contribution to one's present" (p. 54). Although an individual may attempt to deny or bury his or her grief, its presence is "patiently awaiting our notice" (p. 56).

No matter how people may attempt to suppress private hurts and sadness, Adam Phillips (2006) warns that "memories always have a future in mind" (p. 131). One's inner grief "often does insinuate itself into our [outer] lives" (May, 2017, p. 57). While grieving the passing of his wife, C. S. Lewis (1961/1996), for instance, comments that "the act of living is different all through. Her absence is like the sky, spread over everything" (p. 11). Grief teaches that the perceived boundaries between one's public and private identities are ultimately unreliable and easily broken.

When inner pain is too long left unattended and neglected, its weight and shadow can eventually extend over all aspects of a person's life. An individual's public and private lives are affected. Parker Palmer (2007) writes there is a danger of becoming disconnected "from our own truth, from the passions that took us into teaching, from the heart that is the source of all good work" (p. 21):

> If we have lost the heart to teach, how can we take heart again? How can we re-member who we are, for our own sake and the sake of those we serve?... If identity and integrity are found at the intersection of the [personal and professional] forces that converge in our lives, revisiting some of the convergences that called us toward teaching may allow us to reclaim the selfhood from which good teaching comes. (pp. 21–22)

When the reader first meets high school English teacher Tom Wingo, the protagonist of Pat Conroy's (1991) novel *The Prince of Tides*, Tom is living in precisely the space Palmer describes. Rather than grieve unspoken tragedies from his childhood, Tom grows up suppressing his memories and pain. Over time, he learns to separate his private grief from his public roles as teacher, husband, and father.

Tom lives two separate lives: a public one (as professional teacher and family man) and a private one (as a survivor of childhood trauma). He has secured his grief and emotional duress within what Adam Phillips (2006) calls a "forgetting museum" (p. 129) and sets out, in effect, to live parallel lives (an inner and an outer one). To the outside world, Tom is a well-liked teacher with a loving wife and two daughters. Inwardly, however, the memories of childhood trauma remained unattended.

In the course of the novel, Tom discovers that grief—no matter how deeply personal—cannot be kept hidden away. Eventually, his public and private lives intersect. Tom comes to realize that his professional identity as teacher and his personal one as husband and father cannot be separated from past injuries to his spirit nor from the hurts he endured to his self-esteem. During the subsequent grief journey, Tom learns that "grief is an unusually harsh teacher" (Nesse, 1991, p. 35).

As a novelist, Pat Conroy uses creativity and imagination to dramatize Tom's inner and outer journeys through grief. In this way, he creates a literary portrait of grieving that acknowledges and explores the many nuances and complexities inherent to grief as a learning experience. He presents grief as a natural process of experiencing, reflecting, and growing. Like the tides of the ocean, Tom's grief experience ebbs and flows through cycles, tempests, and seasons.

This chapter explores the capacity of *The Prince of Tides* (1991) to (1) demonstrate how the public and private strands of one's identity are intricately interwoven; (2) explore the extent to which an individual's personal challenges can both reflect on and inform his or her professional life; and (3) indicate the importance of honest self-understanding to expose what Palmer (2007) calls "*the personhood from which good teaching comes*" (p. 25).

WHEN PUBLIC AND PRIVATE LIVES CONVERGE

When Tom Wingo began his teaching career, he was confident that the pain and grief of his unspoken childhood trauma were safely hidden away (buried and repressed). His twin sister, Savannah, reminds Tom to focus on what she has observed to be his greatest assets:

> Teach them this, Tom, and teach them very well: Teach them the quiet verbs of kindness, to live beyond themselves. Urge them toward excellence, drive them toward gentleness, pull them deep into yourself, pull them upward toward manhood, but softly like an angel arranging clouds. Let your spirit move through them softly, as your spirit moves through me. (Conroy, 1986, p. 76)

These qualities became hallmarks of Tom's early work as teacher. He is respected by his peers and admired by students. Despite this, Conroy reveals that beneath Tom's professional success "was a sadness so overwhelming that I could barely move or speak.... For two years I managed to function even though I carried this sorrow around in my heart" (Conroy, 1986, p. 205). Tom was silently suffering what Adam Phillips (2010) calls phantom histories: memories, losses, and sadness "that are severed and discarded, but linger on as thwarted possibilities":

> We live in a double life, a doublethink in relation to this absence.... The phantom history is known and not known at the same time. It lives on as a strange kind of unfinished and unfinishable business. (p. 105)

The public Tom Wingo (teacher, husband, brother, and father) was adept at "run[ning] away from the things that hurt him" (Conroy, 1986, p. 403). The phantoms of his past, however, remained. Eventually Tom became so adept at running away from his inner life that without realizing it he also began running "from the people who loved him, and from the friends empowered to save him":

> But where do we run when there are no crowds, no lights, no end zones? Where does a man run? [Tom] said, studying the films of himself as a boy [playing football]. Where can a man run when he has lost the excuse of games? Where can a man run or where can he hide when he looks behind him and sees that he is only pursued by himself? (p. 403)

It was as if Tom's public life was becoming a kind of shell underneath which the emotional wounds of his personal life were left to fester. Emotionally, he could not run from his hurt and grief because the trauma of his childhood had become his inner landscape no matter where he stood. This left him personally and professionally vulnerable:

> I had suffered a terrible loss and I was simply inconsolable. I coached three sports and I taught English five classes a day and my work held me together. Then I could no longer bear the weight of my sadness. (Conroy, 1986, p. 205)

The heaviness Tom feels is the weight of his inner suffering. L. Thomas Hopkins (1954) writes that the "heart of the [learning] process" is "what takes place inside of [a person]" (p. 66). This requires what Hopkins calls "creative assimilation" (p. 51) —a two-way process within which a person learns to integrate his or her inner and outer worlds (p. 66). Tom Wingo never learned to reconcile these two parts of his one self.

Hopkins (1954) insists that without this kind of reckoning, a person cannot achieve what he calls a genuine "unity of self" (p. 63). Twenty-five years earlier Tagore (1933/2004) similarly remarked that "the object of education is to give man the unity of truth" (p. 153). Hopkins (1954) adds that "the quality of [this] process is found in the kind of self which the individual becomes" (p. 67).

Despite his efforts to deny and repress his inner hurt, the weight of Tom Wingo's grief begins to impact his outer life. Tom increasingly feels isolated and disconnected from his wife and children. But it is in his role as teacher that the inner pain surfaces most explicitly:

I was teaching one day and reading *Fern Hill* by Dylan Thomas to one of my classes; I became so moved by the poem that it brought tears to my eyes. The poem is beautiful and it moves me every time I read it but this time was different. I couldn't stop crying.... That was when they fired me. (Conroy, 1986, p. 205)

Although in the physical world he was reciting *Fern Hill* (Thomas, 1945) to his students, inwardly he was addressing his ten-year-old self. Thomas's poetic words act as a kind of talisman that awaken the grieving child within Tom's heart:

In the sun born over and over, / I ran my heedless ways, / My wishes raced through the house high hay / And nothing I cared, at my sky blue trades, that time allows / in all his tuneful turning so few and such morning songs. (Thomas, 1945, p. 196, lines 39–43)

Within Tom Wingo lives the ten-year-old boy who desperately (and unceasingly) longs for compassion and solace. The adult Tom, however, keeps "running heedlessly away" (line 40) from this inner suffering. Of remembering and grieving, "nothing he cared" (line 42). Although dismissed from his conscious mind, the child Tim remains alive in the subconscious:

Before the children green and golden / follow him out of grace, / nothing I cared, in the lamb white days that time would take me up to the swallow thronged loft by the shadow of my hand, / in the moon that is always rising. (Thomas, 1945, p. 196, lines 44–48)

The imagined innocence and splendor, "green and golden," respectively (line 44), of his "lamb white" (line 46) childhood continue to be "swallowed up in shadows" (line 47) of his memories. Child Tom has been "patiently awaiting [adult Tom's] notice" (May, 2017, p. 56). Thomas's *Fern Hill* (1945) beckons Tom Wingo's inner child forward. The images in the poem tug on the emotional chains that fetter Tom to what has become his "phantom history" (Phillips, 2010, p. 105):

I should hear him fly with the high fields / and wake to the farm forever fled from the childless land. / Oh as I was young and easy in the mercy of his means, / time held me green and dying / though I sang in my chains like the sea. (Thomas, 1945, p. 196, lines 50–54)

The farm represents Tom's youth. The truth of how it transformed from "green and golden" (line 44) to "green and dying" (line 53) is what Tom has been "forever fleeing" (line 45). As Conroy earlier observed, Tom's efforts to run away from his grief are ultimately futile because in reality, Tom Wingo "is only [being] pursued by himself" (Conroy, 1986, p. 403).

The mechanisms of his outer life helped Tom feel a sense of power and control over his inner suffering. They appeared to keep him a safe distance from his childhood pain. Adam Phillips (2010) cautions, however, that "our sense of power is [oftentimes] a function of our helplessness" (p. 121):

> Once trauma is the issue, helplessness is the heart of the matter... Our lives are always threatening to be too much for us.... We are always at risk of being overwhelmed by ourselves. (p. 121)

Deep in Tom's heart there was a nagging helplessness that eventually would not be silenced. Tom could no longer separate the personal from the professional. Being a teacher, as Jeffrey A. Kottler and Stanley J. Zehm (2000) point out, "involves a special blend of personal dimensions combined with technical and instructional expertise" (p. 6). Teaching his students this Dylan Thomas poem became for Tom Wingo the moment when his parallel public and private lives converged.

The classroom, as an arena of authenticity, epitomizes Parker Palmer's (2007) belief that "the courage to teach is the courage to keep one's heart open in those very moments when the heart is asked to hold more than it is able" (p. 12). Tom now resides fully within this emotional and spiritual space.

OUTER TIDES AND INNER STORMS

Tom recalls thinking "my class was distraught. I was distraught, but I couldn't stop myself" (Conroy, 1986, p. 205). To the outer world, there seemed to be nothing discernable in that moment to have elicited such an uncontrollable emotional outburst. But as Arne Johan Vetlesen (2004) observes, "human nature is not restricted to what can be observed" (p. 38):

> History must always be taken into account when the individual's actual situation is to be understood, with the sufferings it may contain. An individual's earlier experiences are of invaluable importance for getting 'behind' the present sufferings and afflictions. (p. 38)

Although the school administration expressed concern for his emotional well-being, Tom explained that he felt this was "a normal response to great sadness" (Conroy, 1986, p. 205). Phillips (2006) cautions that when grief and bereavement are too-long denied, "trauma becomes another word for living a life" (p. 19):

> We are in shock; in shock, but wishing our way through. It is as though there is a design flaw in the human animal; our childhood is more than our development can cope with. We are all in recovery from having been children. (p. 19)

It took being dismissed from his teaching position for Tom to realize that he needed to acknowledge and confront his inner demons. This would require a depth and intensity of introspection unlike Tom had ever experienced. Instead of repressing his emotional hurts, he set out to reflect upon them. Kottler and Zehm (2000) advocate that "reflection is a critical dimension of what it means to be an effective teacher" (p. 120):

> The reflective person has taken the time to educate him-or herself about many different aspects of human existence.... It is absolutely crucial to have structured time alone to recover from the demands placed on you by others, to consider where you are headed in your life, simply to make time for you to be able to reach deep inside yourself to find what you think and feel about what is taking place around you. (p. 123)

Tom begins seeing a psychologist. With her guidance and support, he confronts what up until now had been his unspeakable and repressed emotional and spiritual suffering. He tells his doctor that "rape is a crime against sleep and memory; its afterimage imprints itself like an irreversible negative from the camera obscura of dreams" (Conroy, 1986, p. 495). Ten-year-old Tom was home alone with his mother and sister when three armed intruders broke into the house and raped his mother and sister as Tom stood helplessly by with a gun pointed in his face. One of them then raped Tom. Twenty-five years after the attack, he acknowledges that the criminals had "defiled my image of the universe" (p. 495):

> [They] had mortgaged a portion of my boyhood, had stolen my pure sanction of a world administered by a God who loved me and who created heaven and earth as an act of divine and scrupulous joy. (p. 495)

Tom tells his psychiatrist "though our bodies would heal, our souls had sustained a damage beyond compensation. Violence sends deep roots into the heart; it has no seasons; it is always ripe, evergreen" (Conroy, 1986, p. 495). Tom eventually admits to his private shame at being helpless against the intruders and his guilt of not being able to protect his mother and sister. He describes how his older brother returned home and killed the intruders with a shotgun. Tom remembers "for fifteen minutes, we lay on the floor of the slaughterhouse that had always been our home and sanctuary" (p. 495).

Insisting that "this didn't happen" (Conroy, 1986, p. 496), Tom's mother sent Tom and his brother to bury the bodies while she and Tom's sister scrubbed down the house. Tom recalls his mother demanding that the children vow "to never tell a living soul what had happened to our family that day" (p. 500). The adult Tom admits "in silence we would honor our private shame and make it unspeakable" (p. 501). He also came to understand that "throughout our lives these three dead and slaughtered men would teach us over and over of the abidingness, the terrible constancy, that accompanies a wound to the spirit" (p. 495).

These sessions of deep introspection represent Tom Wingo visiting his personal "forgetting museum" (Phillips, 2006, p. 129). The museum's collection of sufferings (i.e., guilt, shame, regret, fear, and helplessness) were carefully preserved. Because grieving and healing were not allowed into the museum, the emotions stored there remained as real, painful, and urgent as they were twenty-five years earlier when the museum was constructed at his mother's behest ("This did not happen").

These spaces of concealed inwardness are what Ralph Harper (1965) describes as "metaphysical tension(s) within the soul" (p. 25) that create what Harper calls a perpetual "source of disquietude" (p. 25). Suffering these inner wounds left Tom "avoiding the present that he is really made for" (p. 25) and rendered him unable to be truly present to himself and to those around him (p. 33). Thus, his closest relationships (wife, daughters, students) became increasingly strained.

Palmer (2007) warns "when teachers dismiss inner truth and honor only the external world, students as well as teachers lose heart" (p. 19). The more the emotional hurt within Tom Wingo remained unacknowledged and unattended, the more his passion for all aspects of his outer life (personally and professionally) diminished. As he continued his sessions with the psychiatrist, Tom further grieved his past and began to take steps toward healing and forgiveness. Tom realizes that "for the first time in a year, I started to have dreams of teaching again" (Conroy, 1986, p. 282):

> I was in a classroom and the subject was Tolstoy and I was telling a class composed of all those students who had ever loved me as a teacher that the reason Tolstoy was great was because he was passionate. Why was it, I wondered, that I was most passionate talking about books I had loved? In the dream it was easy. Those books honored me; those books changed me.... When I woke from the dream I realized that I had no classroom to enter whenever a new book took possession of me. I needed students to complete myself. (p. 282)

In his treatise on public education, Leo Tolstoy (1860) identifies two figures in a classroom: one is "vivacious and curious" with "a sparkle in his eyes and on his lips" as he "strongly express[es] his thoughts" (p. 176); the other he describes as "a worn-out, retiring being, with an expression of fatigue, terror, and ennui, mouthing strange words in a strange language—a being whose soul has retreated, like a snail, into its house" (p. 176). Of these two descriptions, Tom recognizes himself as having become the latter. As he relates his dream to his psychiatrist, he realizes that "as a teacher, I had been a happy man. Now, I was only a diminished one" (Conroy, 1986, p. 282).

For Tom, grieving the tragedies of his past was difficult, yet critical work. Facing his trauma meant reflecting on what Jeff Golliher (2008) calls "the dark night of the soul":

> To sense darkness within ourselves is supposed to be troubling—disquietude, restlessness, the feeling that something isn't right, fear of the unknown.... Difficult inner struggles, grief, personal tragedies—these might trigger it... a difficult nest of emotions involving fear: the fear of being blamed, for example, or wrongly accused, and the feeling that I won't be met with approval. (pp. 113–115)

Golliher (2008) writes that "movements through grief are not about survival or maintaining a status quo" (p. 118). Instead, he describes them as opportunities for transformation wherein "some part of us dies; another part lives on" (p. 118). Throughout *The Prince of Tides* (1986) is a repeated motif that captures the movements from *diminishment* to *remembrance* and from *recovery* to *reidentification*. These fluid stages of growth and development reinforce the idea that grieving and healing are not found in solutions and cures. They are to be experienced in a continual process of reflection and renewal.

Tom Wingo's emotional recovery starts from a place of *diminishment* (where suppressed memories were left alone to fester) and moves to a place where personal tragedies are *remembered* and grieved. Although the emotional scars would remain, Tom was beginning to *recover* and heal. He could start to *reidentify* with the values and beliefs from which he had become disconnected. These terms represent movements of emotions as they ebb and flow throughout Tom's personal and professional lives.

The charts below demonstrate how Conroy (1986) uses words and images to portray these inner tides of growth and change. These dynamic processes defy linear framing as they integrate cognitive, emotional, and spiritual concerns. The chart format is intended only as tool in terms of ascertaining qualities and traits of the various emotional movements that often occur simultaneously. The chart format itself does not speak to the organic and oftentimes unexpected course that these intrinsic movements, experiences, and epiphanies take. Nevertheless, it offers a starting point for further reflection.

Navigating the Tides of Our Identities	
Diminishment	The island boy, Tom Wingo, had cut himself off from all who loved him and set himself adrift in the sea lanes of a long and dreamless attrition. (p. 663)
Remembrance	Why don't you try to find out who inhabits that soul beneath the shoulder pads? (p. 478)… I'm sick of hiding what I really am, what I feel inside. I'm going to New York where I don't have to be afraid to find out everything there is to know about myself. (p. 481)
Recovery	I tried to marshal the fragments of wisdom I had learned as an island child and put them in order like some undiscovered archipelago I could return to at will. (p. 485)
Reidentification	I had taught myself to listen to the black sounds of the heart and learned some things that would serve me well. I had come to this moment with my family safely around me and I prayed that they would always be safe and that I would be contented with what I had. (p. 677)
Reflection	Where is the "soul beneath the shoulder pads" of our personal and professional identities?

Navigating the Journeys of Time

Diminishment	My body had not felt like an instrument of love or passion for such a long time; it had been a winter of deadening seriousness, when all the illusions and bright dreams of my early twenties had withered and died. I did not yet have the interior resources to dream new dreams. (p. 25)
Remembrance	There were things to be learned on the tangents and the extremities.... Once you have traveled, the voyage never ends, but is played out over and over again in the quietest chambers, that the mind can never break off from the journey. (pp.151–152)
Recovery	It was not [my sister's] tears or my father's tears that caused this resonance, this fierce interior music of blood and wildness and identity. It was the beauty and fear of kinship, the ineffable ties of family, that sounded a blazing terror and an awestruck love inside of me. (p. 675)
Reidentification	My character [has risen] to the surface.... I [choose] to honor my history. (p. 671)
Reflection	In what ways do our future dreams honor our past experiences?

Navigating Waves of Contemplation

Diminishment	I began to run down the beach. At first it was controlled, patient, but then I started to push myself, letting it out, until I was sprinting, breaking into a sweat, and gasping for air. If I could hurt the body, I would not notice the coming apart of the soul. (p. 31)
Remembrance	His death forced me to acknowledge the secret wisdom that issues from the contemplative life.... As an adult I would envy forever the simplicity and grandeur of [my grandfather's] vision of what it was to be a complete and contributing man. His whole life was compliance and a donation to an immaculate faith. (p. 572)
Recovery	I've got to try to make something beautiful out of the ruins. (p. 672)
Reidentification	Lord, I am a teacher and a coach. That is all and it is enough. (p. 672)
Reflection	Imagine how concepts such as simplicity, contemplation, and faith can influence a teacher's work.

Despite the outward gestures of affection and respect Tom received from his family and students, an inner wave of hurt, distrust, and self-deprecation washed over his inner landscape and diminished his self-esteem. Conroy's choice of descriptors (i.e., withering, gasping, breaking, coming apart) evoke this inner despair. No one suspected that underneath Tom's façade of success was a power-keg of emotional and spiritual despair and self-loathing. Although he kept his past locked in his "forgetting museum" (Phillips, 2006, p. 129), waves of self-hatred and regret managed to still wash over his heart. When this happened, Tom felt undeserving of happiness and love; hence, he pushed himself away from his family and career.

Feeling diminished from the inside out, Tom eventually succumbs to his inner grief while reciting *Fern Hill* (Dylan Thomas, 1945) to his high school students. For Tom, in that moment the classroom became a space of remembrance. Other descriptions Conroy uses for spaces of remembrance include: the soul beneath the shoulder pads, the sea lanes of attrition, emotional tangents and extremities, and locales of simplicity and grandeur. This event convinces Tom to seek help from a psychiatrist who eventually guides him to other spaces of remembrance. It is significant that his initial breakthrough occurs while teaching. After all, the classroom is a living space that ultimately demands authenticity, courage, and honesty if it is going to nurture the levels of transformation it has the capacity to procure.

As Tom begins remembering life-changing events from his childhood that he has long suppressed, he comes to understand some of the reasons for his self-imposed diminishment and low self-esteem. Emotionally and spiritually, Tom was teaching from a space of spiritual hurt. Guilt (of not protecting his mother and sister when criminals invaded their home), shame (at having been sexually victimized), and helplessness (to stop the violence) were slowly tearing away at his emotional core. Although he was able to function for many years by relying on his intellectual and cognitive abilities, eventually the emotional, spiritual, and moral components of his humanity demanded attention, healing, and nurturing.

Whereas remembrance implies looking backward, recovery is forward-looking. Although these may sound like opposing ideas, Conroy's text shows not only that they coexist, but that they are reliant on each other. Kay Chang (2017) expounds on the emotional partnership of grieving and healing in which "there is a need to cry and a need to fly":

> Grieving takes time.... There is both a need to respectfully acknowledge the on-going burden of living without loved ones or the familiar ways of life and to thoughtfully foster new ways of building on the communal strengths of the survivors.... One can neither keep on mourning about the past indefinitely nor can one create a future without looking back at the past from time to time. Most survivors of trauma will come to make sense out of the recovery process—the pain never completely goes away, it gets to be part of life. (p. 4)

The Prince of Tides (1986) reminds us that the inner truths that anchor our identities and values (as individuals and as teachers) need to be reflected on and revisited lest we lose sight of that which nourishes and supports the integrity of our work. Engaging in a grieving teacher's curriculum, like so much of the teaching profession, takes courage, perseverance, and meaningful introspection. Tom Wingo demonstrates that the rewards of working through grief lie in the potential to transform loss into meaningful personal and professional growth. It is worth repeating that "grief is an unusually harsh teacher" (Nesse, 1991, p. 35). For Tom, grief is a truly transformative learning experience.

The curriculum of grief for Tom Wingo was Tom Wingo himself. Only by better understanding himself, his values and beliefs, and the experiences that both challenged and sustained them was Tom able to remember, recover, and reidentify with his teacher's heart. Tom Wingo's story illustrates the highly personal nature of teaching. As William Ayers (1993) points out, "greatness in teaching requires a serious encounter with autobiography" (p. 129):

> Who are you? How did you come to take on your views and outlooks? What forces helped to shape you? What was it like for you to be ten? What have you made of yourself? Where are you heading? An encounter with these kinds of questions is critical to outstanding teachers because teachers, whatever else they teach, they teach themselves. (p. 129)

ASCERTAINING WHAT'S REAL WITHIN THE SURREAL

While external measurements of a teacher's effectiveness are important, they do not tell the complete story. Ernst Cassirer (1954) suggests that ascertaining the quality of a teaching and learning experience relies more on examining and reflecting on the "varied threads which weave the symbolic net, the tangled web of human experience" (p. 42). Because many of these threads are emotional and spiritual in nature, Cassirer reminds us that when reflecting upon them, individuals are "no longer in a merely physical world" as much as "a symbolic universe" (p. 42).

Cassirer asserts that images from myth, art, and religion are better suited than discernible facts and measurements in terms of understanding and reflecting on one's values, aspirations, and emotions. For instance, rather than trying to quantify Tom Wingo's despair, Conroy (1986) describes it by comparing its intensity to "the dark music of crucifixionists" (p. 572). Cassirer writes that the situation of grief "is the same in the theoretical as in the practical sphere":

> Even here [in the natural world] man does not live [exclusively] in a world of hard facts, or according to his immediate needs and desires. He lives rather in the midst of imaginary emotions, in hope and fears, in illusions and disillusions, in his fantasies and dreams. (pp. 42–43)

Tom's twin sister, Savannah, shared the same harrowing experience on that violent evening twenty-five years earlier. Of the family agreement to never speak about the incident, Tom reports "only Savannah broke the agreement, but she did it with a wordless and terrible majesty. Three days later she cut her wrists for the first time" (Conroy, 1986, p. 501). Savannah would survive three other suicide attempts. When she was well enough, she wrote (and published) poems that captured the reality of her desperation. Poetic images and language allowed Savannah to give voice to her suffering.

One of the symbols Savannah draws on for her poetry is that of the Infant of Prague. Traditionally the figure represents blessings bestowed on the innocence of childhood. Since Savannah's youth was devastated by violence and silence, to her mind the Infant of Prague failed in its role as protector. In Savannah's poetry the Infant is depicted having joined forces with "black dogs of suicide and the angels of negation" (Conroy, 1986, p. 462). She articulates a surrealist vision in which these dark spirits chant a "withering litany she had heard since childhood, taunting her with her worthlessness" and "regaling her with murderous hymns and chants" (p. 462).

Whereas scholars such as John Gray (2003) support the idea that "some truths cannot be told except as fiction" (p. 131), others disagree. Donald Davidson (1978) asserts "we must give up on the idea that a metaphor carries a message, that it has a content or meaning (except, of course, its literal meaning)" (p. 45). Richard Rorty (1989) argues that although metaphors may draw people's attention to certain feelings or thoughts, they are not "truth-telling devices" (p. 17). By this thinking, Savannah's images that include "dogs hanging on meat hooks from her apartment wall, their bodies twisted in agony" and of "hundreds of these crucified dogs screamed out, their voices sibilant and intertwined" (Conroy, 1986, p. 462) might be regarded as "irrational ruptures" (Rorty, 1989, p. 17) without further semantic meaning or depth.

On the other hand, Daniel Chandler (2002) purports that "any representation is more than merely a representation of that which it represents: it also contributes to the construction of reality" (p. 66). Through her poetry, Savannah turns her unspeakable childhood experience into a narrative through which she can impose some sense on it. George Lakoff and Mark Johnson (1980) argue "the essence of metaphor is understanding and experiencing one kind of thing in terms of another" (p. 5).

To Savannah's mind, invaders breaking into her childhood home and raping her, her mother, and her brother is no less surreal than the "disfigured angels with their fluted, encircling voices" (Conroy, 1986, p. 462) in her poetry. Having what was the "living" room of her home transformed into a "slaughterhouse" (p. 495) is no less real to her rational mind than "the small feet of the Infant of Prague, lynched from the ceiling, demanding of Savannah [in the voice of Savannah's mother] that she maintain her silence" (p. 462).

Lynn Butler Kisber (2014) asserts that these kinds of artistic representations are helpful in terms of their capacity to "evoke emotion and metaphoric meaning, and reveal unspoken and unintentional understandings that otherwise may remain hidden" (p. 50). Tom and Savannah's mother's response to the crimes committed in their home all those years ago was to deny them completely: "this didn't happen. Do you understand? Do you all understand? This did not happen" (Conroy, 1986, p. 496). When Savannah writes that "black dogs of suicide" are "calling for her death" should we respond in the same way, that it "didn't happen"?

The images Savannah uses to describe the inner devastation she and Tom experienced as children (i.e., angels whose "eye sockets were black holes flowing with pus" and "menstruating angels hanging from shower rods" [Conroy, 1986, p. 462]) embody fear, grief, and despair that for Tom and Savannah are all too real. Imagine trying to role play a "normal" outer life when it is as if "hundreds of crucified dogs" are "screaming out" in your mind (p. 462).

Tom's and Savannah's outer sadness were only a fraction of the much darker desperation they experienced internally. Gray (2003) muses that an individual's conscious thoughts are only a tiny percentage of the vast storehouse of intrinsic images, memories, and understandings. Although the nightmarish images Savannah uses may defy the laws of the natural world and surpass the boundaries of the physical environment, their emotional resonance is genuine.

Tom's emotional reality, suppressed for so many years, had subconsciously become the lens through which he started to perceive the outer world. Zygmunt Bauman (2006) calls this "diverted fear" (p. 3)—when the apprehension of uncertainty yields heightened insecurity and vulnerability. One of the outer-world manifestations of these diverted fears is Tom's gradual emotional distancing from his students and family. Lars Svendsen (2007) writes that "fear prevents precisely that which could cause it to diminish: human contact" (p. 98):

Fear and mistrust become self-perpetuating.... A fear culture is, then, a culture where trust disintegrates. In a world that is increasingly perceived as dangerous, it is difficult to have trust—you want assurances instead. (p. 98)

Trust is integral to healthy relationships. As Tom's inner pain and fear increased, his ability to maintain relationships with his wife and children diminished. He later came to understand more clearly how his inner life was impairing his outer one:

I became tentative, suspicious, and dull. I learned to hold my tongue and mark my trail behind me and to look to the future with a wary eye. Finally, I was robbed of a certain optimism, that reckless acceptance of the world and all it could hand my way that had always been my strength and deliverance. (Conroy, 1986, p. 539)

Tom Wingo's personal and professional lives had reached an impasse. Fear replaced his capacity for trust. Bertrand Russell (1921/1950) describes fear as "the main source of superstition, and one of the main sources of cruelty. To conquer fear is the beginning of wisdom, in the pursuit of truth as in the endeavor after a worthy manner of life" (p. 96). If Tom aspired to a lead a life of integrity as a teacher, husband, and father, he needed (as Russell articulated) "to conquer fear in the pursuit of truth." Conroy's novel illustrates how the consequences of not attending to inner suffering can affect many aspects of one's outer life.

Without grieving and coming to terms with his loss and sadness, Tom Wingo could no longer be the individual—personally or professionally—that he had the potential to be. Tom's courage to comfort and forgive his inner ten-year-old self eventually lead him to spiritual catharsis and a transformation of spirit:

I had taught myself to listen to the black sounds of the heart and learned some things that would serve me well. I had come to this moment with my family safely around me and I prayed that they would always be safe and that I would be contented with what I had.... Lord, I am a teacher and a coach. That is all and it is enough. (Conroy, p. 677)

In Conroy's (2002) epilogue to *My Losing Season*, he writes that "there is no teacher more discriminating or transforming than loss" in its capacity "to invite reflection and reformulating and a change of strategies" toward living a more worthwhile life (p. 395):

Losing prepares you for the heartbreak, setback, and tragedy that you will encounter in the world more than winning ever can. By licking the wounds, you learn how to avoid getting wounded the next time. (p. 395)

Conroy (2002) reminds us that throughout an individual's life, public and private identities, values, and aspirations are challenged by events (often unexpected) that have the potential to derail or significantly alter his or her mission and vision. These are moments of personal and professional reckoning:

Loss hurts and bleeds and aches. Loss is always ready to call out your name in the night. Loss follows you home and taunts you at the breakfast table, follows you to work in the morning. You have to make accommodations and broker deals to soften the rabbit punches that loss brings to your daily life. (p. 395)

Even as teachers assume exterior personas that embody the title, role, and exterior manners of professional educators, their inner realities always "follow [them] to work in the morning" (Conroy, 2002, p. 395). Like Tom Wingo, teachers may ignore or suppress personal grief and loss as they persevere in their professional capacity. Nevertheless, one's inner life "is always ready to call out [our] name" (p. 395).

Conroy reminds us that throughout one's life, our personal and professional identities will need varying degrees of attention, grieving, and healing. Individuals, however, are often left on their own to persevere through times of personal or inner crisis. Nevertheless, Tom Wingo, albeit a literary character, challenges us to acknowledge, honor, and embrace the integration of our personal and professional identities; warns us about the risks of denying or ignoring our inner pain and grief; and teaches us that through reflection and grieving, catharsis and renewal are possible.

TOPICS FOR REFLECTION

1. To what extent is your professional life more or less following a linear trajectory—a measurable, map-like series of professional experiences ostensibly marked by promotions, career advancement, and tenure? Can you recall times when this professional cartography has not aligned with the nonlinear events of your inner life? What resources and supports do you turn to for sustenance during these kinds of moments when the geography of your inner life has upset the more anticipated cartography of your professional life?

2. What are some of the beliefs and values that define and sustain the intrinsic quality of your teaching? In what ways are these reflected in your classroom interactions and discourse? Can you recall examples or stories that reveal the ways in which you believe these qualities have transformed your instruction from mundane to extraordinary and from mechanical to transformational?

3. Although in the physical world Tom Wingo is reciting a Dylan Thomas poem to his students, on a spiritual level he is reading the words to his ten-year-old self. Can you recall a similar experience in which outer words and actions unexpectedly resonated with you on personal and/or emotional levels? Reflect upon times when your professional (outer) being became closely aligned to your inner self.

   Have there been times when personal concerns could not be separated from your professional work? Can you remember times when (whether you realized it at the time or not) you stood at the precipice "where personal and public meet" (Palmer, 2007, p. 18)? Have you ever considered moments when your students may have experienced this same sort of intersection between outer events and inner beliefs or values?

4. Parker Palmer (2007) writes that good teaching comes from a teacher's identity and integrity (p. 13); and that meaningful instruction has as much to do with a teacher's wounds, fears, and shadows as with his or her strengths and talents (p. 13). From this, Parker observes that "teaching is a daily exercise in vulnerability" (p. 17). Reflect on moments throughout your life as a teacher (and as a student) when your inner personal vulnerabilities impacted your outer work. What can be gained by reflecting on these kinds of experiences?

5. Pretend the theme for your next professional development session is: How a teacher's personal and professional vulnerabilities can serve to strengthen his or her practice. What are some of the issues you think might be addressed? What kinds of responses or discussion points might be and/or should be raised? If you were asked to prepare a brief presentation pertaining to this theme, what might you say or present to the audience?

6. Consider Tom Wingo's epiphany: "Lord, I am a teacher and a coach. That is all and it is enough" (Conroy, 1986, p. 677). To what extent and in what ways does this reflect your self-perception (personally and professionally) as an educator?

7. Reflect on this Bertrand Russell (1921/1950) quotation: "Fear is the main source of superstition, and one of the main sources of cruelty. To conquer fear is the beginning of wisdom, in the pursuit of truth as in the endeavor after a worthy manner of life" (p. 96).

   What are some of the superstitions that students (and teachers) have about teaching and learning? Can you name some of the fears that arise from them?

CHAPTER 5

How can educators counter these fears and superstitions and forge a path toward truth and wisdom?

8. Kottler and Zehm (2000) advocate that "reflection is a critical dimension of what it means to be an effective teacher" (p. 120). What opportunities for individual and collective reflecting do you have as a professional teacher?

If you were given the opportunity (and a budget) to plan a weekend reflective retreat for you and your peers, what topics, challenges, and/or activities would you like to see on the agenda? To what degree do we believe that by better understanding ourselves (i.e., values, conflicts, fears, aspirations) we educators can in turn better serve our students? If you could invite anyone to speak as an advocate for reflective practice, whom would you invite? (Since it is a "magical invitation" your selections do not need to be restricted by space and time.)

9. In his prologue to *The Prince of Tides*, Conroy (1986) observes "my wound is geography. It is also my anchorage, my port of call" (p. 1). *Port of call* (its first recorded use dates to 1880–1885) began as a nautical term meaning a place where a ship stops during its voyage usually to take on or discharge passengers and cargo or to undergo repairs (OED, n.d.). Extending that metaphor to your contemporary public and private lives, what are your metaphorical ports of call? At what time or place have you paused to evoke or channel mentors, friends, or family members whose values, inspiration, or examples have been integral to your personal and professional mission and vision?

Consider life/career moments when your values have been tested, your integrity questioned, and/or when your mission and vision needed to be re-examined. These are examples of times when we return to our ports of call for reflection, healing, and renewal. What have these kinds of experiences taught you about yourself as a teacher—and as a person? In what ways have they impacted your life as educator and the lives of your students?

CHAPTER 6

MOMENTS OF RECKONING

The Aeneid, *Virgil*

Whether mourning the passing of a loved one, the loss of a long-held aspiration, or the failure of a vision to be fulfilled, grieving has the potential to emotionally reverberate to the core of one's humanity. Aeneas (*The Aeneid*, Virgil, 19 BCE/1990) is an archetype of humanity's struggle to reckon with inner trials that impact one's public and private lives. His public responsibilities are vast. His mission calls him to unite a multitude of tribes, to coordinate a dangerous journey across the Mediterranean Sea, and to establish a nation that is destined to become the Ancient Roman Empire. While executing these momentous tasks, Aeneas suffers an intense grief that interrupts and threatens to debilitate his public vocation.

While his ships are shored on the Northeastern African coast to replenish needed supplies, Aeneas falls in love with Dido, the Queen of Carthage. Within a spell of love, Aeneas proposes marriage. A prophetic dream, however, reminds Aeneas that his public duty is to leave Carthage and establish Rome. Hundreds of men are looking to him for leadership. The history of the Western world itself is relying on Aeneas to return to his public mission.

In short, Aeneas chooses duty over love. Deciding to sacrifice his personal happiness (and Dido's), he hardens his heart and immediately returns to prepare his ships to continue the voyage. As he and his men sail away, Aeneas sees in the distance the red glare of a fiery funeral pyre burning on the shore of Carthage. Suffering despair, heartache, and public humiliation, Queen "Dido's heart beat wildly at the enormous thing afoot. She rolled her bloodshot eyes. Her quivering cheeks were flecked with red as her sick pallor grew before her coming death" (Virgil, Book IV, p. 119, lines 892–896).

As Aeneas and his crew sail further from Carthage, the flames continue to rise. While Queen Dido is being consumed by the flames, she cries for "the cold Trojan, far at sea, [to] drink in this conflagration and take with him the omen of my death!" (Virgil, 19 BCE/1990, Book IV, p. 120, lines 917–191). Once he realizes the repercussions of his decision, Aeneas is consumed with flames of another sort: those of guilt, remorse, and shame. His public mission, which fueled his decision to leave, will also be jeopardized by the emotional conflagration.

Although Aeneas the Character existed 2,000 years ago, Aeneas the Archetype remains contemporary. It embodies the emotional complexities inherent to human beings and demonstrates in dramatic fashion the intricate entanglement of an

© KONINKLIJKE BRILL NV, LEIDEN, 2020 | DOI: 10.1163/9789004422506_006

individual's public and private lives. Aeneas personifies what Paulo Freire (2008) calls a person's capacity to *create* and *recreate* his or her relationship to the world (p. 3). In order to reconcile himself with the past, find solace in the present, and recommit himself to the future, Aeneas learns that he must "transcend a single dimension" in order to "reach back to yesterday, recognize today, and come upon tomorrow" (p. 3).

As Aeneas's grief journey moves across relevant spaces of the past, present, and future, he experiences what Freire (2008) identifies as a process of integration: "the capacity to adapt oneself to reality *plus* the critical capacity to make choices and to transform that reality" (p. 4). He reckons with his past and present so that he can *recreate* for himself a future path that more closely aligns his inner values and beliefs with his public duties. Freire (2008) describes this depth of introspection as a means of operating "not only *in* the world but *with* the world":

> This shock between a yesterday which is losing relevance but still seeking to survive, and a tomorrow which is gaining substance, characterizes the phase of transition as a time of announcement and a time of decision. (p. 6)

Aeneas's grief journey teaches the importance of placing oneself in "consciously critical confrontation" (Freire, 2008, p. 12) with his or her own spiritual and emotional challenges. Previously, Aeneas's work was narrowly focused on accomplishing outer tasks. His journey of grief and introspection teaches him that *how and why* one goes about this is equally important. In this way, an individual becomes "the agent of his own recuperation" (p. 12).

This chapter examines Aeneas's journey of grief, which in many ways is "an education of 'I wonder,' instead of merely, 'I do'" (Freire, 2008, p. 32). As a man of action, Aeneas is called to build cities. But as a man of character, Aeneas has the potential to construct communities of compassion and empathy. Similarly, as teachers of action, we are called to raise assessment scores. But as teachers of character, we, too, have the potential to create spaces of understanding and fellowship.

MOVEMENTS OF MOURNING

Aeneas hastily focuses exclusively on his mission and sails away from Carthage (and Dido) with his crew. By refusing to "reach back to yesterday or recognize today" (Freire, 2008, p. 3), he leads his crew "through the waves blown dark by a chill wind, [and] held his ships firmly on course for a mid-sea crossing" (Virgil, 19 BCE/1990, Book V, p. 125, lines 1–3). His men, on the other hand, "kept [their] eyes upon the city far astern, now bright with poor Dido's pyre" (lines 4–5). They "knew of a great love profaned" that led their "hearts into foreboding" (lines 8–9).

Nine days later, Aeneas is suddenly shaken with "grieving and [overcome] in tears" (Virgil, 19 BCE/1990, Book VI, p. 159, line 1). Unable to ignore or deny his grief—and its related guilt, remorse, and shame—Aeneas sets out on new course, an inner one. He lands his ship ashore and navigates a different kind of journey through what Jacques Derrida (2001) calls a "world suspended by some unique tear" (p. 107). For the first time since leaving Dido, Aeneas cries out in heartfelt lamentation. His conscience (embodied in the voice of the mythological Sibyl) scolds him:

> "Slow, are you, in your vows and prayers? / Trojan Aeneas, are you slow? Be quick, / the great mouths of the god's house, thunder-struck, / will never open until you pray" (Virgil, 19 BCE/1990, Book VI, p. 161, lines 84–87)

> "Boldly, more boldly where your luck allows, / Go forward, face them" (p. 163, lines 144–145)

Aeneas is drawn into an inner journey to face his grief and regret. The depth of his sorrow is deep. It is dramatized in his movements across the ancient underworld. Virgil uses the underworld as an extended metaphor. This landscape represents his emotional geography. The underworld personifies the expanse of Aeneas's introspection as he revisits pivotal individuals from his past, recognizes his present emotional despair, and *recreates* his path forward. Despite the many battlefield enemies and physical altercations he has faced, Aeneas is about to discover that confronting grief, remorse, and shame will require an even higher degree of courage and fortitude.

His first reckoning with grief is dramatically imagined within the Fields of Mourning. Here Aeneas encounters the spirits of "those whom pitiless love consumed with cruel wasting, hidden on paths apart by myrtle woodland growing overhead. In death itself, pain will not let them be" (Virgil, 19 BCE/1990, Book VI, p. 175, lines 596–598). Aeneas now confronts Queen Dido "with her fatal wound still fresh" (line 599):

> He wept and spoke / tenderly to her: "Dido, so forlorn, / the story then that came to me was true, / that you were out of life, had met your end / by your own hand. Was I, was I the cause?" (Book VI, p. 175, lines 612–116)

Aeneas literally and figuratively comes face to face with his decision to prioritize public duty over personal honor and private commitments:

> "I left your land against my will, my queen. / The gods' commands drove me to do their will, / as now they drive me through this world of shades, / these moldy waste lands and these depths of night. / And I could not believe that I would hurt you / so terribly by going. Wait a little. / Do not leave my sight. Am I someone to flee from? The last word / destiny lets me say to you is this." Aeneas with such pleas tried to placate / the burning soul, savagely glaring back. / And tears came to his eyes. (Virgil, 19 BCE/1990, Book VI, p. 176, lines 620–630)

Grief has much to teach Aeneas. This exchange demonstrates how his understanding of the relationship between duty and love is evolving. His worldview is expanding to include an empathy and compassion he has never known before. Years later, Aeneas will be a more compassionate, empathic leader due to the lessons

99

he is now receiving. By opening himself up to his vulnerabilities, he is fortifying his strength of heart.

As a middle school language arts teacher, I had the opportunity to bring students to a local young-adult adaptation of the Henry Purcell and Nahum Tate (1688) opera *Dido and Aeneas*. The Aeneas-Dido relationship especially resonated with students. When Aeneas suffers the pangs of conscience at having left Dido behind, some students criticized his guilt and shame as weaknesses. Others argued that he was wrong to treat Dido cruelly, reasoning that personal commitment (and love) should outweigh his work-related mission. Some students argued strongly that the needs of the hundreds of thousands of citizens who would benefit from Aeneas's public mission far outweighed his commitment to a single individual. Others insisted that without Dido's support and affection, Aeneas's leadership and victories would be hollow.

I was struck by my students' thoughtful deliberation as they contemplated the relationship between private and public commitments and some of the related ethical nuances. It reminded me of the capacity of visual and performance art to reflect, inspire, and challenge an individual's fundamental understandings of his or her world. Just when I had become convinced of the remarkable success of my curriculum planning and implementation, the students, as is often their custom, turned the proverbial tables on me: If I were Aeneas, what would I have done? Had I ever been in a situation like this? Would I *really* choose my professional life over my personal one?

Oh, dear. Crossing the existential bridge between inner truths and outer performance was intimidating. I felt that I was standing at the very precipice Parker Palmer (2007) described wherein a teacher "must stand where personal and public meet" (p. 18). Aeneas's interaction with Dido's spirit is a reminder that being true to one's inner emotional commitments is difficult and courageous work. To be honest, I admit that I retreated from the situation—proclaiming that our time was up and we needed to move on.

I wonder whether anyone having stood in my teacher shoes at that moment would ever question the relevancy of Virgil's *Aeneid* to contemporary life. Aeneas's crisis of integrity is *our* crisis; his wrangling with guilt and loss is *our wrestling*; and his grieving is *our* grieving. Pascale-Anne Brault and Michael Naas (2001) note that these crises represent the kinds of emotional and spiritual intricacies which are fundamental to our lives. They identify them as essential components of a larger "rhetoric of mourning"—when an individual "interiorizes the status of the other in us" (p. 21). Brault and Naas assert that the "metonymic force of mourning" (p. 18) embody movement of intrinsic and emotional *gestures* to larger-scale *citations* and, eventually, to a universal *metonymy*.

This movement from *gesture* to *citation* to *metonymy* embodies the movements of mourning. Gesture implies the internalizing of the "other." Consider persons who have moved out of our day-to-day lives but remain fixed in our memories and hearts; or dreams and aspirations that are no longer within our reach but nevertheless remain hidden and/or protected within our minds; or values or ideals that have come up short in our personal or professional lives but whose idealized roots remain protected deep in our core. Cherished individuals and beliefs remain a part of us through gestures of thought and remembrance. In this way, we move forward while retaining the spirit of the loved ones that have touched us on our journey.

Gestures of grieving can be emotionally intense because they tear down the walls of our secular lives that often prevent a person from experiencing the intensity of his or her emotions. When Aeneas faces the underworld spirit (gesture) of Queen Dido, its tearful eyes, burning soul, and savage glare are unfiltered and raw. It cuts to the very core of his being and breaks down the wall that separated Aeneas from his emotions. Until this moment, he mostly acted from a space of apathy: passive, detached, and indifferent to the feelings of others. Aeneas felt no ethical commitment towards Dido. His apathy had become a barrier that separated Aeneas from the portion of his humanity that felt things deeply. His grief journey through the underworld essentially tears down apathy and exposes Aeneas to a set of emotions he had previously denied, repressed, or devalued.

Apathy can also affect our work as teachers. To enact the business of teaching and learning while keeping compassion and sympathy behind a wall of apathy may increase productivity and efficiency—but at what cost? Leo Buscaglia (1982) warns that the opposite of teaching from a place of compassion is to teach from a space of apathy. How effective can even the most efficient of teachers be when his or her demeanor, attitude, outlook, or discourse are coming from a space of apathy? Buscaglia (1982) goes so far as to issue an explicit directive:

It's too bad when you go to work and you don't love it, especially in our profession. If you don't get excited every morning about getting into that room with all those little kids with their bright eyes waiting for you to help them, then get *the hell out of education!* Do something where you're not going to be coming into contact with little kids and killing them at an early age. (p. 36)

Aeneas leaves the Fields of Mourning and visits the Blessed Groves of the underworld. Here Virgil demonstrates movement from *gesture* to *citation* as Aeneas interacts with the spirit of his deceased father. His father's words (his father's *citation*) represent the substance of Aeneas's emerging personal realizations:

Son, refrain! You must not blind your heart / to that enormity of civil war, / turning against your country's very heart / her own vigor of manhood. / You above all / who trace your line from the immortals, you / be first to spare us. Child of my own blood, throw away your sword! (Virgil, 19 BCE/1990, Book VI, p. 189, lines 1120–1126)

His father's words (*citation*) expand the narrow confines of Aeneas's grief. Aeneas's discernment of life's larger meaning, purpose, and context is beginning to emerge:

First, then, the sky and lands and sheets of water, / the bright moon's globe, / the Titan sun and stars, / are fed within by Spirit, and a Mind / infused through all the members of the world / makes one great living body of the mass. (Virgil, 19 BCE/1990, Book VI, p. 185, lines 973–977)

Aeneas is beginning to grasp the reverence and import incumbent to serving something larger than his individual self. These sentiments help him understand that he can best honor those whose lives he has impacted (negatively or positively) by aspiring to a more altruistic mission and vision:

You are the only soul who shall restore / our wounded state by waiting out the enemy. / Others will cast more tenderly in bronze their breathing figures, I can well believe, / and bring more lifelike portraits out of marble; / argue more eloquently, use the pointer / to trace the paths of heaven accurately / and accurately foretell the rising stars. / Roman remember by your strength to rule / earth's peoples- / for your arts are to be these.... Child of our mourning, if only in some way / you could break through your bitter fate. (Virgil, 19 BCE/1990, Book VI, p. 190, lines 1143–1152; p. 191, lines 1197–1198)

These words (*citation*) demonstrate Aeneas reconciling his inner grief with the continuance of his future public endeavors. He is beginning to realize that, in great part due to his personal losses and grief, he is now capable of better understanding the suffering and hardships of the people he serves as leader. His suffering has informed his mission and vision with an empathy through which he can now better appreciate the lives of the individuals to whom he is responsible.

In this way, Aeneas is maturing developmentally and emotionally. Similarly, L. Thomas Hopkins (1954) writes that a major purpose of education is for its participants (teachers and students) to grow and become the best version of themselves possible (p. 49). By choosing to confront his grief, loss, and regret, Aeneas is transforming into a leader who considers more than his personal gain and public image. He is gaining a deeper awareness and sensitivity toward how his decisions and actions impact the lives of others. Aeneas is already well-trained in the ways of battle and self-defense. Now he is being educated in a curriculum of compassion, empathy, and humility.

Hopkins (1954) elaborates on education's capacity to inspire not only growth of behavior but also "maturity of behavior" (p. 55). Aeneas's transformation demonstrates that although inner suffering can suspend a person's personal and professional growth, it also contains within it seeds of transformation. Tragedies, which can turn one's passion and enthusiasm into apathy, also have the potential to reinvigorate one's values and beliefs.

The third wave of this movement from *gesture* to *citation* to *metonymy* is when the source of one's grief is expressed as more than a quotation or citation. Metonymy happens when that which is particular and specific to an individual assumes a more expansive presence, meaning, purpose, and impact (Brault & Naas, 2001, p. 18).

What was once personal to a few is now meaningful and purposeful to many. Singular pain takes on broader significance.

For example, Aeneas travels safely through the underworld (i.e., through his despair and grieving) and returns to the physical world because he is guided by the spirit (i.e., metonymic symbol) of his mother embodied in the shape of doves:

> Two doves / in casual flight out of the upper air / came down before the man's eyes to alight / on the green grass, and the great hero knew / these birds to be his mother's. Joyously / He prayed: "O be my guides, / if there's a way. / Wing on, into that wood land where the bough, / the priceless bough, shadows the fertile ground. / My divine mother, do not fail your son / in a baffling time." Then he stood to see / what signs the doves might give, or where their flight / might lead him. (Virgil, 19 BCE/1990, Book VI, p. 166, lines 272–285)

The doves are a symbol of maternal love. Instead of being isolated in a silo of personal grief, the spirit of Aeneas's mother has become timeless yet tangible, boundless, and immeasurable. Clifford Mayes (2005) describes these kinds of experiences "as moments of transcendence" and asserts that a teacher's work can effect the same transformation:

> With *this* particular teacher, with *these* very students, in *this* ordinary classroom, our personal and collective histories [can be] reconciled and redeemed and the goal of spiritual teaching [i.e., transcendence] can finally be attained. (p. 93)

BOUNDARIES OF GRIEVING

When the boundaries of one's grief are narrow, its hurt is felt most singularly. Brault and Naas (2001) identify this concentrated point of pain as the *punctum* (Latin). When an individual's *punctum* is pluralized (what Brault and Naas call the *studium*), the boundaries of its pain are expanded to be understood (and its load shared) by a larger community (p. 25). The intensity of grief is diminished when its singularity is pluralized.

For example, consider the mourning associated with the public assassination of American President Abraham Lincoln. Grieving Lincoln's sudden, violent death began with intimate *gestures* (unique and personal to his immediate family and friends). As *gestures* of individual mourning (*punctum*) expanded into national grieving (*studium*), the narrow yet deep boundaries of sadness broadened in scope and depth. They eventually transformed into national mourning articulated through expressions (*citations*) that pluralized the grief. The personal mourning of Lincoln the individual is expanded to a collective grieving of Lincoln as a celebrated and honored American icon.

The words (*citation*) of Lincoln's secretary of war, Edwin M. Stanton, capture this movement from *punctum* to *studium*. Historians Benjamin P. Thomas and Harold M. Hyman (1962) recount the oft-repeated description of Stanton at

Lincoln's deathbed: "openly weeping at last, [Stanton] murmured that Lincoln now belonged to the ages" (p. 399). The immediacy of mourning Lincoln the individual is pluralized as he is now being honored more broadly as an emblem of the national values he had come to represent. *Lincoln the Man* is now *Lincoln the Crusader*—a living representation of America's commitment to end the institution of slavery.

The final stage of Brault and Naas's (2001) "rhetoric of mourning" (p. 21)—from emotional *gestures* to larger-scale *citations* to a universal *metonymy*—is demonstrated with Walt Whitman's (1865) elegy to Lincoln, *O Captain! My Captain!* Lincoln's spirit is expanded into a metonymic emblem, thereby transforming *Lincoln the President* into *Lincoln the Captain*. Collective mourning is now transfigured into a celebration of achievement: the nation has "weather'd every rack" (Whitman, 1865, p. 300, line 2) of war and injustice, and "the prize [formal declaration ending institutionalized slavery in the United States] we sought is won" (line 2):

> O Captain! My Captain! Our fearful trip is done.... For you the flag is flung—
> for you the bugle trills; / For you the bouquets and ribbon'd wreaths—for you
> the shores a-crowding; / For you they call, the swaying mass, their eager faces
> turning.... Exult, O Shores, and ring, O bells! (Whitman, 1865, pp. 300–301,
> lines 1, 10–12, 21)

As a middle school literacy/social studies teacher I have shared Whitman's poem with my students many times. I can attest that personal life experiences have deepened and, I believe, strengthened my instructional presentation. Teaching this poem as a twenty-two-year-old, I dutifully emphasized the mechanics of its rhythm, rhyme, and structure as well as its historical significance. As a thirty-year-old, however, I began sharing the poem from a place of grieving. Just as Lincoln died before he would see the reality of post-slavery America, my father and high school teacher mentor died before seeing how deeply my life had been affected by the seeds they had planted within my teacher heart.

Whitman created an iconic space of linguistic metonymy within which my personal grieving could be similarly transformed into a celebration of the "captains" in my life—in all our lives. Instructionally, my students and I could now move past the mechanical construction of the poem, look more deeply into its heart, and reflect upon the ways it resonates with us on personal levels.

Whitman's elegy expands the singular grieving (*punctum*) for Lincoln's death into a larger sphere (*studium*) through a kind of substitution/replacement. The power, potentiality, and expanse of its resonance are dramatically increased. My students and I were able to connect in personal ways to its images, framing, and articulation of grief. During teaching moments like this, I feel that my role advances from teacher to what Mayes (2005) describes as a "teacher-philosopher" (p. 65).

As teacher, I discussed Whitman's poem in terms of its meter, rhyme, vocabulary, and figurative language. As teacher-philosopher, I challenged my students (and myself) to reflect upon who the "captains" of our lives might be, what voyages or challenges s/he had helped us through, and how we might embody the lessons they imparted to us. Whitman's elegy became more than a just a piece of nineteenth-century literature to be revered. I was no longer teaching it because only because it was mandated by the curriculum; and students no longer studied it only in terms of eventually passing a content exam.

O Captain! My Captain! (Whitman, 1865) came to be studied and analyzed in my classroom because of its personal relevance to students' lives. It was a text used to inspire introspection as a means to better understand ourselves and our values. The immediacy and emotional resonance of examining the elegy in our twentieth-century public school classroom in Chicago is a living testimonial to Whitman's ability to capture the timelessness and universality of humanity's capacity to grieve.

EMOTIONAL EXPANSIVENESS OF GRIEVING

Initially Aeneas saw the underworld as "a place apart—a dark, enormous cave" (Virgil, 19 BCE/1990, Book VI, p. 159, lines 15–16). The image represented the isolation he felt within the heart of his *punctum*, or individual pain. But the more he explored the larger geography of grief, the more he realized that it extends far beyond the limits of his understanding. He came to realize that his mourning was at once specific to himself and simultaneously shared by others.

Once Aeneas steps outside the cavern of his individual grief, he begins to see (and empathize with) the broader landscape of suffering. The spaces of grief he encounters include

- the River Styx ("the river over which no soul returns" [Book VI, p. 174, line 574]);
- the Fields of Mourning ("Here are those whom pitiless love consumed with cruel wasting… In death itself, pain will not let them be" [p. 175, lines 596–597, 599]);
- the Cliffs of Orcus ("Grief and avenging Cares have made their beds, / and pale Diseases and sad Age are there, / and Dread, and Hunger that sways men to crime, / and sordid Want" [p. 169, lines 377–380]);
- and Cocytus ("all in the nearby crowd you notice here are pauper souls, the souls of the unburied" [p. 171, lines 439–440]).

Having been born into royalty, Aeneas never expressed sympathy or compassion for individuals who fell victim to the monsters of poverty, disease, and prejudice. This changed when his underworld journey of grief lead him to the Courtyard of Giant Elms ("where dreams, false dreams, the old tale goes, beneath each leaf / cling and are numberless. / There, too, about the doorway forms of monsters crowd" [p. 169, lines 387–390]). The legion of abominations Aeneas encounters included

Centaurs, twisted Scyllas, hundred-armed / Briareus, and the Lernaen hydra / hissing horribly, / and the Chimaera / breathing dangerous flames, and Gorgons, Harpies, / Huge Geryon, triple-bodied ghost. (Virgil, 19 BCE/1990, p. 169–170, lines 391–395)

This passage was one of my students' favorites when we studied ancient Greek and Roman mythology. Not only did they enjoy visualizing the odious features of the creatures themselves, but they also joined me in imagining what contemporary moral revulsions the monsters could be representing. For example, we imagined that the Scylla embodied gang members trying to coerce new recruits into their ranks, while Harpies embodied modern day gossip-mongers spreading salacious, tabloid-like rumors.

Until Aeneas looked beyond the walls of his apathy, he did not understand the depravity that these creatures they fed on or the despair they left in their wake. Nor did he pause to consider how the creatures themselves suffered alone in their own moral repugnance. When he witnesses the kinds of hopelessness and powerlessness that trap people in such appalling predicaments, his compassion and empathy grows exponentially. Aeneas is beginning to realize that beneath the outer appearances of those who are marginalized and judged by their station in life lies a humanity that is not as different from himself as he had been taught to believe.

The exterior features of these mythological creatures are like scars that mark the emotional and spiritual wounds beneath. Aeneas is realizing that it is too easy for someone to "jest at the scars that never felt a wound" (Shakespeare, 1597, *Romeo and Juliet,* Act 2, Scene 1, line 43). After all, even Aeneas will forever bear the emotional scars of regret and guilt (his abandoning Dido and her subsequent suicide respectively) which will never fully heal. These griefs will serve as perpetual testimonials against the dangers of apathy. They will also be constant reminders that a person's external words and actions can have deeply emotional repercussions.

Aeneas has extensive knowledge of a variety of political, economic, and military subjects. But now he is being schooled on inner realities that lie beneath the veneer of public life. As an aristocrat destined for leadership roles, he has long been trained in the mechanisms and protocol of government. He is now receiving an education on the importance of looking beneath the surface of his public duties to the beliefs, values, and personal aspirations that also demand his attention.

Educators are similarly well-trained in the mechanisms and procedures of teaching and learning. Most have extensive knowledge of content-based information and adhere to the outer protocol of their public role. But in what ways are educators attuned to the inner realities critical to their work? To what extent do teachers take the time to reflect on their beliefs, values, and aspirations—and of those of their students as well?

John Dewey (1916) asserts "there is a valid distinction between knowledge which is objective and impersonal, and thinking which is subjective and personal" (p. 295). He warns that when learning becomes rote and prescribed, "teaching then ceases to be an educative process" (p. 304). Genuine learning happens when the individual humanity of the teacher and the student is allowed to flourish:

> Thinking... starts from doubt or uncertainty. It marks an inquiring, hunting, searching attitude, instead of one of mastery and possession. Through its

critical process true knowledge is revised and extended, and our convictions as to the state of things reorganized. (p. 295)

An authentic learning experience is rooted in more than convention and process alone—it is aligned to the thoughts, beliefs, and values of its participants—students and teachers. How content is communicated, experienced, discussed, explored, and reflected on relies on the individual hearts and minds of those participating.

In his grief, a period filled with "doubt and uncertainty" (Dewey, 1916, p. 295), Aeneas was inclined to isolate himself from others, and from his own feelings. How often and in what ways are educators (for personal and/or professional reasons) similarly tempted to isolate themselves in their classrooms or within the confines of a prescribed curriculum? In the underworld of his private thoughts, Aeneas "inquires, hunts, and searches" (Dewey, 1916, p. 295) through his heart and conscience to better understand the "uncanny powers of mind and soul" (Virgil, 19 BCE/1990, Book VI, p. 159, line 18). Imagine what wisdom or insights teachers and students might gain by embarking on such philosophical inquiries or imaginative searches.

Aeneas returns to the world of the living with scars of grief that will never fully heal. What kinds of personal and professional scars are educators (and their students) carrying? In what ways might these scars challenge—or strengthen—a teacher's mission and vision? Perhaps, like Aeneas, the more deeply teachers grapple with these kinds of introspective questions, the more his or her teaching has the capacity to be increasingly real, meaningful, and transformative.

FROM RECKONING TO REVELATION

Bellah et al. (1985) mark the contrast between teaching as a calling versus teaching as a job. They observe that an authentic calling represents "a crucial link between the individual and the public world" (p. 66). One *works* to receive a paycheck, health care benefits, and a retirement package. But what does the work of teaching *call* educators to do? What ideas, beliefs, or values are they *called on* to enact through their teaching? Bellah et al. (1985) reflect that teaching in its highest incarnation can be a living testament to an educator's mission, vision, values, and aspirations (personal and professional):

In the strongest sense of a "calling," work constitutes a practical ideal of activity and character that makes a person's work morally inseparable from his or her life.... However we define work, it is very close to our sense of self. What we "do" often translates to what we "are." (p. 66)

As was customary in the oral tradition of epic ancient storytelling, the essence of Aeneas's character is summed up in an epithet. His epithet *pius* (pious) is more than a descriptor. It defines the moral commitment and ethical duty that Aeneas comes to personify. His experiences with loss and grief have brought him to an awakening toward a deeper purpose for living and a stronger commitment to carry on the tradition of honor and service established by his ancestors. Unlike other classical heroes (e.g., Odysseus the *"poikilios"* [wily], Diomedes the "master of the war cry," "man-killing" Hector, and "war-like and spear-famed" Menelaus), Aeneas as hero represents strength of heart rather than strength of muscles or weapons. Vases, murals, gemstones, coins, peace altars, and terra cottas use Aeneas's image as an icon for duty, piety, and service.

As an impressionable high school Latin student reading *The Aeneid* for the first time, I was fascinated with this idea of personal strength and integrity rooted in piety. In many ways, my decision to become a teacher was influenced by this concept. For me, this notion has come to represent the integration of my personal values with my professional life. My calling as a teacher is to embed my efforts with piety. To my mind and heart, teaching as an act of integrity elevates education from the mundane to the sacred. In many ways, it is the difference between the asking ourselves *What are we making?* (i.e., salaries, pension contributions) and *What are we making of ourselves?* (and of our students).

As someone sets out on a career or life path, he or she is told to "make something of yourself." It is equally important to follow up on that advice throughout one's career and life. As educators, as individuals, and as communities, *what are we making of ourselves?* What are we making of our students? To what extent is what we are creating of ourselves and others aligned with our values, beliefs, and aspirations?

Aeneas's transformation in the underworld culminates in a prophetic glimpse into the future. Having faced his regrets and persevered through his grief, Aeneas comes to realize that if his work is rooted in honor, so, too, will be his legacy: "Famous children in your line will come, souls of the future, living in your name... who shall bring once again an Age of Gold" (Virgil, 19 BCE/1990, Book VI, p. 186–187, lines 1017–1018, 1065).

The outer structures of the Roman Empire that Aeneas helps create (i.e., the architecture, palaces, temples, roads, towns) are not destined to be his lasting legacy. In the underworld, he sees that what endures beyond his lifetime are the values he lives by, models, and consequently passes on to future generations. Brick and mortar will not last—but his piety will. Although Aeneas's work is calculated extrinsically per his accumulation of land and wealth, his intrinsic achievements are measured by his capacity to show mercy, spread justice, and heal the ills suffered by the masses (Virgil, 19 BCE/1990, Book VI, p. 190, lines 1152–54).

Similarly, although an educator's work is measured by extrinsic criteria (i.e., assessment scores, observation criteria, school and district statistical data), his or her lasting legacy has the potential to far exceed these temporal measures. When test scores are long-forgotten, it is teacher-student relationships, especially those based on trust and respect, which will endure. It is neither the information learned nor knowledge acquired that matters so much as the values modeled and compassion shared.

These are spaces where public work and private values can intersect. Knowledge can be gained within environments grounded in mutual respect. Information can be learned as relationships of trust are forged. Test scores can demonstrate cognitive achievement that was nurtured in classroom spaces of compassion. This demonstrates the critical role relationships and values play in transforming teaching and learning from the mundane to the sacred. Nel Noddings (2005) observes:

> When we discuss teaching and teacher-learner relationships in depth, we will see that teachers not only have to create caring relations in which they are the carers, but that they also have a responsibility to help their students develop the capacity to care. (p. 18)

Caring was never a part of Aeneas's professional life. During his grief, however, he entered into "regions not for the living" (Virgil, 19 BCE/1990, Book VI, p. 165, line 225) where he struggled against "all silent shades; and Chaos and infernal Fiery Stream, and regions of wide night without a sound" (p. 169, lines 363–365). These experiences engaged him in a caliber of personal introspection from which he gleaned a "fiery energy from a heavenly source" (p. 185, line 981). This spiritual energy served as a balm which would heal his inner suffering that otherwise would remain "imprisoned in the darkness of the body" (p. 185, line 987).

Aeneas emerges from his mourning with newfound empathy and compassion for others: "Let me scatter lilies, all I can hold, and scarlet flowers as well" (Virgil, 19 BCE/1990, p. 191, lines 1199–1200). His public mission becomes more grounded in his heart as he comes to understand his professional undertaking as a sacred mission. His duty to lead his people to Rome is no longer work—it is now his calling. His public mission, previously driven primarily by material gain, now aligns to his personal vision: to establish a just and equitable nation whose piety would outlast and outshine his own life.

For example, upon leaving the underworld of his grief and rejoining his crew to resume his sea voyage, Aeneas sends out a group of crewmembers to explore a distant shore prior to the rest of the crew landing there. Encountering hostility, the men are killed. Prior to his time in the underworld, Aeneas would likely have stayed true to his public mission and sailed on without any delay in the schedule. But Aeneas has learned firsthand the importance of acknowledging and reckoning with the weight of grief. His introspection taught him to think more deeply, listen more carefully, and act more purposefully and compassionately.

Aeneas's story teaches that there is more to grieving than perpetual pain and heartache. Its journey can lead to a deeper understanding of the values and beliefs a person is called to champion. And so, instead of immediately moving forward, Aeneas and his crew take time to mourn their comrades. Grieving collectively tears down the siloes of sadness so that no one needs to carry the entire emotional weight alone. Aeneas learned that despite how singularly one is impacted by grief, the boundaries of its scope and depth are deeper than one may suspect:

> All who were there / clamored around the body in lament, / Aeneas, the good captain, most of all.… Racing to pile up logs for the altar-pyre / and build it

sky-high.... Aeneas himself went first in all this labor, / cheering his fellows on, with implements / like theirs in hand. (Virgil, 19 BCE/1990, Book VI, p. 166, lines 252–254, 257–258, 263–265)

This episode indicates one way in which Aeneas's mission and vision as a leader has been transformed. Instead of focusing on issues related to scheduling and overall efficiency, Aeneas decided to delay the voyage in terms of the emotional needs of himself and his crew. Although it did profit him materially, Aeneas and his crew took the time to create a sacred space in which to grieve and honor the lost crew members. Mayes (2005) writes that an educator's work contains the same potential for transformation. He asserts that teaching and learning as "means of transcendence" can lead to an educational experience that "inhabits a sacred space" (p. 88):

To be spiritual, the curriculum does not have to deal with explicitly "spiritual" topics. However, it must be spiritually grounded in the teacher's heart—or else it will become the mere transmission of data and theories for the sake of some imposed political or economic goal.... But the pedagogies that grow from the fecund soil of the love of others and the sacred are—despite the teacher's formal religious commitments or lack thereof—spiritual pedagogies. (p. 89)

This elevates education (and one's work as an educator) to spaces of integrity. The dignity of teaching, Maya Angelou (2014) suggests, lies in the moments when students and teachers find the time, space, opportunity, and compassion to give the best of themselves to each other. Angelou (2014) beautifully frames humanity's potential to move from tragedy and grief to spaces of dignity:

Tragedy, no matter how sad, becomes boring to those not caught in its addictive caress. You may not control all the events that happen to you, but you can decide not to be reduced by them. You shouldn't go through life with a catcher's mitt on both hands; you need to be able to throw something back.... Dignity doesn't just mean always being stiff and composed. It means a belief in oneself, that one is worthy of the best. Dignity means that what I have to say is important, and I will say it when it's important for me to say it. Dignity really means that I deserve the best treatment I can receive. And that I have the responsibility to give the best treatment I can to other people. (pp. 77–78, 82)

How often do we go through life, as Angelou warns, "with a catcher's mitt on both hands"? Once a hand is freed, what are we returning to each other? When upset, do we throw back anger? When uncertain, do we throw back fear? Is living a life wherein one strives toward dignity and integrity a worthwhile aspiration? When grieving, do we throw back hopelessness? If on one hand (with the catcher's mitt) we receive and hold on to feelings, values, and beliefs and with the other hand we are free to disperse these kinds of things outside of ourselves, from which does integrity and dignity derive: from what we hold on to or what we share?

In many ways grief is about these two components: letting go and holding on. How much of what (or whom) one grieves ought an individual hold on to? How much to let go? What memories, habits, belongings, and dreams do we preserve within our emotional catcher's mitt? Which ones do we release? Returning to Schubert's (1986) curriculum questions, what memories, habits, belongings, and dreams are most critical and worthwhile to leading lives of dignity and integrity?

TOPICS FOR REFLECTION

1. As teachers, we work to earn paychecks, receive health care plans, and accrue tenure toward retirement packages. But what does your work as an educator *call you* to do? What ideas, beliefs, and values define and inform your teaching? In what ways are these values similar to those that "called you" to education in the first place? Where in your work are glimmers of the mission and vision that inspired you early in your career?

2. At one point, Aeneas's grief and loss threaten to isolate his spirit behind a wall of personal and professional apathy. Reflect on times and events (as a teacher or student) that were impacted by apathy. Can you recall teachers who were teaching from a space of apathy? What noticeable qualities, actions, or words indicated what you understand as apathy and what effect(s) did that have on learning?

   How effective can even the most efficient instruction be when a teacher's demeanor, voice, attitude, or outlook are coming from a space of apathy? Now rethink past educational experiences you have had (as a teacher or student) that were impacted by compassion and/or empathy. What noticeable qualities, actions, or words indicated what you understand as these qualities? What effect did they have on learning?

3. The new school district superintendent is scheduled to speak at your school. She announces to the faculty that anyone suffering with apathy or disinterest toward their students or their work in general should "get the hell out of education" (Buscaglia, 1982, p. 36). On hearing this, what might be going through your mind or the minds of your peers? Are these words too harsh? Would they inspire, motivate, or frighten you (and your peers) to be a more compassionate teacher? How might you respond to her? What follow-up questions or comments would you like to ask?

4. Clifford Mayes (2005) describes a *teacher-philosopher* as one who inspires his or her students to question what they read, and to consider alternate possibilities, explanations, and solutions. In what ways do you consider yourself a *teacher-philosopher*?

   Mayes asserts that a *teacher-philosopher* uses techniques and strategies to "defamiliarize the world" (p. 72) so that students can make sense of themselves and their lives on their own terms. What kinds of strategies and techniques might accomplish these goals? Have you ever had a teacher who operated according to this kind of thinking? What is gained and what is lost by "defamiliarizing" the world for our students?

5. In Walt Whitman's 1865 elegy for President Abraham Lincoln, he addresses Lincoln as "O Captain! My Captain!" Who have been the "captains" in your life as an individual and as a teacher? In what ways have they inspired you? How do they continue to inspire your work as a teacher ?

6. A time machine has been configured that can transfer you back to your first day as a teacher. This is your chance to "make something of yourself." As the novice teacher ready to meet your first class of students, what were you hoping to "make of yourself"? Write those words down. Now step back into the time machine to the present day. Look at the words you recorded. In the years that have passed since your first day, what *have* you made of yourself? In what ways have you become the teacher you aspired to be?

7. Brainstorm responses to this follow-up question: As a professional educator, what are you "making of your students"? For example, to what extent are they becoming retainers of information or independent thinkers and problem solvers? What activities, projects, and assignments are guiding students toward being more empathic, ethically conscious, or socially aware?

8. What personal and professional "scars" have you incurred during your years as a teacher and/or a student? How have these experiences infuenced your role as educator? What kinds of losses, hurts, or regrets do those scars represent? In what ways do you carry them with shame and/or honor?

Consider how moments of grief, anger, regret, or similar emotions can affect one's outlook, values, or attitudes. In what ways have these scars strengthened your mission and vision—or weakened them? Do you believe it is possible that personal and professional disappointments and losses can inspire positive and life-affirming transformation?

9. How often do we go through our teaching lives, as Maya Angelou (2014) warns, "with a catcher's mitt on both hands" (p. 77)? Can you recall any "catcher-mitt" moments? Once your hand is free from the metaphorical "catcher's mitt," what have you thrown back to your students? Can you recall moments when (intentionally or not) you have thrown back hope or hopelessness? Anger or reconciliation? Fear or courage?

10. An epithet is commonly used in ancient epic storytelling to briefly capture the essence of a character. Greek hero Odysseus's epithet, *wily*, reflected his cleverness. Other famous characters and their epithets include: *man-killing* Hector, *pious* Aeneas, and *spear-famed* Menelaus. As teacher, what epithet do

you aspire to? What epithet do you think best captures the essence of your day-to-day work? If your students were asked to devise your epithet, what ideas do you think they would come up with? What would happen at a teacher workshop if you and peers were assigned to create epithets for each other? Would this be a good idea?

11. Congratulations! You have been invited to deliver a ten-minute talk at the school board end-of-year public forum. The topic is: *the dignity of a teacher's work*. What might you say? What stories will you recall? What lessons will you impart? Consider incorporating these reflections by Maya Angelou (2014):

> Dignity doesn't just mean always being stiff and composed. It means a belief in oneself, that one is worthy of the best. Dignity means that what I have to say is important, and I will say it when it's important for me to say it. Dignity really means that I deserve the best treatment I can receive. (p. 82)

12. In what ways have your personal values expanded the scope and depth of your professional work? Try to recall classroom moments when ethical considerations (such as acting upon mercy or kindness) out-prioritized the intellectual aspects of your curriculum. Can you think of any circumstances in which you believe they should?

FROM THE EXISTENTIAL TO THE METAPHYSICAL

Pet Sematary, *Stephen King*

HANNAH THE BEST DOG THAT EVER LIVED 1929–1939. Although sandstone was relatively soft—as a result the inscription was now little more than a ghost—Louis found it hard to conceive of the hours some child must have spent impressing those nine words on the stone. The commitment of love and grief seemed to him staggering. (King, 1983, pp. 31–32)

How often do educators pause to consider a child's "commitment of love and grief" toward those they love? Or toward learning? Or toward life itself? Whether or not their thoughts are expressed in words, a child's emerging emotional and spiritual commitments are real, as indicated in this tombstone dedication for a family pet. Doctor Louis Creed, the protagonist of Stephen King's (1983) novel *Pet Sematary*, never gave these kinds of thoughts much attention, let alone acknowledged or validated them. After all, children are too young to understand or feel such things deeply... or are they?

Trailing down a lovely pathway through a wooded area near his family's home, Louis passes beneath "an arch made of old weather-stained boards" where he discovers "written on these in faded black paint, only just legible... the words Pet Sematary" (King, 1983, p. 29). The hours children must have spent carving epitaphs for their pets are a testimonial to their emotional attachments and grief:

Smucky the Cat. He was obedient. 1971–1974.
Gen. Patton. (Our! Good! Dog!). Died 1958.
Marta our pet rabbit dyed. March 1, 1965.
Trixie, Kilt on the highway. Sept 15, 1968.
Biffer. A helluva sniffer / until he died he made us richer. (pp. 30–31)

Although some words (*sematary*, *dyed*, *kilt*) are misspelled the depth of feeling is authentic. This sacred space attests to emotional connections and deeply felt bonds that often go unnoticed in the busy day-to-day flutter of activities. Hours after discovering this pet graveyard, Louis reflects further on a child's capacity to feel things deeply. He ponders, "death was a vague idea" but "the Pet Sematary was real. In the texture of those rude markers were truths which even a child's hands could feel" (King, 1983, p. 39).

© KONINKLIJKE BRILL NV, LEIDEN, 2020 | DOI: 10.1163/9789004422506_007

This visit to the pet sematary foreshadows Creed's metaphysical journey beyond the familiarity of the outer world. He will soon come face-to-face with those "truths which even a child's hands could feel" (p. 39). His previously unchallenged views and beliefs will be stripped down to their emotional essence. Like a child who feels trapped and powerless inside a nightmare, Louis will experience emotions (fear, despair, sadness) more deeply than he thought possible. King dares his readers to join Louis Creed as he travels behind the veil of outer reality to those spaces (and truths) hidden beneath. Louis's grief will challenge his understanding of *the way things are supposed to be* as he emotionally and spiritually journeys through *things are as they are.*

As fiction, *Pet Sematary* operates in a world where an individual is forced to face inexplicable fears and unimagined grief. As a work of meta-fiction, the novel blends elements of gothic literature ("*I am following a dead man up to the Pet Sematary and this is no dream*" [King, 1983, p. 72]) with images and reflections of philosophical depth ("death is where the pain stops and the good memories begin" [p. 153]) and emotional authenticity:

> His grief came for him fully, like some gray matron from Ward Nine in purgatory. It came and dissolved him, unmanned him, took away whatever defenses remained, and he put his face in his hands and cried, rocking back and forth on his bed, thinking he would do anything to have a second chance, anything at all. (p. 265)

The challenge of using *Pet Sematary* as a tool to examine a curriculum of grief is that readers are asked to temporarily suspend their disbelief. The novel considers possibilities that lie beyond the natural world and extend into the realm of the supernatural. It includes events that defy the laws of the physical world as science understands them. As educators whose profession prioritizes rational knowledge, facts, and carefully assessed outcomes, teachers are challenged to consider emotions felt at depths immeasurable and to reflect on inexplicable events. In short, *Pet Sematary* offers a surreal depiction of grief and mourning. Like grief itself, the novel describes metaphysical spaces that simultaneously circumvent rationality *and* reveal otherwise hidden truths—whether readers want to face them or not.

An examination of grieving as a teacher's curriculum cannot ignore these kinds of dark, nightmarish experiences wherein an individual's understanding of life becomes unclear at best or, at worst, obliterated. This chapter explores how the journey of grief leads individuals to reexamine previously unchallenged views, beliefs, and values.

THE BALANCE BEAM OF RATIONALITY

In their research, Larry Cochran and Emily Claspell (1987) observe that individuals who are grieving often describe life as having become hollow. Instead of searching for meaning *in* life, grief leads a person to search for the meaning *of* life. Cochran and Claspell characterize this aspect of grieving as "highly and necessarily imaginative":

Imagination concerns what is not. The sense of loss immerses a person in the "not-ness" of life.... For example, one might sense a loved one's presence, all of which are a part of an "as if" reality, at least as we ordinarily define reality. Imaginative activity is heightened by isolation, wretchedness, helplessness, and memory. Meaningful contact with the world is broken and the person is directed inward. Imagination also concerns what is. Part of the struggle is pretense. (p. 119)

Louis Creed's expertise as a doctor is rooted in his knowledge and application of scientific laws of the physical world. There is no room in his life for this kind of imaginative activity. Rational thinking defines his daily experiences—until a speeding semitruck strikes and kills his four-year-old son Gage. The random cruelty and cosmic unfairness are inexplicable. Louis is overwhelmed with grief. By the standards of his logically organized and rationally-sound conception of the world, this reality is unjustifiable and unimaginable.

The death of his child sends Louis on an existential journey through what Cochran and Claspell (1987) describe as the "not-ness of life" (p. 119). Louis's medical training had impressed on him an urgency to search for solutions and to fix problems. When he refuses to accept what his rational mind presents to him, Louis searches for solace outside rationality: "*What comes when you're too slow wishing away the thing that knocks on your door in the middle of the night is simple enough: total darkness*" (King, 1983, p. 379).

On the morning of Gage's funeral, Louis's thoughts turn uncharacteristically philosophical ("It's probably wrong to believe there can be any limit to the horror which the human mind can experience" [King, 1983, p. 215]). When choosing a coffin to contain his son's body, Louis ponders the depth of his grief: "Just how much horror [can] the human mind stand and still maintain a wakeful, staring, unrelenting sanity?" (p. 215). Emotionally isolated from family and friends, Louis feels that the world as he has known it is broken. As he struggles with "wretchedness, helplessness, and memory" (Cochran & Claspell, 1987, p. 119), Louis now turns to imagination:

Gage was not killed; all of that had only been a hellishly detailed moment of imagination as Louis outraced his son's death across a green lawn on a sunshiny May afternoon. (King, 1983, p. 263)

Stephen King (2002) writes that the mystery of death "is probably the single greatest subject of horror fiction: our need to cope with a mystery that can be understood only with the aid of a hopeful imagination" (p. 511). Louis continues to imagine that "none of those things happened" (King, 1983, p. 261). When reality does not align to his rational view of the world, he turns to his imagination to correct the "mistake":

Gage was running down the gentle slope of lawn that merged with the soft shoulder of Route 15, his husky little legs pumping, and by all rights of the world he should have fallen over sprawling but he just kept going and now

117

the sound of the truck was very loud.... Just as Gage's forward motion carried him into the road, Louis's fingers brushed the back of his jacket... and then snagged it. He yanked Gage backward and landed on the ground. (p. 262)

Louis escapes to an "as if" reality: *as if* Gage attended grammar and high school; *as if* he is accepted to Johns Hopkins University Medical School; *as if* he competes with the United States Olympic swimming team (King, 1983, p. 263). Even as Louis imagines he and his wife one day in the future watching "their son win a gold medal for the U.S.A." (King, 1983, p. 264), all the while he "felt that in truth he was walking along a narrow beam over a gulf of insanity" (p. 295):

They watched when the NBC cameras moved in for a close-up.... "I guess this caps everything," he [Louis] said huskily and turned to embrace his wife. But she was looking at him with dawning horror, her face seeming to age before his eyes as if whipped by days and months and years of evil time; the sound of the national anthem faded and when Louis looked back at the TV he saw a different boy there, a black boy with a head of tight curls in which gems of water still gleamed.

This caps everything.
His cap.
His cap is...
... oh dear God, his cap is full of blood. (p. 264)

Louis is trapped between two worlds: the rational one that his physical senses are relaying and the metaphysical one hiding beneath a veil of propriety. Louis is struggling to find meaning in a life that no longer abides by the rules he had been taught to expect. His grieving impacts both his conscious and subconscious mind.

John Dewey (1934) writes that an authentic education teaches individuals to make sense of the world through one's mind *and* imagination. He asserted that one's *consciousness* changes rapidly due to external events, while one's *mind* evolves slowly. When long-standing views of the world are abruptly interrupted, an individual's way of seeing and understanding the world becomes disconnected from the outer reality. The mind (our *intuitive* system of belief and organization of thought) continuously but only gradually readjusts to data received by one's consciousness. *Imagination* lies in the space between one's fast-thinking consciousness and his or her more slowly evolving mind.

Inasmuch as it affects people's understanding of themselves and the world around them, grieving is a critical learning experience. Dewey's description of meaning-making that entails mind *and* intuition and of understanding the world in ways that utilize consciousness *and* imagination are especially relevant at such times when a person struggles to process suffering and tragedy that he or she deems unimaginable. Louis now embodies the space Dewey (1934) describes as "fanciful and unreal." He is floundering somewhere between consciousness and imagination.

Gordon Reddiford (1980) observes that as a tool of education, imagination teaches that not all *why* questions are supposed to have definitive answers. He concludes that some beliefs and values are not meant to be tested or sacrificed "at the bar of reason" (Reddiford, 1980, p. 212). When a person's rational mind is suddenly "baffled and arrested," Dewey (1934) writes that "the stream of meanings aroused into activity by the present contact remains aloof" (p. 284):

> Then it forms the matter of reverie, of dreams; ideas are floating, not anchored to any existence.... Emotions are equally loose and floating to these ideas. The pleasure they afford is the reason why they are entertained and are allowed to occupy the scene; they are attached to existence only in a way that, as long as sanity abides, is felt to be only fanciful and unreal. (p. 284)

Building on what Kenneth Burke (1937) calls "the bureaucratization of the imaginative" (p. 225), Paul Lynch (2013) warns against what he labels an "unprincipled pedagogy" (p. 97) when curriculum and instruction "become so bureaucratized that they lose their original imaginative character" (p. 101). Anders Schinkel, Doret J. de Ruyter and Aharon Aviram (2016) assert that education's potential to help students find and construct meaning in their lives depends on nurturing more than one conceptual framework.

This means exploring and understanding the world through a variety of lenses beyond a cognitive one. Schinkel et al. (2016) describe the importance of enhancing children's creative sensitivities and of providing critical opportunities for imagination (p. 412):

> Put negatively, just as education (or something supposed to be education) may detract from or obstruct meaningfulness by impeding understanding or filling children's heads with 'inert ideas' (Whitehead, 1962, p. 1), it may do so by blunting children's sensibilities, feelings, imagination, and creativity. (p. 412)

Beyond the more prosaic tasks included in a teacher's day-to-day work, educators need to look for opportunities to create pathways through which students can learn to search for meaning in their lives (Schinkel et al., 2016, p. 413). Building on Dewey's (1934) premise that authentic teaching and learning rely on the learner's mind, consciousness, intuition, and imagination, Schinkel et al. (2016) assert that the ways in which educators organize and prioritize a traditional school curriculum can "*add to* or *detract from* the meaningfulness of children's lives (and then the lives they will live as adults)" (p. 411):

> There is obviously much about life and the world—and some of the most important things among them—that children will not learn through the curriculum; yet it may reveal to children something of the richness and complexity of the world.... Apart from the transmission or construction of knowledge of the various subjects on the curriculum, an important function of education (for meaning) would be to stimulate wonder, attentiveness, and appreciation. (pp. 411–412)

Instead of conceiving of an education in which students are *informed* about what constitutes reality (which defined Louis's educational experiences), imagine an educator's capacity to lead students toward *constructing* meaning in their lives. Joseph Campbell (1991) writes about the importance of individuals learning to create, identify, and secure what he calls their sacred space. He describes this as "any space set apart from the usual context of life" (p. 180). It is neither secular nor pragmatic because one "does not have anything in your sacred space that's not of significance to you for the harmonization of your own life":

> In your sacred space, things are working in terms of *your* dynamic —and not anybody else's. Your sacred space is where you can find yourself again and again.... [Here is] a joy that comes from inside, not something external that puts joy into you. (Campbell, 1991, p.180)

In what ways are educators familiar with the sacred spaces within themselves from which their passion, joy, and inspiration for teaching emanates? When personal and professional demands and crises threaten the harmony of their outer (personal and professional) lives, how many educators turn to that sacred inner space where they "can find [themselves] again and again" (Campbell, 1991, p. 180)? Consider the possibilities of a curriculum that helps children discover their own sacred spaces. Imagine lessons, resources, and activities with the potential to transform classrooms themselves into sacred spaces where teachers and students could "find [themselves] again and again" (Campbell p. 180).

These kinds of imaginings defy traditional logic and scientific principles. They speak instead to the affective aspects of our humanity. Similarly, emotional and ethical qualities of teaching and learning are difficult to measure or quantitatively confirm. The landscape of a person's inner life is not readily verified with linear assessment tools. Neither is imagination. And neither is grief.

Pet Sematary immerses readers in spaces that defy traditional logic, science, and religious dogma. Through a gothic lens, the novel explores the meaning of life in its least mundane and most metaphysical incarnation. The narrative invites individuals to search those parts of themselves normally hidden from conscious or rational thinking. James Goho (2014) describes the use of gothic literature to delve beneath the outer layers of our lives:

> Gothic literature tells the hidden stories of a people. Hidden because they tell darkly of dark things. They look underneath beds, go into attics, wander through graveyards, and go deep down into cellars and caves... [and into] the darkness of a forest, or a city, or in our houses, and in our heads. (p. 1)

Louis is beginning to imagine the depths of emotional and spiritual realities that lie beneath the rational veil of the physical world. He enters into what G. R. Thompson (1974) describes as the "drama of the mind engaged in the quest for metaphysical and moral absolutes" (p. 6). At Gage's funeral, outer reality is comprised of "neat rows of folding chairs"; a "dwarf coffin no more than four feet long" that is "lined with plushy pink silk"; and the smell of flowers that "made [Louis] want to gag" (King, 1983, p. 222). But the inner reality that reveals itself to Louis's heart is comprised of a movie in his mind "replaying the accident over and over and over" (p. 216); the "mystery sound of pigeons in his ears" (p. 225); the "malignantly acidic content rising through his digestive works" (p. 227); and "some malign jack-in-the-box" rattling in his skull (p. 230).

In his grief, the images of malignant acid, screeching pigeons, and evil jack-in-the-boxes are no less real than the neat rows of chairs in front of the coffin. At Gage's burial site, the mourners comment on the softness of the damp ground and the sweet aroma of fresh flowers. But all that Louis notices is "damp moss growing" so darkly (p. 327); and a "landscape of stony soil" (p. 327). Is the newly laid grass any less real than this inner landscape of stone? Where is the line between the outer cemetery of the physical world and the inner burial ground within Louis's mind and heart? His son is not only buried deep in the ground—he is also buried deep in his father's soul.

Grief has shattered Louis Creed's conception of the world. It has blurred the lines of reality within which he framed his understanding of life. Tragedy has brought Louis to a new place within which, as Reddiford (1980) describes, "reality makes inescapable demands" that are not "uniquely satisfied by scientists" (p. 211). A frightened Louis now asks: "*Is the line so thin, then... so thin you can simply step over it with this little fuss, muss and bother... that simple? Is it lunacy?*" (King, 1983, p. 318).

Grief has shaken Louis's understanding of life and undermined his meaning *in* life. He feels that all that remains is a treacherously narrow bar of reason on which he hovers precariously over a "gulf of insanity":

Madness was all around him, softly fluttering as the wings of night-hunting owls with great golden eyes: he was heading into madness.... Madness. Madness all around, close, hunting him. He walked the balance beam of rationality. (King, 1983, p. 295)

Describing grief through an empirical lens, George Engel (1961) cites physical symptoms including loss of appetite, chronic fatigue, tight throat, and digestive irregularities. For Louis, however, grief is beyond description; and so King reveals Louis's despair in metaphysical terms. King's balance beam metaphor embodies what is emotionally genuine (albeit rationally unimaginable). Louis's personal reality is now in a space wherein "all thoughts ceased and exhaustion dragged him down to black dreamless unconsciousness" (King, 1983, p. 359).

DREAMS, NIGHTMARES, AND REALITIES

The field of time is the field of sorrow.... If you try to correct the sorrows, all you do is shift them somewhere else. Life is sorrowful. How do you live with that? You realize the eternal within yourself. You disengage, and yet, reengage. You—and here's the beautiful formula—participate with joy in the sorrows of the world. You play the game. It hurts, but you know that you have found the place that is transcendent of injury and fulfillments. You are there, and that's it. (Campbell, 1991, p. 120)

Joseph Campbell's scholarship explores ways that myths, traditions, and belief systems (as expressed in storytelling) contribute to our understanding of ourselves and the world around us. He writes that "in our schools is not the wisdom of life. We're learning technologies, we're getting information… there is a tendency to specialization" (Campbell, 1988, p. 11). Although knowledge and information have fortified Louis in knowing the world, they have not prepared him to accept it.

What Campbell (1988) calls the "wisdom of life" (p. 11) is lost within the cleverness of Louis's specialized knowledge and buried somewhere beneath the collection of facts and information he has amassed throughout his life. For example, shortly before Gage's death, Louis's daughter Ellie asks Louis what happens to people after they die. Louis shares a brief encyclopedic-like litany of popular systems of faith (i.e., reincarnation; Hindu and Buddhist beliefs of Nirvana; Catholic conceptions of heaven, hell, and purgatory).

Dissatisfied with this intellectual response to her philosophical question, his daughter then asks "Which do you have faith in, Daddy?" (King, 1983, p. 185). Louis in turn summarizes the scientific concepts of metabolism and entropy. He explains that due to these physical laws of nature, dying is "perfectly natural.… Clocks run down—that's all I know" (p. 38). This knowledge-based explanation elicits a purely emotional response: Ellie wept. Louis reasons that her crying "was a necessary first step on the way to making an uneasy peace with a truth that was never going away" (p. 39).

His matter-of-fact response to his daughter's tears indicates that while his education and training schooled Louis in the science of the physical world, it failed to enlighten him about the range and depth of a person's emotional realities. Nel Noddings (2005) observes that an individual can be "awashed in information but impoverished in the kind of advice that requires sound moral judgment" (p. 39). She maintains that caring for each other is the "ultimate reality of life" (p. 15) and therefore should not be disregarded in our teaching and learning.

Paul Lynch (2013) suggests that teachers need to occasionally "step off the assembly line" (p. 28) of teaching facts and information. He describes the need to "teach for uncertainty" (p. 38) and proposes that educators occasionally move from a prescribed curriculum to one that acknowledges and explores the unexpected and unexplainable:

Teaching is what responds, not what elicits response. To teach—to be a professor, an academic doctor—is to be a nurse of experience. A Deweyan teacher helps students turn their experience-as-data into experience-as-method. This is what reflection means, and it is the most demanding pedagogical work. (p. 95)

To what extent are educators "nurses of experience"? The Oxford English Dictionary (OED) traces the etymology of *nurse* to Late Middle English: to nourish, protect, and promote well-being. While knowledge may nourish a person's cognitive capacity, in what ways does it fortify a person's personal and emotional health? Although information may protect a person from intellectual ignorance, how successful is it in providing comfort in terms of dealing with life's tragedies and griefs? Whereas external data and facts may inform a person about the physical world, in what ways are they promoting one's emotional, spiritual, and personal well-being?

Tu Weiming (2011) reminds us "human beings are not merely rational animals" (p. 97). He writes that "cool speculation of the mind alone" cannot educate us on "matters of the heart" (p. 97). Thomas Rickert (2007) similarly calls for educators to disrupt the fantasy that equates scientific data with wisdom by acknowledging and exploring the unorthodox, unexpected, and oftentimes troublesome realities that silently exist beneath knowledge-based and fact-driven curricula (p. 196).

Louis is experiencing emotional anguish and personal suffering which lie outside the neatly ordered sphere of rationality. He refuses (or is unable) to "participate with joy in the sorrows of the world" (Campbell, 1991, p. 120). His life, once governed by the logic of nature, is now following a logic of grief. He exists within a hypothetical space Sam Harris (2010) calls "the moral landscape":

A space of real and potential outcomes whose peaks correspond to the heights of potential well-being and whose valleys represent the deepest possible suffering. Different ways of thinking and behaving—different cultural practices, ethical codes, modes of government, etc.—will translate into movements across this landscape and, therefore, into different degrees of human flourishing. (p. 7)

Grief has turned Louis's thoughts (normally neatly organized and logical) inside out. He now operates in what Harris (2010) describes as spaces of "intuitive morality" where "a clear boundary between facts and values simply does not exist" (p. 11). Although adhering to his reliance on rationality, grief has replaced facts with inklings, data with premonitions, and information with hunches. His intuition, again, tells him to "fix this problem." Louis had heard the supernatural stories his neighbors told about the mysterious powers of resurrection found in the pet sematary. Of course, he immediately dismissed them as foolishness... until now.

The notion of reburying Gage's dead body inside a pet sematary with the intention of resurrecting him (using the mystic powers to which the local folk lore attests) reveals (for maybe the first time in his life) a Louis Creed who thinks and acts according to his emotions and intuitions. All his intellectual cleverness will not change the past, resurrect his son, or assuage his despair. Louis rationalizes that the pet sematary folklore must be the solution to his problems. He reasons that, like Lazarus in the *New Testament*, Gage will live again: "so Christ brought Lazarus back from the dead... that's fine with me. If I have to swallow it, I will" (King, 1983, p. 186). The chart below demonstrates how Louis's emotional despair aligns to what Harris (2010) describes as "the illusory divide between facts and values" (p. 14):

Intuitive morality (The Moral Landscape, Harris, 2010)	Intense grieving (Pet Sematary, King, 1983)
Regarding the relationship between human knowledge and human values... truth has nothing, in principle, to do with consensus: one person can be right and everyone else can be wrong. (p. 31)	His grief came for him fully... took away whatever defenses remained.... He put his face in his hands and cried... thinking he would do anything to have a second chance. (p. 265)
...certain facts about human experience cannot be readily known, or may never be known. (p. 31)	What was beyond the Pet Sematary? The idea had a deadly attraction. It made a balance of logic which was impossible to deny. (p. 240)
Is it possible that certain people are incapable of wanting what they should want? Of course... (p. 21)	*So, Louis, what do you say.... Would you like to keep your dead son or go for what's behind Door Number One, Door Number Two, or Door Number Three?* (p. 242)
The division between facts and values is intellectually unsustainable... (p. 24) A belief—to be actually believed—entails the corollary belief that we have accepted it *because* it seems to be true. (p. 136)	"Gage," he muttered. Gage was in there, behind that wrought-iron fence, unjustly imprisoned... *Gonna break you out, Gage*, he thought. *Gonna break you out, big guy, or die trying.* (p. 312)
Extraneous information... situational variables... strongly influence our judgment. (p. 140); wishful thinking, self-serving bias, in-group loyalties, and frank self-deception can lead to monstrous departures from the norms of rationality. (p. 123)	*Climb a tree, shinny along a branch, drop into a graveyard, watch lovers... dig holes? That simple? Is it lunacy? I spent eight years becoming a doctor but I've become a grave robber in one simple step—what I suppose some people would call a ghoul.* (p. 318)

Louis's despair is what Eliezer J. Sternberg (2010) describes as a "*boundless problem*" that "cannot be expressed mathematically, using equations and probabilities.... There are too many unknowns, too many scenarios that cannot sensibly be expressed as simple probabilities" (p. 46). Louis rationalizes that even during his early medical training he sometimes needed to accept what initially sounded inexplicable:

> I mean I had to buy the concept that the fetus of one twin can sometimes swallow the fetus of the other *in utero*... and then show up with teeth in his testes or in his lungs twenty or thirty years later to prove that he did it, and I suppose if I can but that I can buy anything. (King, 1983, p. 186)

To his mind the pet sematary offers the remedy he needs: resurrection. Louis is familiar with the stories some of his neighbors told about pets who were reburied in the ancient Indian burial ground just beyond the pet sematary—and came back to life. King (1983) describes the lure of this idea as "a kind of seductive lullaby, the voice of possible comfort, and a dreamy sort of power" (p. 304): "How could he refuse to take the chance available to him—this one, unbelievable chance" (p. 274):

Perhaps this is what people do with the inexplicable, he thought. *This is what they do with the irrational that refuses to be broken down into the normal causes and effects that run the Western world.* Maybe it was not how your mind coped with the flying saucer you saw hovering over your back yard one morning.... You simply passed terror intact, like a kidney stone... *that's what you do all right*, he thought with immeasurable relief. *You pass it like a stone, and that's the end of it.* (pp. 78–79)

Ever the medical clinician, Louis evaluates his options: he can leave his son forever buried in the cold earth, or he can take action and re-bury him in ancient soil. Like Lazarus in the *New Testament*, Gage will live again:

I'm like Thomas saying he'd only believe Jesus had risen when he could look through the nail holes and stick his hands in the guy's side. As far as I'm concerned, he was the real physician of the bunch. (King, 1983, p. 186)

Dealing with tragedy on a cognitive level without acknowledging its emotional and spiritual reverberations amounts to what Sternberg (2010) calls "a tempest in the brain" (p. 43) wherein "there is no rational way to quantify experiences, intuitions, emotions, or personal values" (p. 46). Sternberg writes that individuals suffering this kind of "tempest in the brain" (p. 43) are likely to "reorganize [their] thoughts by moving them from one region to another and by making connections between disparate concepts" (p. 46).

Unwilling or unable to embrace his grief, Louis finds the pet sematary to be "a deadly attraction [that] made a balance of logic which was impossible to deny" (King, 1983, p. 240):

When are you going to do it? When are you going to bury Gage in the annex to the Pet Sematary?... Lazarus, come forth.... The teacher said if he'd just said "Come forth," probably everybody in that graveyard would have come out. (p. 239)

Overwhelmed by despair, Louis's obsession to resurrect Gage replaces his grief: "*But I could bring Gage back to life! Gage could live again!*" (King, 1983, p. 240). Joseph Campbell (1991) cautions that "the death of one for whom you feel compassion shouldn't [become] an affliction":

Your attachment is the temporal aspect of the relationship; your compassion is the eternal aspect. Hence, you can reconcile yourself to feelings of loss by identifying with that which is not lost when all is lost: namely, the consciousness that informs the body and all things. (p. 105)

Louis is unschooled in these kinds of spiritual or philosophical considerations. At this point he represents the human condition at its most emotionally distraught, intrinsically frail, and spiritually irreconcilable. His ensuing actions are a metaphorical journey into the depths of grief and despair: Louis decides to retrieve the body of his dead son from his burial lot and rebury him just beyond the pet sematary.

Many literary critics have analyzed this pivotal moment. Bernadette Bosky (1986), for example, observes that "the tragedy of *Pet Sematary* is that Louis Creed begins to follow his intuitions only when he should begin to doubt them" (p. 268). Vernon Hyles (1987) laments Louis's "attempt to create order out of chaos and strength out of weakness" that intentionally "creates monstrosities" (p. 59). Leonard Mustazza (1992), meanwhile, writes:

> What cannot be put aside so easily, however, what lingers in memory long after the gory details have faded is the artist's rendering of the human mind's capacity or incapacity for dealing with death…. King manages to show us that chaotic vision stripped of all consolations of philosophy, science, and reason. (p. 81)

As Louis heads to Gage's burial site, in his mind he continues "to place all the known components [of his plan to resurrect Gage] in an order as rational and logical as this dark magic would allow" (King, 1983, p. 273). Louis's habit of using rationality and logic to justify events is now used to rationalize the illogical. He reasons that the spiral of graves in the pet sematary align with ancient religious symbols associated with ancient Egyptians, Phoenicians, Mycenaens, the buildings of Stonehenge, and apocalyptic images in Judeo-Christian writings. Therefore, it must be valid.

Whether the pet sematary is real, a surreal nightmare, or a metaphoric representation of Louis Creed's grief, the fear and desperation it embodies are akin to Louis's inner reality—the landscape of his grief:

> [Louis] got Gage under the arms, aware of the fetid dampness, and lifted him that way, as he had lifted him so often from his evening tub. Gage's head lolled all the way to the middle of his back. Louis saw the grinning circlet of stitches which held Gage's head onto his shoulders.
>
> Somehow, panting, his stomach spasming from the smell and from the boneless loose feel of his son's miserably smashed body, Louis wrestled the body out of the coffin. At last he sat on the verge of the grave with the body in his lap, his feet dangling in the hole, his face a horrible livid color, his eyes black holes, his mouth drawn down in a trembling bow of horror and pity and sorrow.
>
> "Gage," he said and began to rock the boy in his arms. Gage's hair lay against Louis's wrist, as lifeless as wire.
>
> "Gage, it will be all right, I swear, Gage, it will be all right, this will end, this is just the night, please, Gage, I love you, Daddy loves you."
>
> Louis rocked his son. (p. 328)

The pet sematary wherein Louis now resides is the antithesis of the his neatly ordered world. The carefully constructed boundaries of his rational thinking that defined his understanding of life could not contain the fear, grief, and despair Louis is now experiencing. There was no space for the ghosts of regret, confusion, and anger within his measured understanding of the world.

In the pet sematary, however, superstitions exist alongside facts, lore in company with information, and leaps of faith apace with calculated certainties. This is a space where emotions defy categorization, faith baffles logic, and intuition eclipses knowledge. In her scholarship on haunting and the educational imagination, Barbara Regenspan (2014) questions the extent to which education itself "is becoming a ghost story" (p. 121). To what extent, for example, is too great a focus on intellectual concerns making ghosts of the spiritual, ethical, and emotional dimensions of student and teacher lives?

Louis Creed's emotional desperation reminds us that a human being's thoughts, actions, and emotions are informed by much more than his or her cognitive or intellectual capacities. Louis's medical acumen and academic cleverness are rendered powerless (and meaningless) once Gage's unimaginable death occurs. Grief, Louis learns, extends far beyond the four corners of a medical book or scholastic tome.

The illogical and irrational ghosts of tragedy defy the expanse of knowledge. No amount of data or rational explanation can sooth the spiritual, ethical, and emotional upheaval they leave in their wake. Similarly, Benjamin Hoff (1982) questions the extent to which schools prioritize knowledge and information while tacitly diminishing opportunities to nurture spiritual, moral, and emotional growth and development. He asks "but is Brain all that important? Is it really Brain that takes us where we need to go?" (Hoff, 1982, p. 153):

> Or is it all too often Brain that sends us off in the wrong direction, following the echo of the wind in the treetops, which we *think* is real, rather than listening to the voice within us that tells us which way to turn?
>
> A Brain can do all kinds of things, but the things that it can do are not the most important things. Abstract cleverness of mind only separates the thinker from the world of reality, and that world, the Forest of Real Life, is in a desperate condition now because of too many people who think too much and care too little. (pp. 153–154)

When faced with unimaginable grief, Louis Creed's cleverness of mind further "separates [him] from the world of reality" (Hoff, 1982, p. 153). Louis's rational mind offers no consolation: "never in his life had his mind felt so alone and disconnected; he felt like an astronaut who has floated away from his ship during an EVA and now only drifts in a great blackness" (King, 1983, p. 322).

In what ways are schools preparing students for their inevitable journeys into these "forests of real life" (Hoff, 1982, p. 154)? Grieving reminds us that there is much to be learned and reflected on beyond retaining, processing, and analyzing information. Hoff (1982) observes that "people are easily led away from what is right for them because people have Brain, and Brain can be fooled.... The Way of

Self-Reliance starts with recognizing who we are, what we've got to work with, and what works best for us" (p. 57).

As educators, in what ways are we lead away from our personal values and beliefs, while prioritizing professional (and oftentimes bureaucratized) goals and outcomes? To what extent is the school curriculum helpful in leading students toward better understanding themselves and recognizing who they are and what is most worthwhile to their lives? To what degree does education contribute to the kind of emotional and spiritual desperation Hoff (1982) describes as inherent to "too many people who think too much and care too little" (p. 154)?

FROM POOH TO POE

He stood in this modest suburb of the dead, looking around. *Louis, what are you doing here? You're looking up a road you don't want to travel.* He pushed the voice aside. If he was torturing anyone, it was only himself... [This is] a kiddie story with gruesome undertones—Winnie the Poe. (King, 1983, p. 273)

Stephen King's juxtaposition of *Winnie* and *Poe* (i.e., the Pooh and Edgar Allan respectively) captures the dissonance inherent to grief: a childlike vulnerability (i.e., emotional fragility, feelings of helplessness or powerlessness) coupled with an adult's inclination to control or rationalize the emotional intensity (Cochran & Claspell, 1987, pp. 60, 70). Representing the child-like end of the spectrum, Pooh admits "I am a bear of No Brain at all" (Milne, 1926, p. 60). Nevertheless, he is famously the only friend who can find Eeyore's missing tail. Although Owl, recognized as the most intelligent of Eeyore's friends, lays several elaborate and cunning traps, only Pooh sees that the bell-rope attached to Owl's front door is Eeyore's missing tail—to which Eeyore had become quite attached, of course (Milne, 1926, pp. 73–74).

Despite the depth of his knowledge, Owl was unable to see what was right before his eyes. For all his cleverness, the simple truth eluded him. Only Pooh's uncomplicated and unsophisticated mind (uncluttered with facts and theories) saw the solution with clarity. How often and in what ways do teachers acknowledge, validate, and celebrate the simple wisdom of children? Consider how much wisdom is sacrificed to make room for the prescribed information and designated skill sets of our curricula.

When things do not seem to be moving forward in the way others expect, Pooh accepts reality rather than trying to change it. He works with circumstances rather than trying to control them. For example, when his friend Eeyore complains on his birthday that "we can't all, and some of us don't. That's all there is to it" (Milne, 1926, p. 100), Pooh, although "being a Bear of Very Little Brain" (p. 102) observes that "a fly can't bird, but a bird can fly.... A fish can't whistle and neither can I" (p. 102).

In other words, instead of devising some clever scheme to eradicate Eeyore's sadness or attempting to alter the reality of Eeyore's feelings, Pooh simply stops to listen. In turn, he realized what everyone else had not—Eeyore was sad that although it was his birthday, he received no presents. Hence, a simple solution to what seemed like a complex problem emerged. One only needs to *recognize and accept* what was right before his or her eyes and resist the temptation (and the audacity) to *change or control* the circumstances.

In Pooh's world, clever schemes intended to control circumstances sooner or later fail. Benjamin Hoff (1982) points out that "cleverness, after all, has its limitations. Its mechanical judgments and clever remarks tend to prove inaccurate with passing time, because it doesn't look very deeply into things to begin with" (p. 37). Consider Pooh's friend Rabbit who often "felt important, as if everything [and everyone] depended upon him" (Milne, 1928, p. 74). When problems arose, Rabbit felt compelled to fix them. Despite his good intentions, however, he oftentimes tried to fix things that did not need repairing or that could not be repaired.

For example, when Kanga and her baby, Roo, visit the forest one day, Rabbit immediately believes that he sees a problem that needs getting rid of. After all, since he had never seen, heard, or read anything about marsupials, he assumed that they must be troublesome. Instead of seeing Kanga and Roo for the friendly creatures they are, Rabbit ignored the reality right before his eyes, and devised an elaborate plan to chase them away. He was quite proud of his scheme as it was filled with several trademarks of academia: multiple intricate steps, elaborate strands of logic, an abundance of long vocabulary words, and a running commentary. In the end, the futility of the endeavor becomes apparent to everyone—including Rabbit who comes to be accepted as known far and wide as "Roo's great friend" (Milne, 1926, p. 152).

Similarly, Louis Creed cannot see the stark (albeit tragic) reality that is right before his eyes. Like Rabbit, he tries to repair the unrepairable by concocting a scheme. Although the futility of his plan is obvious to the readers, Louis is bewitched by its cleverness. Ignoring the physical reality of death, Louis reburies his dead son in the infamous pet sematary ("*Louis, I think this is it. Your last chance. You're right. It's my last chance and I'm damned well taking it*" [King, 1983, p. 321]).

He buries the helplessness associated with his grief beneath a dogged determination to take control of the situation at any cost. Louis had heard the lore that described dead creatures coming back to life "look[ing] damned" (King, 1983, p. 255) as if something inside [them] "was screaming, really... something inside... screaming... and screaming... and screaming" (p. 258). In one story, the person resurrected from the pet sematary is said to have been transformed into "a monster. Maybe it was a zombie or a dybbuk or a demon" (p. 259).

But to Louis, the lore of the pet sematary "made a balance of logic which was impossible to deny" (King, 1983, p. 240). The idea of a logical scheme designed to erase tragedy and thereby obliterate grief mesmerizes Louis. His struggle to change reality perverts his shock and grief into a false hopefulness. Because the truth would render his plan irrational, he clings to the false narrative. Recalling Campbell's (1991) prophetic words from earlier in this chapter, "if you try to correct the sorrows, all you do is shift them somewhere else" (p. 120). As Louis sat by his son's grave ready to enact his clever scheme, the narrator tells readers that Louis was "trying to place all the known components in an order as rational and logical as this dark magic would allow" (King, 1983, p. 273). When "dark magic" is mistaken as "rational and logical," the movement toward the macabre world of Edgar Allan Poe's fiction is complete.

Poe begins his short story *The Murders in the Rue Morgue* with a brief narrative comparing an analytical mind with a scheming one. He muses that "the mental features discoursed of as the analytical, are, in themselves, but little susceptible of analysis" (Poe, 1841, p. 117). He posits that although the analytical are "fond of enigmas, of conundrums… to calculate is not in itself to analyze" (p. 117). Whereas one who schemes and plots relies upon a wide expanse of knowledge and has a capacity for being clever, one who analyzes is engaged in thinking deeply and reflecting on truths as opposed to facts.

Poe writes that thoughtful introspection elevates intellect into "recesses of thought altogether inaccessible to the ordinary understanding" (Poe, 1841, p. 118). In other words, it removes an individual's thoughts and beliefs from mundane concerns and into a higher ethical space. From this perspective, Louis Creed is headed further down on a path of desperation and tragedy: he calculates a clever scheme, but does not think deeply; he focuses on facts without regard for larger truths. As the narrator observes, "it is a path [Louis] hoped for blindly" (King, 1983, p. 296).

In the world of Pooh, characters tend toward realizing larger truths. For example, after Piglet gathers an assortment of violets to decorate his home, Milne (1928) describes how Piglet's thoughts turn outward beyond himself:

> It suddenly came over him that nobody had ever picked Eeyore a bunch of violets, and the more he thought of this, the more he thought how sad it was to be an Animal who had never had a bunch of flowers picked for him. So he hurried out again, saying to himself, "Eeyore, Violets," and then "Violets, Eeyore…." (p. 86)

Louis's thoughts, by contrast, turn further inward—away from larger truths. In fact, as he transports his dead son to the pet sematary, the narrator describes Louis as acting "as if hypnotized" (King, 1983, p. 329) and as a person "who has been called from a mesmerist's trance" (p. 329). Poe's short story *Mesmeric Revelation* (1849) describes a character, Mr. Vankirk, similarly drifting further and further away from a reality he can no longer control. Vankirk is fatally ill but refuses to accept the emotional and personal realities of his own mortality (similar to how Louis denies the finality of his son's death).

Louis, like Vankirk, is "suffering with acute pain in the region of the heart" (Poe, 1849, p. 41). Both characters struggle with emotional and spiritual ambiguities that defy their rational understanding of how the world should work. Despite their worldly knowledge, both characters are emotionally conflicted by their current life circumstances. They deny the reality of their emotional vulnerabilities by clinging to the linear and encyclopedic knowledge that they have always relied on. It is as if they are mesmerized by information and data that no longer adheres to the realities right before their eyes. Their situations recall John Dewey's (1938) prophetic words: "What avail is it to win prescribed amounts of information about geography and history, to win ability to read and write, if in the process the individual loses his own soul" (p. 49).

The *Pet Sematary* (1983) narrator observes that Louis's story is akin to "a kiddie story with gruesome undertones—Winnie the Poe" (King, 1983, p. 273). Winnie-the-Pooh embodies child-like wisdom. His perspective of the world is a simple one, uncomplicated by deep thoughts or complex reasoning. Although he is intuitively aware of emotional and moral considerations, most of the time he would prefer to simply whistle. Conversely, Poe's (1849) protagonist Vankirk (*Mesmeric Revelation*) ascertains the meaning of life in terms of scientific concepts as well as the principles and laws of nature and the physical world. He is disinterested in emotional, spiritual, and ethical realities which are not bound by laws of science. King suggests that Louis has become a hybrid of what these characters represent.

Like Pooh, Louis adopts a child-like simplicity to his thinking. Rather than face the complications of his grief-filled world, Louis would prefer to whistle. Like Vankirk, Louis is transfixed on what he sees as a rational plan based on irrefutable truths. In Louis's grief, however, he has replaced his faith in science with myth and his adherence to natural laws with superstition.

The charts below highlight relevant excerpts from *Winnie-the-Pooh* (Milne, 1926) and Poe's *Mesmeric Revelation* (1849) to highlight these divergent frameworks of thought. The third column of each chart uses related excerpts from *Pet Sematary* (King, 1983) to show the metamorphosis from Pooh and Poe to Winner-the-Poe. Each chart includes its own mini-commentary for further consideration and reflection.

From Pooh	*To Poe*	*To "Winnie-the-Poe"*
"Yes," said Winnie-the-Pooh. "I see now," said Winnie-the-Pooh. "I have been Foolish and Deluded," said he, "and I am a Bear of No Brain at All." "You're the best bear in all the World," said Christopher Robin soothingly. "Am I?" said Pooh hopefully. And then he brightened up suddenly. (Milne, 1926, p. 60)	[My] intellectual faculties are wonderfully exalted and invigorated.... reason had nothing to do [with them]. (Poe, 1849, pp. 42–43)	Louis stared down into the ditch as if hypnotized. At last he dragged his gaze away with a little gasp—the gasp of one who has come to, or who has been called from a mesmerist's trance (p. 329).... [he] ignored that part of his mind which whispered constantly that he had gone mad. (King, 1983, p. 331)

Vankirk (in the Poe story) exalts in his own intelligence to the point where he is blinded to how much he does not actually understand the emotional and spiritual realities that exist outside of books and encyclopedias. Similarly, Louis, mesmerized by his own clever plan, enters so far into his own version of reality that any hope of comfort or healing is lost to a kind of madness.

131

Pooh's self-knowledge, on the other hand, is tempered with a humility that allows him to understand and accept that in certain matters he is "foolish and deluded." Although he admits that he is a bear of little brain, he is not inclined to see that as a problem which needs to be fixed. Instead, he seeks out and finds comfort in simple and genuine friendship.

What might happen if we teachers invested even a fraction of time spent on classroom discipline to prioritize and model kindness and humility? While school curriculum is strongly based in complex thinking (e.g., applying the scientific method, solving algebraic algorithms) and enhancing cleverness (e.g., expanding vocabularies, using the newest technologies), to what extent does it value what is simple and uncomplicated? Unless we remain vigilant, imagine the sorts of simple wisdom that can become lost within the tomes of information, data, and facts dispensed.

From Pooh	To Poe	To "Winnie-the-Poe"
Pooh hasn't much Brain, but he never comes to any harm. He does silly things and they turn out right. There's Owl. Owl hasn't exactly got Brain, but he Knows Things. He would know the Right Thing to do... (Milne, 1926, p. 184)	The atmosphere, for example, impels the electric principle, while the electric principle permeates the atmosphere. These gradations of matter increase in rarity or fineness, until we arrive at a matter unparticled— without particles—indivisible—one. (Poe, 1849, p. 43)	*Louis had re-discovered his dream and was in its grip....* *Faith is accepting gravity as a postulate,* he thought... (p. 344)... *he accepted the ability of the [pet sematary] to resurrect the dead.* (King, 1983, p. 345)

Pooh and Owl live with humility, kindness, and a sense of morality through which they "would know the right thing to do" without relying on intellect and cleverness. As he is dying, Vankirk's thoughts are neither spiritual nor moral in nature; they narrowly focus on the physiology of his condition. Louis equates his grief and emotional despair with the clinical trappings and rational logic of his medical training. Once he conflates gravity and resurrection as comparable postulates, to his mind the pet sematary becomes a logically valid plan. Unlike Pooh, he is emotionally aloof and morally indifferent. Unlike Vankirk, whose analytic thinking remains scientifically-sound (although unfeeling), Louis's thinking is rational in form only—but no longer in substance.

For all their intelligence, imagine what Vankirk and Louis could learn from Pooh and his friends. Then imagine what we teachers can learn from our students. What if we talked less and listened more? Examining the movement from Pooh to Poe to Winnie-the-Poe reveals the dangers inherent to filling our students with information at the expense of nurturing their emerging understanding of themselves and the world around (and within) them.

From Pooh	To Poe	To "Winnie-the-Poe"
Sometimes he [Eeyore] thought sadly to himself, "Why?" and sometimes he thought "Wherefore?" and sometimes he thought, "Inasmuch as which?"—and sometimes he didn't quite know what he *was* thinking about. So when Winnie-the-Pooh came stumbling along, Eeyore was very glad to be able to stop thinking for a while, in order to say "How do you do?" (Milne, 1926, p. 62)	And here the law of impulsion and permeation is modified. The ultimate or unparticled matter not only permeates all things, but impels all things. (Poe, 1849, p. 43)	His thoughts dissolved into the inarticulate, droning mutter of prayer (p. 350)... but it was that thought [to resurrect his son], so falsely comforting, that got him to his feet and moving again. (King, 1983, p. 353)

Eeyore has no problem asking thought-provoking questions that prompt thinking but guarantee no answers. At the same time, he also appreciates friendship, especially as it provides a means "to be able to stop thinking for a while." As Vankirk approaches death, there is no mention of any human connection expressed in his words or thoughts. Neither does he pontificate ethically or spiritually. His concerns remain limited to facts and physical phenomena that verify and describe his physical deterioration.

Louis has detached himself from human connection (he sent his wife and child out of town while he executes his plan to resurrect his son). Without the courage to acknowledge that some of life's questions do not have answers, Louis now emotionally and morally "unplugs his connections to reality." For all the complexities of science and higher knowledge, Louis cannot see the simple truths (i.e., of death, unforeseen tragedy and grief) that surround him. He continues to look for explanations and solutions to questions and problems for which there are none.

From Pooh	To Poe	To "Winnie-the-Poe"
"Now then, Pooh," said Christopher Robin, "where's your boat?" "I ought to say," explained Pooh, as they walked down to the shore of the island, "that it isn't just an ordinary sort of boat. Sometimes it's a Boat, and sometimes it's more of an Accident. It all depends."	The only consideration which restrains us is our conception of its atomic constitution; and here, even, as we have to seek aid from our notion of an atom, as something	Nothing seemed to matter. He felt like something less than human now, one of George Romero's stupid, lurching movie-zombies, or maybe someone who had escaped from T.S. Eliot's poem about the hollow man.... "Headpiece full of straw," he said in his croaking voice. "That's me." (King, 1983, p. 356)

From Pooh	To Poe	To "Winnie-the-Poe"
"Depends on what?" "On whether I'm on the top of it or underneath it"... [this] wasn't what Christopher Robin expected, and the more he looked at it, the more he thought what a Brave and Clever Bear Pooh was, and the more Christopher Robin thought this, the more Pooh looked modestly down his nose and tried to pretend he wasn't. (Milne, 1926, p. 62)	possessing in infinite minuteness, solidity, palpability, weight. Destroy the idea of the atomic constitution and we should no longer be able to regard the ether as an entity, or, at least, as matter... (Poe, 1849, p. 44)	

When Christopher Robin acknowledges that Pooh has shared a clever observation, Pooh again responds with humility. Many of the qualities and values Pooh displays (i.e., humility, kindness, honesty) are not measured on standardized assessments, awarded top academic honors, or even required for a variety of high-paying jobs. Formal skills-based assessments (often linked to teacher accountability and performance ratings) and similar curricula initiatives prioritize measureable increases in content knowledge, expanse of information, and other cognitive-based criteria.

How would Pooh score on such standardized measurements of teaching and learning? What about Vankirk or Louis Creed? Based on the expanse of their knowledge and vocabulary, I suspect Vankirk and Creed would rank high while Pooh, "being a Bear of Very Little Brain" would place low. Pooh would likely be labeled a low-achieving student and perhaps his teachers would be identified as underperforming. And yet, based on the analysis of the three characters, Pooh is the only one wise enough to understand that not all questions are intended to be answered; to realize that the companionship of others is more comforting than a brain full of knowledge; and to accept that sometimes things happen that we cannot change or control.

The sorts of simple wisdom and values Pooh expresses have less to do with intelligence and cognitive capacity than with emotional awareness and ethical considerations both of which are indispensable during moments of personal crisis and emotional intensity.

From Pooh	To Poe	To "Winnie-the-Poe"
Pooh tried to think of something he would say, but the more he thought, the more he felt that there is no real answer....	For although we may admit infinite littleness in the atoms themselves, the infinitude of littleness in the spaces between them is an uncertainty. There will be a point—there will be a	*I love you, Tigger! I love you! I believe in you, Tigger! I will always love you and believe in you.... Thinking such troubled half-dreaming thoughts, Louis Creed slipped away,*

From Pooh	To Poe	To "Winnie-the-Poe"
"I shan't say anything," said Pooh at last. "I shall just hum to myself, as if I was waiting for something." (Milne, 1928, pp. 45–46) Where am I going? I don't quite know. / Down to the stream where the king-cups grow— / Up on the hill where the pine-trees blow— / Anywhere, anywhere. / *I* don't know. (Milne, 1924, p. 36)	degree of rarity at which, if the atoms are sufficiently numerous, the interspaces must vanish, and the mass absolutely coalesce. (Poe, 1849, p. 44)	unplugging his connections to waking reality line by line, until all thoughts ceased. (King, 1983, p. 359)

Pooh is honest enough to admit when he has run out of things to say and has the modesty to then stop talking. His unpretentious humming indicates his acceptance of his limitations and his being content with the fact that sometimes there are no answers. As Vankirk nears his death, he never stops speaking. Although the substance of his dialogue is intellectually impressive, one might question its relevance to the immediate situation of his imminent death. Louis is determined to talk his way out of tragedy, grief, and death. Without the humility to accept that he cannot undo his loss, he defies death itself. Henceforth, he continues with his scheme (no matter how incoherent) to resurrect his son in the pet sematary.

Unlike Pooh, Louis lacks the humility to ask of himself: "Where am I going? I don't quite know" (Milne, 1924, p. 36). There is much that the University of Maine physician Louis Creed can learn from a "Bear of Very Little Brain" (Milne, 1926, p. 140). A few to items to consider include: (1) Not all questions can be neatly answered, no matter how much time we spend thinking about them or how clever we are; (2) Kindness, modesty, and honesty can sooth a person's distress; and (3) Sometimes it is wise to stop talking and just listen, be with a friend, or hum.

Imagine if, like Pooh, Louis had the humility to accept life's mysteries without demanding an explanation or insisting on a solution. Instead of closing himself off to others, imagine if Louis had the capacity to welcome and confide in a friend with whom he could grieve. What if Louis, like Eeyore, stopped asking "Why?" "Wherefore?" "Inasmuch as which?" and admitted that he "didn't quite know what he *was* thinking about" (Milne, 1926, p. 62). Imagine if Louis stopped calculating, rationalizing, and hypothesizing long enough to listen to his grief and accept what he could neither control nor explain... or to simply hum.

As teachers, how often do we take the time with our students to ponder questions just for the sake of wondering? To what extent is our practice invested in binary choices (right or wrong, correct or incorrect)? Once information is learned, how often do classrooms regard the real-world moral consequences of the information? Once facts are collected, how much time is given to consider in what ways those facts align with or run counter to others' beliefs or values? In what ways do we teachers take the time to appreciate a child's sense of wonder and imagination?

AUTOMATONS, ZOMBIES, SLEEPWALKERS... NO MORE!

Although an important part of humanity involves our cognitive capacities, we are not automatons. Consider how tragedy and grief reduce Louis Creed, an intelligent and successful doctor, to feeling like "a movie-zombie, or maybe someone who had escaped from T.S. Eliot's poem about the hollow man.... [with a] "headpiece full of straw" (King, 1983, p. 356). As educators, imagination, morality and values, humility and kindness, compassion, and our capacity to grieve and to comfort each other should not be discounted or set aside from our work.

In Poe's (1849) short story, a medical attendant describes Vankirk's intellectual ramblings in his final moments before death as a kind of "colloquy occurring between a sleepwalker and [him]self" (p. 41). Early in his deliberations over using the pet sematary to resurrect his son, Louis remarks that it was as if "he had experienced an isolated incident of sleepwalking, brought on by the unexpected and extremely upsetting happenstances" (King, 1983, p. 83). When he later decides to execute his scheme, he observes "*if I was awake I'd no more head* [*into the Pet Sematary*] *than I'd get drunk and go skydiving. But I'm going to do it.... So I must be dreaming. Right?*" (p. 114).

In what ways are teachers sometimes sleepwalking through their work? Consider the following: (1) When educators drill facts without taking the time to wonder about them; (2) Ask students to focus on the mastery of rote skills without considering their merit or real-world value; and (3) Enforce adherence to rules and regulations (i.e., walking in straight lines, raising hands to ask permission for a Kleenex) without calling on other traits such as kindness, honesty, or integrity. Are there not some features of sleepwalking happening here?

Ralph Ellison (1947) warns that "sometimes it is best not to awaken them; there are few things in the world as dangerous as sleepwalkers" (p. 5). Louis awakens from his sleepwalking to find his son, newly resurrected from the pet sematary, wielding his father's medical scalpel (once a tool for healing) as a weapon of slaughter. "Sounds came from [Gage's] swollen throat like the bells of hell" (King, 1983, p. 384) that shook Louis from his mesmerized state. Only now does Louis see what is right before his eyes. While metaphorically sleepwalking, Louis believed that ingenuity and cleverness could remedy any problem—even death. He was bewitched by the idea that he could manipulate reality with his cleverness. He could not imagine creating and living a life without his son. Now, sleepwalking no longer, he realizes how dangerous this thinking (and his hubris) were.

The more Louis endeavors to reverse death or deny the truths of tragedy or grief, the more spiritual harmony and emotional balance are destroyed. The resurrected but murderous incarnation of Gage personifies that destruction. Instead of sowing seeds of healing, solace, and hope, all that emerges is more tragedy and death. Stephen King's prose paints a surreal window through which to glimpse the far-reaching valleys of despair and inner suffering.

It takes the nightmare of a psychotic Gage (whose reanimated corpse murders his mother and neighbor) for Louis to understand that some tragedies and misfortunes, no matter how incomprehensible or unimaginable, exist beyond his human capacity to understand or fix. Louis's emotional journey takes him from denying an unthinkable tragedy, to challenging death itself, to eventually experiencing a violent epiphany of humanity's limitations and frailties.

Louis may have been an expert medical diagnostician, but he misread the conditions of his son's tragedy and the depth of his own grief. For lacking emotional foresight and being disconnected from others, he chides himself: "How could I have been so stupid?" (King, 1983, p. 379). His epiphany is reminiscent of Pooh admitting "I have been Foolish and Deluded," said he, "and I am a Bear of No Brain at All" (1926, p. 60). Louis subsequently admonishes himself:

> Grief, not stupidity, Louis. There is a difference… small, but vital. The battery that burying ground survives on. Growing in power… it has fed on your grief… no, more than that. It's doubled it, cubed it, raised it to the nth power. And it just isn't grief it feeds on. Sanity. It's eaten your sanity. The flaw is only the inability to accept, not uncommon. It's cost you your wife, and it's almost surely cost you your best friend as well as your son. This is it. What comes when you're too slow wishing away the thing that knocks on your door in the middle of the night is simple enough: total darkness. (King, 1983, p. 379)

Louis comes face to face with his nightmare: the resurrected Gage, "his mouth smeared with blood, his chin dripping, his lips pulled back in a hellish grin" (King, 1983, p. 385). Ironically, Louis is now forced to kill the very child he so cleverly and painstakingly worked to bring back. Stripped of his intellectual hubris and fully embracing the depth of his humanity, he can begin grieving;

> Louis got up and sauntered down the hall to a far corner. He crouched there, pulling himself into a ball, cramming himself into a corner, tighter and tighter. He found he could make himself smaller if he put a thumb in his mouth and so he did that.

> He remained that way for better than two hours… and then, little by little, a dark and of-so-plausible idea came to him. He pulled his thumb from his mouth. It made a small pop. Louis got himself

> (hey-ho let's go)
> going again.

In the room where Gage had hidden, he stripped the sheet from the bed and took it out into the hall. He wrapped his wife's body in it, gently, with love. He was humming but did not realize it. (King, 1983, p. 386)

In grief, we are all children again. Thomas Attig (1996) identifies a variety of vulnerabilities that individuals of all ages experience while grieving, including: "emotional fragility, unusual sensitivity, weak self-confidence, low self-esteem, instable identity or pre-existing psychological or emotional conditions such as separation anxiety, depression, or mental illness" (p. 85). Nevertheless, as Hoff (1982) points out, hope exists within a person's innate child-like resiliency, hopefulness, and imagination:

Return to the beginning; become a child again.... Why do the en*light*ened seem filled with light and happiness, like children? Why do they sometimes even look and talk like children? Because they are. The wise are Children Who Know. Their minds have been emptied of the countless somethings of small learning, and filled with the wisdom of the Great Nothing, the Way of the Universe. (p. 151)

How much of our work as teachers validates and celebrates the innate gifts of children? In what ways do we nurture, cultivate, and learn from child-like tendencies to dream, wonder, imagine, cry, and (of course, like Pooh) hum? John Dewey (1916) wrote that it is critical to remember "the educator, like the farmer, has certain things to do, certain resources with which to do, and certain obstacles with which to contend" (p. 106):

The conditions with which the farmer deals, whether obstacles or resources, have their own structure and operation independently of any purpose of his.... It would be absurd if the farmer set up a purpose of farming, without any reference to these conditions of soil, climate, characteristics of plant growth, etc. His purpose is simply a foresight of the consequences of his energies connected with those things about him. (pp. 106–107)

It would be equally absurd for teachers to set purposes for teaching and learning that did not align intellectually, emotionally, and ethically with their students. After all, how else will their (and our) humanity be nurtured and cultivated? To what extent do schools tend to the emotional and spiritual gardens of its students and teachers? Within the confines of a data-driven curriculum that emphasizes facts and skills, how much space do educators afford to nurture emotional and spiritual health and well-being? Where in the life of a classroom are resiliency, hopefulness, and imagination acknowledged and celebrated?

While at the pet sematary to rebury his son, Louis is wearing a gardener's hat and gloves. But the garden he is tending is an inorganic one: it lacks authentic properties of life as it intends to thwart the natural processes of life and defy death. Louis had become so entranced with *inorganic* facts, figures, and hard science that when tragedy beyond reason occurred, he was emotionally and spiritually unprepared.

Because his attention through the years had been directed toward concerns of the outer world, Louis never learned to attend to the garden of his inner spirit and soul. When the physical world provided him no answers or solace, Louis felt lost. Despite his professional knowledge and expertise, he did not know where to turn for comfort or emotional healing:

> He shuddered, but not from the cold. It was a feeling of aloneness that made him shudder. It was strong and persuasive. There was no way to concretize it with a metaphor. It was faceless. He just felt by himself, untouched and untouching. (King, 1983, p. 108)

Parker Palmer (2007) observes that teachers and students "are cultivating a garden together, backs to the sun. The question is a hoe in our hands and we are digging beneath the hard and crusty surface to the rich humus of our lives" (p. 36). Louis never ventures more deeply toward the "rich humus of his life" until further unexplainable and unthinkable tragedy strikes. He reveled in facts, information, and data that flourished on the surface of life and became so narrowly focused on the observable and measurable *outer* world that he ignored the realities and nuances of his *inner* life.

Louis was called to adapt to a new world that was unfamiliar and unforgiving. Embracing a new understanding of life, especially one that in many ways contradicted his previous views, requires mourning. With new thoughts and deeper understandings, previous beliefs and ways of thinking departed. Like life itself, learning involves the growth of new ideas and the passing away of former ones.

TOPICS FOR REFLECTION

1. Grief reminds us that life is more than a set of facts and processes—it is a collection of *experiences*. Paul Lynch (2013) offers a variety of suggestions to guide teachers toward focusing less on information and more on life itself. Imagine that your school administration has decided to adopt the four Lynch belief-statements listed below as priorities for the upcoming schoolyear.

   Priority One: Teachers will occasionally "step off the assembly line" (p. 28) of teaching facts and information.

   Priority Two: Teachers will take the time to "teach for uncertainty" (p. 38).

   Priority Three: Teachers will design lessons and activities that move away from the prescribed curriculum toward exploring the unexpected and unexplainable (p. 38).

   Priority Four: More than dispensers of information, teachers will be "nurses of experience" (p. 95).

Among you and your peers, decide what you believe the priorities listed below are asking of you. How might they be implemented? What would these endeavors look and sound like per your grade level and content area? What might be the potential challenges and benefits?

2. Barbra Regenspan (2014) maintains that "the central haunting of our lives as teachers is the construction of educational philosophy on concerns of power and knowledge, as opposed to connection" (p. 140). In what ways does inequitable distribution of educational resources and opportunities impact your work? How difficult would it be to revise reading lists, modify assignments, or reframe specific lessons to better elicit the voices and aspirations of underserved populations? What would be gained by doing so?

3. John Dewey (1916) compares teachers to farmers and gardeners who have the potential to plant the seeds of life. If the seeds are nourished and allowed to take root, students will receive sustenance of various kinds for years to come. What are some of the thoughts, beliefs, values, or ideas you hope to cultivate in the minds and hearts of your students?

To what extent do you have faith that whether or not the seeds take root during your time with the students, the potential remains for them to bloom in the future regardless of whether you are there to witness it? What are some of the thoughts, beliefs, values, or ideas that your students have planted in *your* mind and taken root in your heart?

4. Can an individual's emotional life truly be separated from his or her professional work? If separated, what is gained or lost? Once he opened up to his emotions, Louis Creed felt that there was "Madness. Madness all around, close, hunting him" and that he sometimes "walked the balance beam of rationality" (King, 1983, p. 295). As a teacher, have there been times when you could relate to this level of emotional distress? How did you deal with these kinds of unsettling feelings? How often do you feel like a teaching machine without any space or time to tend to the emotional needs of the students? Can you recall classroom moments and/or lessons that were impacted or enhanced by the emotional climate of the classroom?

5. Joseph Campbell (1991) wrote "your sacred space is where you can find yourself again and again" (p. 180). He observed "you do not have anything in your sacred space that's not of significance to you for the harmonization of your own life" (p. 180). Consider the sacred nature of your work as teacher. Imagine lessons, resources, activities and projects that have transformed classrooms into sacred spaces. Can you imagine ones that have the potential to do so?

6. As teachers, how often do we take the time with our students to ponder questions and topics just for the sake of wondering? To what extent is our practice invested in binary choices (right or wrong, correct or incorrect) instead? Once information

is dispersed, how much classroom time is spent reflecting on it? What would be gained by investing in additional time for reflective activities and conversation?

7. What lessons, texts, teachers, projects, or related experiences have been pivotal in helping you better understand your values, beliefs, and aspirations? How have they helped shape your personal and professional life? In what ways can teachers help students better reflect upon personal and collective values, beliefs, and aspirations?

8. While school curriculum is strongly based in complex thinking (e.g., applying the scientific method, solving algebraic algorithms) and enhancing cleverness (e.g., expanding vocabularies, using the newest technologies), to what extent does it value what is simple and uncomplicated? As a society, to what extent are we educating a generation in which "too many people who think too much and care too little" (Hoff, 1982, p. 154)? What lessons have you engaged in that focus on caring over thinking and that prioritized emotion over knowledge?

9. Consider the A. A. Milne characters Rabbit, Owl, and Pooh. To what extent can you see yourself or your students reflected in them? When have you or your students acted in ways that resemble personalities embodied in Milne's (1926) characters?

Rabbit: He considers himself the most resourceful of Pooh's friends. He is the self-appointed problem-solver. Sometimes, though, he sets out to solve problems that do not actually exist. Other times he is determined to solve problems for which there are no solutions. Oftentimes, he devises elaborate schemes and intricate plots for problems that, in fact, are quite simple.

Owl: He has the reputation for being the most clever of Pooh's friends; he is the most well-read, and has the largest vocabulary. Oftentimes, however, he is so busy espousing facts, theories, and tomes of information that simple answers elude him. For all his intelligence, he frequently cannot see simple truths that are right before his eyes.

Pooh: Although he considers himself a "Bear of Little Brain," Pooh acts with humility, kindness, and honesty. If he does not know what to say, he simply keeps quiet—or hums.

10. In your experiences, in what ways do parents, teachers, and administrators acknowledge, validate, and celebrate the wisdom of children? How important is it that a portion of instructional time is used to nurture a child's sense of wonder and imagination? How often does it feel as if students are "empty vessels to be filled" with knowledge, figures, and facts? In what ways does this align to your vision of teaching?

11. Describe one or two lessons or classroom experiences that address the immediate lives of the students. Brainstorm ways in which teaching and learning can better align intellectually, emotionally, and ethically with the lives of students.

CHAPTER 8

NUANCES OF GRIEVING: IDENTITY, VULNERABILITY, RESILIENCY, AND GRACE

Oliver Twist, Charles Dickens

Significant change almost always means loss and causes a kind of bereavement. Since the meaningfulness of life depends on predictability, we are bereaved by an actual or potential loss, whether it is caused by a death or by a "discrediting of familiar assumptions" (Marris, 1986, pp. 20–21). We are bereaved if someone we love dies, but we are also bereaved if assumptions we live by and take for granted are devalued…. A major part of our world stops making sense; continuity is disrupted; our connections can no longer be counted on. (Evans, 1996, pp. 28–29)

Although individuals who are grieving often find that day-to-day living feels unfamiliar, even disorienting, Robert Evans (1996) reminds us that grief and bereavement are nevertheless integral parts of our humanity, not separate from it. When accepted as a core element of who we are, grieving can be understood as much more than what an individual experiences when a loved one dies. Kay Chang (2017, p. 3) examines a variety of grief experiences and identifies four categories to consider: loss of innocence (usually related to some form of abuse); loss of a dream (a personal or professional aspiration); loss of stability (i.e., a natural disaster, financial loss); and loss due to a "living death" (i.e., separation by divorce or incarceration). Each of these experiences affects a person's daily life, influences his or her interactions with others, and alters one's views of the world. Hence, they have a great deal to do with teaching and learning.

Marshall Alcorn (2002) observes "all changes in deeply held beliefs involve an experience of loss or mourning…. When people come to change important feelings, something must be given up, and this is a painful experience" (pp. 111–112). He points out that the "enormous and painful work of mourning" that "helps us change our internal representations of the world" (p. 113). When too great an emphasis is placed on cognitive skills and intellectual concerns, educators are often reduced to a status (and a function) of teaching machines which renders these more expansive considerations meaningless.

In a similar way, when students are considered empty vessels waiting for educators to fill their brains with information, their inner emotional lives are diminished. Grief teaches that the cognitive and emotional parts of our identities are intertwined.

© KONINKLIJKE BRILL NV, LEIDEN, 2020 | DOI: 10.1163/9789004422506_008

Jennifer Nias (1989) in her research on teacher identity observes "in teaching, there cannot be a strict separation between the professional and the personal self" (pp. 202–203).

A teacher's personal and professional identities are vulnerable to a variety of external factors, including administrative policy decisions and mandates, interactions with peers, parents, and students, and the pressures inherent to the procure measureable learning outcomes. Based on his biographical studies of teacher lives, Geert Kelchtermans (1993) delineates these vulnerabilities into five categories: self-image, self-esteem, job motivation, task perception, and future perspective. Now, imagine a teacher who, on top of all this, is grieving a personal loss.

Because a teacher's grief is a critical part of who he or she is, it is not something that can be left at the classroom doorstep. Likewise, a student's mourning cannot be set aside on the school playground. It would be like asking teachers and students to rip out their hearts and leave them outside the school building during school hours to be re-collected after the dismissal bell sounds. Like our hearts, our identities are integral to all aspects of our personal and professional lives. David Feldman (2017) observes that grieving individuals are prone to question not what they do so much as who they are:

> We may start to question our faith in ourselves. Some people find themselves wondering, "Who am I without my loved one?"… Grief takes time because it entails accepting the loss of these roles and redefining ourselves. (p. 3)

If the bereavement process were limited to relearning routines and carrying on with outer activities of life, there would be little to consider here. But grieving is complex. Its emotional and spiritual layers extend deep into a person's values, beliefs, aspirations, and fears. Similarly, teaching would be a simpler task if its execution was limited to classroom management and the dissemination of information. As Kelchtermans (1996) concludes in his study of teacher vulnerability, "There is more to teaching than thorough subject knowledge and technical teaching skills…. Teachers' talk about their work immediately reveals that emotions are at the heart of teaching" (p. 307).

Teachers and students are not merely on a journey to give and receive information. Thomas Newkirk (2017) writes that they are "fellow travelers" on a path towards better understanding themselves, each other, and the world they inhabit. Hence, the lives of teachers and students intersect on many levels. In this way, teaching and learning touches upon so much more than intellectual concerns:

> No one likes to have protective layers pulled bare, revealing old scars or sensitive places still raw. To survive the day, we tell ourselves that our truths are THE truths, and they form our version of reality. When we're confronted with their illusory nature, we're no longer on solid ground. We grieve…. [Our] time and energy will be spent changing who we are and [grieving] for the loss of self that was once so sure. (p. 57)

These words reinforce the belief that there is more to teaching than information, method, effectiveness, and efficiency. Gary Fenstermacher (1990) identifies teaching as "a profoundly moral activity" (p. 132) in which the way one teaches is often a reflection of who he or she is (or what he or she is living through). Consider, for example, the expanse of a teacher's deliberation in terms of selecting assignments, activities, and projects. William D. Greenfield (1991) asserts that a teacher's moral inclinations oftentimes become his or her "point of view or reference point for action, influence, or decision that is deeply rooted in an understanding of and a commitment to what is in the best interests of children from an educational and developmental perspective" (p. 191).

A teacher's influence on students' emerging sense of who they are, what they value, and how they perceive the world and their place in it cannot be underestimated— nor should it be undervalued. A teacher's sense of (personal and professional) self (beliefs, values, feelings) is equally critical to the life of a classroom. Thus, it is important to consider ways in which contemporary classrooms accommodate authentic interaction among teachers and students on intellectual, affective, and ethical levels.

Jeffrey Berman (2004) observes "teaching may thus be viewed as a kind of mourning, a working through of grief and sorrow" (p. 131). Together, teachers and students can grieve the passing of ideas no longer viable; mourn the end of beliefs they once thought inviolate; and work through the cyclical transition from one stage of life to another. Imagine what wisdom might be gleaned by aligning the curriculum of school with the curriculum of our lives.

Instead of separating our lives at school from the totality of our experiences, consider classrooms that recognize, validate, and thrive upon the intersection of components that together reflect the expanse and depth of our humanity. After all, when one experiences significant grief, all aspects of life become vulnerable to what Alcorn (2002) calls a *mourning effect* (p. 96):

> It presents a situation in which accepting changes in the world requires a usually difficult change in the self and in those internal representations that make the self comfortable in the world (p. 116).... Mourning, in short, shows itself as part of a system of meaning, or a system of rhetoric, that not only informs the *emptiness* of things we imagine to be lost but also supports the *substantiveness* of the things we imagine to be present. (p. 117)

Oliver Twist (Dickens, 1867/2003) is relevant to this exploration because Oliver's life story is not so much interrupted by grief as it is defined by it. His journey of bereavement begins seconds after his birth. As the newborn lay in his mother's arms "she imprinted her cold white lips passionately upon his forehead... shuddered; fell back—and died" (p. 28). Alone in the world, Oliver Twist grieves the loss of his mother, his family, and his very identity. On emotional and metaphysical levels, his story transcends space, time, location, gender, and race.

Young Oliver's emotional and spiritual journey through bereavement is in many ways *our* journey. This chapter uses relevant excerpts from Dickens's novel to examine grief's influence on an individual's emerging and evolving identity. It further demonstrates the intimate role grief plays in how we come to understand ourselves and the world around us. Oliver Twist's story reminds us of the role people's emotional and moral vulnerabilities play as they endeavor to forge the identities, values, and beliefs that in many ways will come to define their life's story.

IDENTITY

After twenty years collecting individuals' stories of bereavement, researcher Thomas Attig (1996) observes that, to varying degrees, most mourners struggle against feeling an incompleteness within themselves. They are often left questioning their identities, purpose, and place in the world. He remarks that children are especially impacted:

> They lack developed coping capacities. Unprecedented feelings frighten some and leave them at a loss as to what to do or say.... Loss often disrupts or undermines the development of self-confidence, self-esteem, and identity.... Children lack models for, and need guidance and support in finding, appropriate things to do in the mourning period and in putting together new life patterns. (pp. 90–91)

This description aptly describes Oliver Twist upon his mother's death. Without family, he becomes "the victim of a systemic course of treachery and deception" (Dickens, 1867/2003, p. 30). He is moved to a government workhouse wherein Dickens reports "twenty or thirty other juvenile offenders against the poor laws, rolled about the floor all day, without the inconvenience of too much food or too much clothing, under the parental superintendence of an elderly female" (p. 30).

Oliver is later transferred to a local orphanage where he arrives pale, under-nourished, and frail. After making the mistake of asking the scullery matron for more food, Oliver is confined for over a week as a "prisoner in the dark and solitary room" (p. 41) in the orphanage cellar. The portrait Dickens creates of Oliver Twist at this moment embodies the "unprecedented feelings of fear" (p. 90) to which Attig (1996) refers. Symbolically speaking, Oliver is starving for more than food. He has never received spiritual, moral, or emotional nourishment. And he never truly has mourned his mother's death. Without guidance or support, Oliver's grief festers:

> There was a still greater obstacle in Oliver's youth and childishness. He only cried bitterly all day; and, when the long dismal night came on, spread his little hands before his eyes to shut out the darkness, and, crouching in the corner, tried to sleep; ever and anon waking with a start and tremble, and drawing himself closer and closer to the wall, as if to feel even its cold hard

surface were a protection in the gloom and loneliness which surrounded him. (Dickens, 1867/2003, p. 41)

This literal portrait of suffering is heartbreaking. Metaphorically, it represents an inner landscape of grief. Oliver epitomizes vulnerability. Consider how this image of a suffering child is in many ways a mirror to ourselves and the deepest recesses of our humanity. Avery D. Weisman (1993) points out that "anyone is vulnerable to almost anything, regardless of status or position in life" (p. 31):

> The precious core of empathy or the experience of selfhood gives rise to the proposition that we are all fellow sufferers, without exemption, and deserve each other's compassionate consideration. To do otherwise is to dehumanize. What we believe, along with the kind of activity we specialize in, must remain secondary to comprehending the universality of being vulnerable. (p. 31)

Weisman (1993) proposes that the "courage to cope" is more accurately described as the "*courage to become*" (p. 95). He adds that "existential courage, therefore, signifies what the vulnerable self must accomplish in overcoming difficulties" (p. 95). Oliver Twist, like all of us, is faced with the awesome task of becoming the best version of his authentic self that he was meant to be. For teachers, Parker Palmer (2007) points out that "the courage to teach is the courage to keep one's heart open in those very moments when the heart is asked to hold more than it is able so that teacher and students and subject can be woven into the fabric of community that learning, and living require" (p. 12):

> Good teachers possess a capacity for connectedness. They are able to weave a world for themselves, and their students so that students can learn to weave a world for themselves.... The connections made by teachers are not held in their methods but in their hearts—meaning heart in its ancient sense, as the place where intellect and emotion and spirit and will converge in the human self. (pp. 11–12)

Nine-year-old Oliver Twist never felt this kind of connectedness. Where are those who would be his teachers, guiding him toward becoming his true self, fortifying him against his vulnerabilities, and nurturing that inner space "where intellect and emotion and spirit and will converge" (Palmer, 2007, p. 12)? Oliver's story takes place during the early days of Western industrialization and the sudden and rapid emergence of cities. There were no laws or provisions securing education (especially for those most vulnerable like the poor, destitute, homeless, and orphaned).

There were, however, several adults who would enter Oliver's life with the means and opportunity to provide Oliver with the emotional and spiritual guidance and sustenance needed for him to "learn to weave a world" (Palmer, 2007, p. 12) for himself. A careful look at three of what I will call the teacher-figures in Oliver's young life underscores this vital work of educators.

CHAPTER 8

Bumble

The parish orphanage, "where one kind word or look had never lighted the gloom of [Oliver's] infant years" (Dickens, 1867/2003, p. 35), only housed children until they turned nine-years-old. Without any other options in terms of family or resources, Oliver is removed to the municipal workhouse "with twenty or thirty other juvenile offenders against the poor-laws" (p. 30). Despite the poor conditions of the orphanage, it was the only life Oliver had ever known. As he departs the orphanage, a "sense of his loneliness in the great wide world, sank into [his] heart for the first time" (p. 35). He grieves as he leaves his fellow orphans behind.

The municipal workhouse where Oliver now resides is operated by civil authority Mr. Bumble (the beadle). Bumble publicly proclaims his commitment to service and charity. In private, however, he is quick to call out each boy as "a naughty orphan which nobody can't love" (Dickens, 1867/2003, p. 46).

Because he regards the orphans in his charge as "audacious young savages" (Dickens, 1867/2003, p. 75), Bumble reasons that overfeeding them would be a waste of public tax revenue. As a result, "Oliver Twist and his companions suffered the tortures of slow starvation" (p. 38). Instead of helping nurture a positive sense of identity and self-esteem among the boys, Bumble teaches self-deprecation. Residing in the workhouse, Oliver remains physically, intellectually, and emotionally homeless.

Poverty, neglect, and social stigma (being poor and orphaned) left Oliver and his workhouse peers much to grieve (i.e., loss of home, family, self-esteem). As the workhouse supervisor, Bumble had the opportunity to help the orphans build a family-like community wherein they might begin to see beyond vulnerabilities. But Bumble lacks what Nel Noddings (2005) calls an ethic of care (p. 21). Noddings describes that an ethic of caring includes modeling and practicing relationships of trust (p. 22) and using dialogue to convey genuine empathy and understanding (p. 23).

Instead of nurturing a community of connectedness, compassion, and hope, Bumble offers lessons in despair and hopelessness. He frequently taunts Oliver and the other workhouse residents that they will never know who their parents are and degrades them by regularly announcing that they are all destined to be criminals and hence, certain "to be hung someday" (Dickens, 1867/2003, p. 41). He increases their emotional vulnerabilities by reinforcing negative self-perceptions that in turn further diminish their self-esteem. Imagine the difference he may have made in the lives of his charges if Bumble as a teacher-figure had modeled empathy rather than cruelty?

Bumble and his public office represent nineteenth-century institutional efforts to intervene in the lives of those economically and socially oppressed by the rapidly changing urban conditions spurred by the Industrial Revolution. Unfortunately, he also represents prevalent societal biases against the less fortunate, implying a kind of Darwinian perspective that some people were destined to be oppressed, others the oppressors.

With "a great idea of his oratorical powers and his importance" (Dickens, 1867/2003, p. 32) Bumble spoke with "a tone of impressive pomposity" (p. 45). He taught the children to submissively follow orders and passively accept their misfortunes as inevitable and, worse, deserved. And yet he was an integral part of the only social structure designed (ironically) to care for those suffering personal and societal hardships.

Although he adhered to the formal laws, Bumble failed to understand how the children's emotional and personal lives suffered beneath the systemic biases and inequities of the municipal citations and bureaucratic protocol:

> Oliver gave way to the feelings which the day's treatment may be supposedly likely to have awakened in a mere child. He had listened to their taunts with a look of contempt; he had borne the lash without a cry; for he felt that pride swelling in his heart which would have kept down a shriek to the last, though they had roasted him alive. (Dickens, 1867/2003, p. 78)

On another occasion, Bumble accused Oliver of being ungrateful and threatened to cast him out of the workhouse. Oliver "wept until the tears sprung out from between his chin and bony fingers" (Dickens, 1867/2003, p. 55). Bumble's reaction ("Well! Of *all* the ungratefullest and worst-tempered boys as ever I see," p. 55) prompted Oliver to equate his moral character with Bumble's words:

> "No, no, sir," sobbed Oliver... No, no, sir; I will be good indeed; indeed, indeed I will, sir. I am a very little boy, sir; and it is so—so... so lonely, sir! So very lonely!" cried the child. "Everybody hates me. Oh! sir, don't, don't pray be cross to me!" The child beat his hand upon his heart; and looked in [Bumble's] face, with tears of real agony.
>
> Mr. Bumble regarded Oliver's piteous and helpless look, with some astonishment... bade Oliver dry his eyes and be a good boy. (p. 55)

This dialogue gives insight into the extent to which Oliver and his fellows are internalizing Bumble's negative lessons. They are learning that they are inherently bad and unlovable. It is no wonder, then, that they begin to believe that they are destined "to be hung someday" (Dickens, 1867/2003, p. 41). This serves as a stark reminder that teaching is a highly moral activity (Fenstermacher, 1990). Andy Hargreaves (1995) writes that although "teachers may or may not have conscious moral intent in their work, almost all of that work has consequences that are moral. There is no escaping this" (p. 15).

Sowerberry

Bumble eventually stumbles upon an opportunity to profit at Oliver's expense. He "sells" Oliver to the highest bidder—Mr. Sowerberry, a coffin maker who agrees to apprentice the boy in his funerary business. Sowerberry is another teacher-figure who happens into Oliver's life. He has the potential to provide Oliver some spiritual, moral, and physical nourishment. What Dickens (1867/2003) describes on the night of the boy's arrival at Sowerberry's, however, foreshadows further loneliness and suffering:

> [Oliver] was alone in a strange place; and we all know how chilled and desolate the best of us will sometimes feel in such a situation…. his heart was heavy, notwithstanding; and he wished, as he crept into his narrow bed, that that were his coffin, and that he could be lain in a calm and lasting sleep in the church-yard ground, with the tall grass waving gently above his head. (Dickens, 1867/2003, p. 58)

This description of Oliver's inner suffering and grief is reminiscent of what Attig (1996) calls "the mystery of living an individual life in which struggles with finiteness, change, uncertainty, and vulnerability recur and persist" (p. 15). He writes "mysteries, and not simply problems, hold center stage in our lives when we grieve":

> Mysteries are ever-present elements of our surroundings, conditions of ongoing living that are too important for us to ignore and that yet persistently challenge and provoke us. We cannot overcome the mysteries or dissipate the challenges that they represent by solving or resolving them…. Mysteries make the limits of our ideas transparent. (p. 15)

Under Mr. Sowerberry's direction, Oliver sets out to "acquire that equanimity of demeanor and full command of nerve which are essential to a finished undertaker" (Dickens, 1867/2003, p. 68). Sowerberry, meanwhile, notices an "expression of melancholy in [Oliver's] face" (p. 61). Rather than trying to understand this sadness or perhaps helping Oliver work through his grief, Sowerberry sees this as an opportunity to increase his monetary profits. He would use Oliver's melancholy as a means to grow his cliental and increase revenue, Sowerberry decides that Oliver should perform all his funerary public duties as a melancholy mute. He figured that an expressionless and emotionless presence would be a comfort to mourners (a comfort they would be willing to pay extra money to have).

Intentional or not, Sowerberry is teaching Oliver that to be successful he must suppress his own voice, hold back his emotions, and minimize his very physical presence. As a silent figure at the funerals of children, Oliver becomes an asset to the business ("in commercial phrase, coffins were looking up…. The success of Sowerberry's ingenuous speculation, exceeded even his most sanguine hopes" [Dickens, 1867/2003, p. 68]). To the outside world Sowerberry is both a successful humanitarian (taking in an orphan no one else wanted) and a savvy businessman. After all, he has the bookkeeping numbers to prove it.

Much like Bumble, Sowerberry views Oliver as a problem that needs to be solved. To assuage the orphan's poverty, he employs Oliver to mutely attend funerals; to "fix" Oliver's homelessness, Sowerberry arranges for him to sleep in the workshop basement ("You don't mind sleeping among the coffins, I suppose?"

[Dickens, 1867/2003, p. 57]); and to rectify Oliver's assumed proclivities toward crime (typical in "these dreadful creatures that are born to be murderers from their very cradle" [p. 73]), he allows Oliver no free time or contact with peers.

Sowerberry believes he is also contributing to Oliver's moral upbringing by teaching him to avoid the sins of gluttony and greed. He is careful not to overfeed Oliver for fear of "raising an artificial soul and spirit in him, unbecoming a person of his condition.... What have paupers to do with soul or spirit? It's quite enough that we let 'em have bodies" (Dickens, 1867/2003, p. 76).

Inwardly, Oliver's humanity continues to be neglected. The boy's outer usefulness is measured by the amount of profit Sowerberry accrues. The more proficient Oliver becomes in remaining silent, following orders, and suppressing his emotions, the more Sowerberry gains. Oliver learns is that he is most valuable to society when he keeps silent and pretends to be practically invisible. Sleeping alone at night among the coffins, Oliver begins to "make a coffin of his heart" (Dickens, 1867/2003, p. 129):

Now, when there were none to see or hear him, he [Oliver] fell to his knees on the floor, and, hiding his face in his hands, wept such tears as, God send for the credit of our nature, few so young may ever have cause to pour out before him! (p. 78)

Oliver learns that he cannot rely upon institutions, laws, or those assigned to implement them to offer care or compassion. He is searching for compassion, hope, and a positive sense of self. The search for these aspects of one's humanity is not limited by age, gender, time, place, or circumstance. On some level all of us— teachers and students—are searching for inner nourishment as well. In this way, grief makes orphans of us all.

Twenty-first-century public education as an institution, despite extensive legal decrees, bureaucratic structures, and teacher licensure protocol cannot ensure emotional, spiritual, and moral growth and development. Noddings (2005) writes "caring is the very bedrock of all successful education and that contemporary schooling can be revitalized in its light" (p. 27). This ethic of care (p. 21) does not require public status (which Bumble personified) or financial savvy (that Sowerberry had). It requires compassion, kindness, and empathy. Fortunately, the next teacher-figure to enter Oliver's life has these inner traits. Although their interaction is brief, its import resonates throughout Oliver's life.

Dick

Oliver Twist eventually escapes Sowerberry's establishment. As he heads toward London, he meets someone who demonstrates the courage to care. In a dark alleyway in the middle of the night he literally runs into Dick, a boy whom he had known from his days at the parish orphanage. Dick seems an unlikely teacher-figure: orphaned, illiterate, penniless, alone, and sickly. Nevertheless, he understands grief. Because he knows firsthand what it means to suffer hunger, shame, guilt, and loneliness, he is filled with the wisdom of compassion, empathy, and a genuine concern for Oliver's well-being.

Dick intuitively sees Oliver's inner humanity. He is the first individual to understand and acknowledge Oliver's suffering. He ascertains the dignity of the person beneath the outer trappings of poverty and neglect. Dick's words are not measured by profit or drawn from bureaucratic mandates. They are genuine. The emotional connection between Oliver and Dick is Oliver's first lesson in compassion and self-esteem:

"I heard the doctor tell them that I was dying," relied [Dick] with a faint smile. "I am very glad to see you, dear... I know the doctor must be right, Oliver, because I dream so much of Heaven, and Angels, and kind faces that I never see when I am awake. Kiss me," said the child, climbing up the low gate, and flinging his little arms round Oliver's neck. "Good-b'ye, dear! God bless you!" The blessing was from a young child's lips, but it was the first that Oliver had ever heard invoked upon his head; and through the struggles, and troubles and changes, of his after life, he never once forgot it. (Dickens, 1867/2003, p. 79)

Up to now, Oliver's grief and misfortunes informed his identity and framed how he experienced the world. In short, grief is all Oliver has known. Dick teaches him that although there is much to mourn, the mourning alone does not need to define him. After more than nine years of being treated as if he were a burden to others and destined for the gallows (lessons Bumble and Sowerberry, intentionally or not, taught well), Dick teaches that Oliver he is worthy of receiving his honest blessing.

Compared to the thousands of words Bumble and Sowerberry regularly spewed upon Oliver (for they liked to hear themselves talk and they thought it their duty to remind Oliver that he was worthless and destined "to be hung someday" [Dickens, 1867/2003, p. 41]), Dick utters less than seventy-five words. But his words were more than a blessing—they were a lifeline. It took a child of grief to save the life of another who was drowning in desperation: "with such kind and gentle words, and such tears of sympathy and compassion, [these words] sank deeper into Oliver's soul, than all the sufferings he had ever undergone" (p. 82).

Consider the hours of discourse students and teachers engage in each week. How much of it demonstrates empathy or compassion? How often do the words validate each other's inner worth? What kinds of messages are our words sending to each other—intentionally or unintentionally?

As teacher-figures, Bumble and Sowerberry saw Oliver as a problem to solve and a means to improve their own personal success and public reputation. How often do teachers perceive students as products to be turned out, or as assessment scores that need to be achieved? On the other hand, empathy and compassion enable Dick to better understand the fullness of Oliver's humanity. Arthur T. Jersild (1955) observes that "it is not extreme to say that one of the basic troubles in education is that as educators we have not had the courage to face the personal implications of our calling" (p. 82):

To help a pupil to have meaningful experiences, a teacher must know the pupil as a person. This means that the teacher must strive to know himself.... Everything in the relation between a teacher and a student has or might have a significant effect on what a child thinks and feels about himself. To have insight into the child's strivings and the problems he faces, the teacher must strive to face the same problems within his own life. These problems are largely emotional in nature. (p. 82)

VULNERABILITY

[Oliver felt] overpowered by the conviction of the bystanders [in his life] that he really was the hardened little wretch he was described to be; what could one poor child do? (Dickens, 1867/2003, p. 143)

With the encouragement (and blessings) he received from Dick, Oliver heads to London to ascertain his identity and place in the world. The awesome process of working to regain authorship of one's life, however, tends to increase an individual's feelings of helplessness (Zembylas, 2003). Lost, cold, and hungry on the streets of the city, Oliver feels especially vulnerable:

Darkness had set in; it was a low neighborhood; no help was near; resistance was useless. In another moment he was dragged into a labyrinth of dark narrow courts, and was forced along them at a pace which rendered the few cries he dared to give utterance to, unintelligible. It was of little moment, indeed, whether they were intelligible or no; for there was nobody to care for them, had they been ever so plain. (Dickens, 1867/2003, p. 143)

In many ways, Dickens gives readers a visual portrait of the emotional landscape of grieving. In a moment, tragedy can transform a well-ordered life into a "labyrinth of dark narrow courts" (Dickens, 1867/2003, p. 143). Once grief's "darkness sets in" an individual's identity and beliefs can seem "unintelligible" (p. 143). His description also lays bare the expansiveness of vulnerability (i.e., "no help was near; resistance was useless... there was nobody to care for them" [p. 143]).

Peter Kaufman and Janine Schipper (2018) write that "when teachers model vulnerability and creative openness" (instead of covering up their vulnerabilities or hiding behind masks of authority or intelligence), "students can begin to see themselves more fully" (p. 52). Expounding on this idea, David Whyte (2014) writes:

To run from vulnerability is to run from the essence of our nature, the attempt to be invulnerable is the vain attempt to become something we are not and most especially, to close off our understanding of the grief of others. (p. 233)

Physically exhausted and emotionally vulnerable, Oliver Twist arrives in London and finds shelter and food from a new teacher-figure: Fagin. He provides Oliver a decent amount of food ("You want grub and you shall have it" [Dickens, 1867/2003, p. 84]); and a "comfortable place" to sleep (p. 84). Sensing Oliver's vulnerabilities, however, Fagin eventually leverages the food and shelter for Oliver's compliance and participation in criminal activities. He senses a moral vacuum or ambiguousness in Oliver and uses his authority as a teacher-figure to fill that space. Hence, an analysis of Fagin offers insights into the moral aspects of teaching and learning.

Fagin

Fagin trains Oliver (and the other boys in his care) in the (morally dubious) work of the pickpocket. To finance their living arrangements and meals, the boys spend their days in the streets of London picking people's pockets and returning the stolen items to Fagin. Years of physical and emotional suffering have made Oliver vulnerable to Fagin's indoctrination into thievery. After all, for the first time in his life Oliver has food, a group friends for companionship, and a teacher-figure who offers him kind words ("draw a tub near the fire for Oliver" [Dickens, 1867/2003, p. 87]) and compliments ("You're a clever boy, my dear.... I never saw a sharper lad. Here's a shilling for you. If you go on, in this way, you'll be the greatest man of the time" [p. 95]).

After ten years of isolation and sadness, Fagin provides Oliver a community of peers with whom he can experience laughter and playfulness. One of Oliver's favorite games involved he and the other boys attempting to pick Fagin's pockets without Fagin knowing ("Oliver laughed till the tears ran down his face" [Dickens, 1867/2003, p. 93]). Without realizing it, Oliver was being indoctrinated into criminal habits:

> In short, the wily old Jew had the boy in his toils. Having prepared his mind, by solitude and gloom, to prefer any society to the companionship of his own sad thoughts in such a dreary place, he was now slowly instilling into his soul the poison which he hoped would blacken it, and change its hue forever. (p. 170)

Bumble and Sowerberry unfairly projected criminality onto Oliver ("I never was more convinced of anything in my life, than I am that that boy will come to be hung" [Dickens, 1867/2003, p. 41]). Oliver now is unwittingly learning the very criminal habits that they unfairly attributed to him. Meanwhile, although Bumble and Sowerberry profess high moral values (i.e., charity, kindness, service) and are respected for their public commission, their cruel mistreatment of Twist contradicted those values.

Fagin professes no such moral high ground. He treats Oliver neither as a burden to society nor as a problem to solve. Perhaps Fagin sees Oliver's humanity because he discerns his own younger self in him. Like Oliver, Fagin grieves the life he could have had if he were born into more privileged social, ethnic, and economic circumstances. He suffers the biases of a larger society that mistrusts Jewish people, resents the poor, and blames society's ills on the uneducated lower classes. In this way, Fagin empathizes with Oliver's sense of helplessness and isolation. The taunts hurled against Oliver (that he and those like him were "born to be murderers and robbers from their very cradle" [Dickens, 1867/2003, p. 73]) were likely used against a young Fagin as well.

Informed by his own grief and suffering, Fagin empathizes and connects with Oliver on an emotional level. Hence, Oliver begins to learn that he is deserving of affection. Ironically, although Fagin's public curriculum involved how to pick people's pockets and steal their valuables, he also teaches the boy what friendship looks and feels like. This evokes what Noddings (2005) describes as "a caring relation, in its most basic form, a connection or encounter between two human beings—a carer and a recipient of care, or cared-for" (p. 15). Who could have imagined that a veteran criminal pickpocket would be the teacher-figure who taught Oliver lessons in friendship and empathy?

Despite this, the curriculum of thieving and criminality that Fagin as teacher-figure offers cannot be overlooked. Horace Mann, a contemporary of Dickens, strongly advocated for the expansion of public education as part of a larger moral enterprise. He believed that the availability of education for all citizens, regardless of economic or cultural background, would help alleviate what he saw as a growing chasm between social classes. His work was explicitly rooted in a moral framework.

In his *Tenth Annual Report* (1846/1957) to the Massachusetts Board of Education, Mann warns that an education without ethical standing "dares the certain vengeance of heaven" (p. 76). Without moral training, he predicted that "the terrible retributions of its delinquency" would be widespread:

… in the squalid forms of poverty and destitution, in the scourges of violence and misrule, in the heart-destroying corruptions of licentiousness and debauchery, and in legalized profligacy—in all the blended and mutually aggravated crimes of civilization and of barbarism. (p. 76)

According to these moral criteria, Fagin is ethically flawed. Despite the physical sustenance and emotional support he provides Oliver Twist and the other boys, Fagin's illegal intentions cannot be denied. Of Oliver's criminal training, he remarks to his band of thieves:

I've—I've had my eye upon [Oliver], my dears, close-close. Once let him feel that he is one of us; once fill his mind with the idea that he has been a thief; and he's ours! Ours for his life. Oho! It couldn't have come about better! (Dickens, 1867/2003, p. 177)

Initially, Oliver accepts life with Fagin without questioning Fagin's motives. He remains blind to the unethical world he is being drawn into and reasons that as "he was too well accustomed to suffering, and had suffered too much where he was, to bewail the prospect of change very seriously" (Dickens, 1867/2003, p. 181). Oliver desires a life without the depravity and humiliation he experienced with Bumble and Sowerberry. Alcorn (2002) warns that "teaching is responsive not simply to knowledge, but also to desire" (p. 6). He also asserts that an individual's vulnerability can allow him or her to be more easily "victimized by curriculum, voices, demands, expectations" (p. 6).

On the eve of what is to be Oliver's first major criminal outing, Fagin cryptically advises Oliver to "take heed" (Dickens, 1867/2003, p. 181) and leaves a book for him to read:

> It was a history of the lives and trials of great criminals; and the pages were soiled and thumbed with use. Here, he read of dreadful crimes that made the blood run cold; of secret murders that had been committed by the lonely wayside; of bodies hidden from the eye of man in deep pits and wells.... The terrible descriptions were so real and vivid, that the sallow pages seemed to turn red with gore; and the words upon them, to be sounded in his ears, as if they were whispered, in hollow murmurs, by the spirits of the dead. (pp. 181–182)

The words leave Oliver in a "paroxysm of fear" (Dickens, 1867/2003, p. 182). He demonstrates the fortitude of his moral compass by reaching out in prayer:

> Falling upon his knees, he prayed Heaven to spare him from such deeds; and rather to will that he should die at once, than be reserved for crimes, so fearful and appalling. By degrees, he grew more calm. (p. 182)

During this quiet moment of prayer and reflection, Oliver reveals something he has never before displayed: hope. He contemplates the possibility that he "might be rescued from his present dangers" (Dickens, 1867/2003, p. 182). His words at this moment show his emerging sense of identity and self-worth:

> [He] asked for any aid [that] was to be raised up for a poor outcast boy who had never known the love of friends or kindred, it might come to mind now, when, desolate and deserted, he stood alone in the midst of wickedness and guilt. (p. 182)

Where did Oliver Twist learn about hope? Certainly not from Bumble or Sowerberry. To what extent has Fagin, despite his criminal ways, schooled Oliver into believing that he deserved to be understood and cared for? Fagin knew how it felt to be treated as a social outcast (suffering bias against his being poor, uneducated, and Jewish). He learned to create a life for himself (albeit a criminal one) that frees him from being passively victimized. It gave him a sense of control in life. Without access to education and being vulnerable in a society that villainizes him, Fagin learned to rely on his wits and resourcefulness to create a life wherein he can survive without relying on the pity, charity, and condescension of those who denigrate him.

In the past, Oliver accepted suffering without a sense that he could be anything other than a helpless and unloved victim. Even his running away from Sowerberry's residence was less about taking control of his life than about escaping from it. It left him vulnerable to the next bully (often in the form of a teacher-figure such as Bumble or Sowerberry) who crossed his path. Fagin was teaching-by-example how to take action against feelings of helplessness rather than passively accepting suffering and feeling trapped by it.

Before Fagin entered his life, Oliver, like many individuals who struggle to learn about the world through a lens of grief, lacked a clear sense of purpose and meaning in life. He embodied the kinds of emotional struggles that Cochran and Claspell (1987) describe as a "passivity of wretchedness" wherein "meaningful contact with the world is broken and the person is directed inward" (p. 119). But Oliver and the other boys felt cared for by Fagin. He provided the closest thing they ever had to a home and family. Oliver no longer felt isolated or disconnected because Fagin and his "family of thieves" looked out for each other.

But sadly, Fagin's lessons lacked moral substance. After Oliver fully understood the criminality of the work he was expected to engage in, he felt isolated once again. He is left to wrangle with his conscience:

> The night was very dark. A damp mist rose from the river, and the marshy ground about; and spread itself over the dreary fields. It was piercing cold, too; all gloomy and black.... [Oliver was] bewildered with alarm and apprehension; and figuring strange objects in the gaunt trees, whose branches waved grimly to and fro, as if in some fantastic joy at the desolation of the scene. (Dickens, 1867/2003, p. 192)

These ominous images describe the landscape of Oliver's soul and spirit (coincidentally the two traits Bumble and Sowerberry denied Oliver of possessing— "What have paupers to do with soul or spirit?" [Dickens, 1867/2003, p. 76]). Reflecting on this excerpt metaphorically, Oliver's intrinsic moral compass is becoming clouded within a "cold and damp mist all gloomy and black" (p. 192). Instead of standing firmly on moral grounds, Oliver now finds himself "on a marshy, damp landscape" (p. 192). The clear view of prayerful humility he expressed in his prayer on just the previous evening is now becoming obstructed by "the gaunt trees whose branches waved" before him (p. 192).

For all the lessons Fagin as Oliver's teacher-figure provides, he never prepares Oliver for these moral crises of soul and spirit. Listening to the wind as it blew across the landscape, Oliver reflects "it seemed like quiet music for the repose of the dead" (Dickens, 1867/2003, p. 192). Oliver at this point is spiritually vulnerable. He is struggling against what Horace Mann (1846/1957) called the "heart-destroying corruptions of licentiousness and debauchery" (p. 76).

Whereas he previously suffered from a lack of physical sustenance, Oliver now searches for moral sustenance. Mann (1848/1957) writes that all education must aim for the highest moral ground, as "a community without a conscience would soon extinguish itself" (p. 98). He asserts in an earlier work that an "*aptness to teach*"

(Mann, 1840/1957, p. 46) requires that educators not only teach subject matter content, but direct their students toward understanding and applying that knowledge in ways that are to the overall benefit and advancement of the entire community.

As Oliver Twist is forcibly lead to the site of the impending robbery, he continues to struggle with his conscience. Dickens presents a dramatic portrait of an individual suffering in an outer world that contradicts inner values and beliefs:

> [They] kept walking on, in mud and darkness, through gloomy lanes and over cold open wastes, until they came within sight of the lights of a town at no great distance. On looking intently forward, Oliver saw that the water was just below them, and that they were coming to the foot of a bridge...
>
> "The water!" thought Oliver, turning sick with fear. "He has brought me to this lonely place to murder me!"
>
> He was about to throw himself on the ground, and make one struggle for his young life. (Dickens, 1867/2003, pp. 192–193)

Is Oliver Twist really the villain that Bumble taught him he was? Does a person sometimes need to do bad things in order to survive? Is one ever justified doing immoral things for the right reasons? When *our* values and beliefs are put to the test, how will *we* respond? These questions speak to the vulnerabilities that lie in what Lama Surya Das (2007) describes as the "tides of existential emptiness":

> Indeed we are constantly engaged in the self-construction business, on both outer and inner levels, through both thought and actions, in our ongoing efforts to convince not only others but ourselves that we really exist. (p. 57)

Lama Surya Das (2007) reflects that teachers and teacher-figures have been instrumental in assisting him "along the spiritual path as well as through life in general" (p. 167). He writes "a masterful teacher can help us progress and develop more than most of us can ever begin to imagine" (p. 168). By contrast, as a teacher and mentor, Fagin foregoes any considerations regarding a spiritual or ethical path. Without what Lama Suyra Das calls self-constructive aspects of teaching and learning, Oliver now faces a kind of self-destructive crisis:

> The night was bitter cold. The snow lay on the ground, frozen into a hard thick crust, so that only the heaps that had drifted into by-ways and corners were affected by the sharp wind that howled abroad: which, as if expending increased fury on such prey as it found, caught it savagely up in clouds, and, whirling it into a thousand misty eddies, scattered it in air. Bleak, dark, and piercing cold, it was a night for the well-housed and fed to draw round the bright fire... and for the homeless, starving wretch to lay him down and die. (Dickens, 1867/2003, p. 201)

The emotional desperation of Oliver's grief is palpable. William Styron (1990) writes that loss and grief, especially when experienced at an early age, are "likely to create nearly irreparable emotional havoc" (p. 79). Styron asserts that "incomplete mourning" increases this vulnerability:

> The danger is especially apparent if the young person has, in effect, been unable to achieve the catharsis of grief, and so carries within himself through later years an insufferable burden of which rage and guilt, and not only dammed-up sorrow, are a part, and become the potential seeds of self-destruction. (Styron, 1990, p. 80)

When grief is repressed or denied, there is little space for solace or healing. William Watkin (2004) asserts catharsis is achieved when this "language of silence" (p. 120) is broken; and suggests "we would do well to listen to the stories and discourse of [those grieving]" (p. 121). Nevertheless, Kieran Egan (1986) laments that "there is little room for our emotional lives" (p. 29) in models of teaching and learning that are largely rational and cognitive. He urges educators to more fully realize the "importance of human emotions and intentions in making things meaningful":

> To present knowledge and intentions cut off from human emotions and intentions is to reduce its affective meaning. This affective meaning, also, seems especially important in providing access to knowledge and engaging us in knowledge. (Egan, 1986, p. 30)

This is a reminder that our public act of teaching has the potential to resonate with the inner lives of students. Deal and Redman (2009) reflect on a teacher's ability to "influence young people by drawing out and nurturing what they have inside" (p. 61):

> Authenticity cuts deeply into the psyche below the intellect. It centers on two often overlooked features of being human—heart and soul.... [This] is an inner journey. It requires us to entertain some penetrating existential questions: "Who am I" "Where did I come from?" "Where am I headed?" "What are my cardinal values and beliefs?" (p. 60)

Despite the intrinsic nature of these questions, this kind of introspection nevertheless affects a person's public life. William Watkin (2004) writes that despite the personal suffering involved in grieving "the reasons for grief are always public" (p. 198): "The subject cannot depress itself; it needs an interaction with the outside world for this to happen. When the subject loses, it loses a sense of itself as much as a beloved person" (p. 198).

RESILIENCY AND GRACE

Oliver Twist is arguably most vulnerable when he faces the prospect that he is doomed to be the "bad one" (Dickens, 1867/2003, p. 355) that so many predicted he was destined to be. Immersed in Fagin's world, he learns to survive despite being "sick with fear" (p. 193)—the fear of becoming, like Fagin, a criminal. In this sense, Oliver is "struggling for his life" (p. 193) physically *and* morally.

At this point of Oliver's story, something unexpected emerges—resiliency. Kay Chang (2017) observes "the key concept of trauma recovery lies in the recognition of a parallel process between vulnerability and resiliency" (p. 4). Of emotional resilience, Andrew Solomon (2012) writes that grieving individuals need to learn how "to rewrite their future without bitterness" (p. 23). He asserts that out of suffering, resiliency can arise.

Although the vulnerability a person feels when experiencing grief seems to leave only sadness and hopelessness in its wake, Solomon (2012) offers that hope and resiliency can emerge. In a visual sense, the ancient myth of the birth of Aphrodite embodies this idea of new life arising from (and often because of) lessons learned during desperate times. The emergence of Aphrodite, the Ancient Greek goddess of love and beauty was born out of bloody violence (D'aulaire, 1962, p. 30). After the Gorgon Medusa is decapitated by the hero Perseus, her severed head explodes in the water below. Out of the chaos, destruction, and disorder, beauty and love (in the form of Aphrodite) emerges.

Kieran Egan (1986) observes that ancient myths such as this were originally intended to contain "the lore of complex tribes" that "encoded all that was most true and significant" (p. 108). Of myths, Joseph Campbell (1991) asserts that they are "educators toward life" (p. 20):

> They are the world's dreams. They are archetypal dreams and deal with great human problems.... The myth(s) tell me about how to respond to certain crises of disappointment or delight or failure or success. The myths tell me where I am. (pp. 19–20)

During times of grief and sadness, individuals may lose sight of who and where they are. The Aphrodite myth teaches us to have faith; although we may feel surrounded by chaos and despair, hope remains. It shows the value of persevering through difficult times. Even at our darkest moments when we feel most surrounded by chaos and despair, we might also be at the precipice of something new, something better. In her research exploring the psychological aspects of grief and trauma, Kay Chang (2017) refers to this dual reality as the "parallel process between vulnerability and resiliency" (p. 4). Learning to recognize that there is sometimes but a thin line between despair and hope is critical in order that grieving individuals can begin "to rewrite their future without bitterness" (Solomon, 2012, p. 23):

> Resilience used to be posited as an extraordinary trait, seen in the Helen Kellers of the world, but cheery recent research suggests that most of us have the potential for it, and that cultivating it is a crucial part of development for everyone. (p. 23)

Who teaches resiliency? For Helen Keller, it was modeled and nurtured by her teacher Anne Sullivan. For Oliver Twist, it is teacher-figure Mr. Brownlow who imparts lessons on building that emotionally delicate bridge between vulnerability and resiliency. Brownlow has no teacher's manual or curriculum guide from which to garner lesson plans on resiliency. He does not defer to intelligence, information, or public decrees. Instead, he relies on compassion and empathy. The deaths of his parents ("The persons on whom I have bestowed my dearest love, lie deep in their graves" [Dickens, 1867/2003, p, 129]) and his fiancée ("the happiness and delight of my life lie buried there too" [p. 129]) remain close to his heart ("Deep affliction has but strengthened and refined [my best affections]" [p. 130]).

Mr. Brownlow

Mr. Brownlow and Oliver Twist unexpectedly meet during one of Fagin's criminal escapades. A public melee ensues wherein Oliver is arrested. He is later arraigned at the courthouse and treated as the abject hoodlum that he had so often been told he was destined to become. One of the citizen-witnesses, Mr. Brownlow, notices "there is something in that boy's face" that is "neither criminal nor unlovable" (Dickens, 1867/2003, p. 102). Whereas others had only seen the boy as "a bad one! I'll eat my head if he is not a bad one," Brownlow sees "a child of a noble nature and a warm heart" (p. 355).

Brownlow's compassion allows him to see beyond outer trappings of poverty and depravity. He intuitively ascertains the vulnerable boy trapped beneath hardships that have been imposed upon him: "that Power which has thought fit to try [Oliver] beyond his years, has planted in his breast affections and feelings which would do honor to many who have numbered his days six times over" (Dickens, 1867/2003, p. 355).

Brownlow decides to care for and protect the boy. He comes to believe that despite his involvement in some criminal activities, Oliver nevertheless embodies "the Angel even upon earth" (Dickens, 1867/2003, p. 208). Brownlow tends to him "with a kindness and solicitude that knew no bounds" (p. 108). Like Oliver, Brownlow was raised in a series of foster institutions following the deaths of his parents. Hence, he empathizes with Oliver's circumstances and understands the importance of Oliver having a safe place to heal and grieve. Through his unconditional care and concern, Brownlow imparts lessons that nurture Oliver's spirit:

> The two orphans, tried by adversity, remembered its lessons in mercy to others, and mutual love, and fervent thanks to Him who had protected and preserved them.... I have said that they were truly happy; and without strong affection and humanity of heart, and Gratitude to that Being whose code is Mercy, and whose great attribute is Benevolence to all things that breathe, happiness can never be attained. (Dickens, 1867/2003, p. 466)

Until now, Oliver Twist had never been allowed emotional space to grieve for his mother or to mourn the life denied him upon her death. Consequently, Oliver became a prisoner to his grief: he neither fully grieved his past nor took ownership of his future. Brownlow gives Oliver the time and space to grieve:

The memories which peaceful country scenes call up, are not of this world, nor of its thoughts and hopes. Their gentle influence may teach us how to weave fresh garlands for the graves of those we loved: may purify our thoughts, and bear down before it old enmity and hatred; but beneath all this, there lingers, in the least reflective mind, a vague and half-formed consciousness of having held such feelings long before, in some remote and distant time, which calls up solemn thoughts of distant times to come, and bends down pride and worldliness beneath it.... Oliver often wandered here; and, thinking of the wretched grave in which his mother lay, would sometimes sit him down and sob unseen; but, when he raised his eyes to the deep sky overhead, he would cease to think of her as lying in the ground, and would weep for her sadly, but without pain... the days were peaceful and serene. (Dickens, 1867/2003, p. 278)

From his own life experiences, Brownlow understood that grief was more than a problem to be solved or a despair to deny or repress. In addition to grieving his parents' deaths (through which he "suffered great pain and sorrow" [Dickens, 1867/2003, p. 130]), we learn that Brownlow had been engaged to a "fair creature... who rejoined her God in youth, and left him a solitary, lonely man" (p. 421). With the death of his parents when he was a young boy coupled with the untimely death of his fiancée, Dickens describes Brownlow's past as "a true tale of grief and trial and sorrow" (p. 423).

Rather than deny his sadness, Brownlow learns to embrace and respect it. He came to understand that remembrance could be both melancholy *and* healing. "Benevolence, mercy, and a humanity of heart" (Dickens, 1867/2003, p. 466) are born from his loss. The solace he sought became the empathy he now extends to others—including Oliver Twist. Oliver is learning that tears of remembrance do not necessarily need to be tears of despair:

Oliver crept away to the old churchyard, and sitting down on one of the green mounds, wept and prayed for [his mother] in silence. There was such peace and beauty in the scene; so much of brightness and mirth in the sunny landscape; such blithesome music in the songs of the summer birds; such freedom in the rapid flight of the rook, careering overhead; so much of life and joyousness in all. (Dickens, 1867/2003, p. 287)

Brownlow's grief taught him that moving forward does not mean denying or forgetting the past. He learns that grief is not something to be left behind in order to persevere toward external aspirations. He now imparts these lessons to Oliver. By embracing memories instead of repressing them, Oliver, too, begins to find solace and peace:

The melancholy which had seemed to the sad eyes of the anxious boy to hang, for days past, over every object, beautiful as all were, was dispelled by magic. The dew seemed to sparkle more brightly on the green leaves; the air to rustle among them with a sweeter music; and the sky itself to look more blue and bright. (Dickens, 1867/2003, p. 295)

Brownlow had faith that time and remembrance could resurrect the "long-forgotten" (Dickens, 1867/2003, p. 208) peacefulness which he believed still resided beneath Oliver's "cares, and sorrows, and hungerings" (p. 208). As a teacher-figure, Brownlow is modeling and guiding Oliver toward emotional resilience. The word *resilience* derives from the Latin *resilire*, meaning to jump back; and its Latin base *salire*, meaning to leap (OED, n.d.). The seemingly opposing images of jumping back and leaping forward are embodied in Brownlow teaching Oliver to nurture forward-looking hope guided by heartfelt remembrance.

Resilience should not be confused with perseverance. Paul Tough (2012) identifies perseverance as that which fortifies individuals toward moving onward and achieving their life goals despite difficulties (p. 75). This forward-looking image implies that the past and its griefs need to be left behind so as not to weigh individuals down or steer them from their goals and ambitions. By contrast, Brownlow's philosophy teaches that to create a meaningful future, one needs to accept and honor the lessons and heartaches of the past.

As a teacher-figure, Brownlow goes beyond "filling the mind of his adopted child with stores of knowledge" (Dickens, 1867/2003, p. 466). He encourages Oliver to recount and reflect upon the experiences of his life. Perhaps more importantly, Brownlow validates Oliver by taking the time to listen to him:

> It was a solemn thing to hear, in the darkened room, the feeble voice of the sick child recounting a weary catalogue of evils and calamities which hard men had brought upon him. Oh! If when we oppress and grind our fellow-creatures, we bestowed but one thought on the dark evidences of human error... if we heard but one instant, in imagination, the deep testimony of the dead men's voices, which no power can stifle, and no pride shut out; where would be injury and injustice, the suffering, misery, cruelty and wrong, that each day's life brings with it! (p. 258)

As members of a larger society, we all have a share in the "weary catalogue of evils and calamities" (Dickens, 1867/2003, p. 258) Dickens describes. Brownlow understood the further misery and cruelty Oliver endured because of the biases others projected onto him. Dickens deliberately alludes to broad and systemic injustices that "oppress and grind our fellow-creatures" (p. 258) in the name of bigotry, misunderstanding, fear-mongering, and a sad litany of other injuries and wrongs.

The more the "Bumbles of our world" ignore the suffering of those they are intended to care for, the greater misery grows. The more the "Sowerberrys of our lives" are driven by greed, the more expansive oppression and social inequalities become. The more the "Fagins of our society" rationalize crime, the greater the disempowered and disenfranchised suffer discrimination and injustice. In this way, lack of empathy and compassion are further "dark evidences of human error" (Dickens, 1867/2003, p. 258).

The crimes Dickens describes are not only of a legal nature but a moral one. Imagine if Oliver's sufferings were allowed to harden his heart. He may have eventually adopted a survivalist mentality. This is reflected in Brownlow's fears that "the cares, and sorrows, and hungerings of the world change [individuals] as they change hearts" (Dickens, 1867/2003, p. 208). A Darwinian "survival of the fittest" mentality motivated Sowerberry to persevere toward greater wealth, garnered Bumble a greater public status, and encouraged Fagin to outrun the law. Grieving has taught Brownlow, however, that "happiness can never be attained" (p. 466) without compassion, kindness, and mercy.

Brownlow's lessons in compassion and resilience help heal Oliver Twist's heart and prevent it from further hardening:

> Oliver rose next morning in better heart, and went about his usual early occupations with more hope and pleasure than he had known for many days. The birds were once more hung out, to sing, in their old places; and the sweetest wild flowers that could be found, were once more gathered. (Dickens, 1867/2003, p. 299)

Oliver's emotional and spiritual growth demonstrates that "the time of greatest gain in terms of wisdom and inner strength is often that of greatest difficulty... The experience of suffering can open our eyes to reality" (Lama Surya Das, 1999, p. 139):

> To the extent that our experience of suffering reminds us of what all others endure, it serves as a powerful injunction to practice compassion and refrain from causing others pain. And to the extent that suffering awakens our empathy and causes us to connect with others, it can serve as the basis of compassion and love.... Unfortunate events, though potentially a source of anger and despair, have equal potential to be a source of spiritual growth. Whether or not this is the outcome depends on our response. (p. 143)

Similarly, Joseph Cardinal Bernardin (1997) reflects that it is only when we "experience redemption, that we find life, peace, and joy in the midst of physical, emotional and spiritual suffering" (pp. 48–49). The redemption he speaks of relies on faith not profit, inner beliefs not material gain, and intangible but life-affirming hope. Where are belief, faith, and hope in our professional lives as educators? Without them, in what ways are teaching outcomes measurable but shallow? To what extent can education be profitable to a person's public life (i.e., job skills, expansive resume items) but inconsequential to his or her private life?

As teachers and students learn, reflect, and grow, imagine the possibilities for transformation that abound. Following this thinking, we can begin to consider Clifford Mayes's (2005) assertion that "curriculum and instruction are means of transcendence" (p. 88). He reflects "to be spiritual, the curriculum does not have to deal with explicitly 'spiritual' topics" (p. 89):

> [Teaching] must be spiritually grounded in the teacher's heart—or else it will become the mere transition of data and theories for the sake of some imposed

political or economic goal. Such goals sometimes constitute a legitimate, if qualified, aim of education; however, they should never be its primary aim. That [would be] education without moral connection to others. (p. 89)

Mayes (2005) implies that within the teaching and learning experience lies potential for authentic moments of transformation and redemption. It is these moments of grace that elevate the work of a teacher from the mundane to the sacred. Paul Tough (2012) describes what he calls the "hidden power of character" in less spiritual terms. He prioritizes the importance of grit, i.e., self-control, zest, will power, competition (pp. 74–76). Synonyms for grit (OED, n.d.) include backbone, toughness, and hardiness.

In the world of *Oliver Twist*, Dickens draws a sharp distinction between grit and grace. For grace, synonyms (OED, n.d.) include decency, thoughtfulness, and respect. In the more secular sphere of grit, Bumble and Fagin are heroes. Their quest for measureable personal gain is driven by materialistic ambition. By contrast, Brownlow is not motivated by physical or material profit. Instead, he acts in a grace mindset that values decency over toughness and respect over power and control.

Given the emotional nuances of an educator's work, these two ideas do not need to be restricted within linear either/or categories. In term of classroom climate and overall instructional purposes, where do teachers fall along the grit-grace spectrum? Can there be too much grit and too little grace? Or vice versa? How well can these two actually coexist?

Grit has the quantitative advantage of being measurable. For example, a school dealing with an elevated student dropout rate could enact a quantitative plan designed to increase student accountability The dropout rate could then be measured at a later time to ascertain how well the problem was fixed. Similarly, grade point averages, assessment scores, and college admission rates also provide some measure of trends in what some educators label as grit (i.e., hard work, perseverance, a disciplined study schedule).

What about grace? Empathy and compassion are not easily quantified. They do not adhere to a protocol that is easily measurable or replicable. Would we even recognize moments of grace if we saw them? Are moments of grace and transformation happening without our being aware of them? Or do they exist only in theory, but not in practice? Do empathy and compassion play no strategic role in the life of a classroom? Are they simply "accidental occurrences" which sometimes occur if you search them out?

Near the end of *Oliver Twist*, Dickens describes an episode that I suggest demonstrates genuine grace and redemption. Far from being a random incident, it is a direct result of lessons Oliver received from two of his early teacher-figures, Dick and Mr. Brownlow. They modeled lessons celebrating the virtues of acknowledging and honoring "humanity of heart" and a "benevolence to all things that breathe" (Dickens, 1867/2003, p. 466).

Fellow orphan Dick was the first to treat Oliver Twist with compassion. Like Brownlow, Dick intuitively saw goodness within Oliver; he acknowledged and validated that virtue by bestowing a heartfelt blessing upon Oliver. Not long after receiving Dick's blessing, Oliver found himself immersed in Fagin's sphere of criminality. Rather than enter willingly into a life of crime, Oliver demonstrated the inner goodness that Dick had sensed and blessed when he pleaded for mercy after realizing the expanse of Fagin's criminal activities:

> Oliver, well-nigh mad with grief and terror, saw that house-breaking and robbery, if not murder, were the objects of the expedition. He clasped his hands together, and involuntarily uttered a subdued exclamation of horror....

> "Oh! for God's sake let me go!" cried Oliver; "let me run away and die in the fields. I will never come near London; never, never! Oh! pray have mercy on me, and do not make me steal. For the love of all the bright Angels that rest in Heaven, have mercy on me!" (Dickens, 1867/2003, p. 197)

Despite his pleas, Oliver is dragged at gunpoint to engage in further crimes at the risk of his own (physical and moral) life. Oliver feels that there is no forgiveness or mercy to be found. Upon being arrested, he meets Mr. Brownlow who, like Dick, senses goodness in him. After accepting Oliver under his care, Brownlow demonstrates that compassion, mercy, and kindness are real—and that all people, including Oliver, can be deserving of them.

These lessons ultimately allow Oliver to stay true to his moral compass; and save him from succumbing to a life of crime. In short, they serve to protect Oliver's inherent goodness. Sadly, however, Dick would not live to see that the blessing and its message of hope had taken take root and prospered:

> "Oliver, my child!... Where have you been, and why do you look so sad? There are tears stealing down your face at this moment. What is the matter?"

> It is a world of disappointment; often to the hopes we most cherish, and hopes that do our nature the greatest honor. Poor Dick was dead! (Dickens, 1867/2003, p. 452)

Despite his short life, Dick enacted a lifetime of difference in Oliver's world. Imagine how differently Fagin's life may have been if he had teacher-figures like Dick and Mr. Brownlow. Without anyone seeing the grieving and suffering person beneath Fagin's trappings of poverty and destitution, he learned to accept a life without mercy or compassion. Without anyone reaching out to teach him as a human being with goodness inside him, Fagin would experience no redemption. He would die a convicted felon, hung on the gallows:

> It was not until the night of this last awful day, that a withering sense of his helpless, desperate state came in its full intensity upon his blighted soul; not that he had ever held any defined or positive hope of mercy. (Dickens, 1867/2003, pp. 456–457)

At Fagin's trial, the jury expressed not "the faintest sympathy or any feeling but one of all-absorbing interest that he should be condemned" (Dickens, 1867/2003, p. 453). Fagin is left alone in the "dark, dismal, silent night" (p. 456) awaiting his punishment in the morning "to be hanged by the neck, till he was dead" (p. 455). He would die without mercy or compassion until Oliver hears of Fagin's fate and insists to see him. Acting upon the lessons he has received from Dick and Mr. Brownlow, Oliver arrives at Fagin's jail cell to offer sympathy and forgiveness:

> "Fagin," said the jailer.
> "That's me!" cried the Jew, falling, instantly, into the attitude of listening he had assumed upon his trial. "An old man, my Lord; a very old, old man!"
> "Here," said the turnkey, laying his hand upon his breast to keep him down. "Here's somebody wants to see you...
> "Oliver," cried Fagin, beckoning to him....
> "I am not afraid," said Oliver in a low voice, as he relinquished Mr. Brownlow's hand...
> "Yes, yes," returned Oliver. "Let me say a prayer. Do! Let me say one prayer. Say only one, upon your knees, with me, and we will talk till morning....
> "Oh! God forgive this wretched man!" cried the boy with a burst of tears.
> (Dickens, 1867/2003, pp. 460–461)

This moment captures teaching as a sacred act. Oliver empathizes with Fagin's grief and suffering. His actions are not motivated by personal gain or profit. He blesses Fagin at this critical moment, just as his teacher-figure Dick had blessed Oliver many years earlier. Oliver learned the redemptive powers of unconditional mercy and compassion from his teacher-figure Mr. Brownlow and now he is living and acting upon those lessons. Forgiving and blessing Fagin are acts of grace. On a spiritual level, Oliver may just have saved Fagin's soul by seeing beyond Fagin's outer life of petty crime to his inner suffering spirit.

Oliver does not randomly arrive in this emotional and ethical space. The seeds of compassion and mercy (planted by Brownlow and Dick) have taken root. This moment of redemption embodies the Henry Adams (1918) adage that "a teacher affects eternity; he can never tell where his influence stops" (p. 300). Phillip Jackson (1986) observes "on such rare and glorious occasions the question of whether a tiny kernel of knowledge is or is not lodged in somebody's head seems trivial" (p. 74):

> Insofar as the farthest reach of a teacher's influence is concerned—the portion receding beyond the limits of human vision—Henry Adams in his famous quotation hit the nail on the head. But, had he been content with a less lofty though more accurate observation, he could easily have used the close at hand as a starting pace. "Near and far," he might have said, "the limits of a teacher's influence remain forever obscure." Therein lie the fate of all who teach—from here to eternity, uncertainties galore. (p. 74)

A TWENTY-FIRST-CENTURY TWIST

Have you ever felt like nobody was there?
Have you ever felt forgotten in the middle of nowhere?
Have you ever felt like you could disappear?
Like you could fall, and no one would hear.
(Levenson, Pasek, & Paul, 2017, p. 88)

These words could have been spoken by Oliver Twist as he sat alone in the orphanage or as he cried during the night in the basement of Sowerberry's funeral establishment amongst the coffins. They could have been uttered by Fagin isolated in his jail cell suffering the "full intensity upon his blighted soul" (Dickens, 1867/2003, p. 460). In fact, they are the words of Evan Hansen, the 17-year-old protagonist of Steven Levenson, Benj Pasek, and Justin Paul's (2017) *Dear Evan Hansen.* Although Evan is journeying through grief in the twenty-first century, his experiences of isolation, low self-esteem, and despair are similar to those of Oliver Twist. Though centuries apart, both texts dramatize the more vulnerable aspects of our humanity. They each offer insights and lessons relevant to an individual's inner growth and development through grieving.

Evan Hansen is grieving changes to his life following his parent's divorce. He is mourning the loss of his father who has relocated and chosen not to communicate with or otherwise remain a part of Evan's life. Despite school and maintaining his electronic presence on the Internet, Evan feels emotionally disconnected from others. He reflects in his journal "there are so many of us, the lonely souls.... Trying to get closer to the center of everything. Closer to ourselves. Closer to each other. Closer to something true" (Emmich et al., 2018, p. 358).

Being seventeen-years old (compared to the ten-year-old Twist), Evan is developmentally more introspective and skilled at explicitly articulating his thoughts and feelings (which he does via his on-line journal). As James Lapine (2017) observes, "the search for 'truth' and 'self' lie at the center of Evan's consciousness" (p. xii). Evan's low self-esteem and acute sense of loneliness, however, render him feeling powerless and unable to assert any meaningful authorship over his own life ("I am broken. A defective piece that has no match and can never fit into the whole" [Emmich et al., 2018, p. 314]):

If the pain is in you, it's in you. It follows you everywhere. Can't outrun it. Can't erase it. Can't push it away; it only comes back. The way I've been thinking, after all that's happened, maybe there's only one way to survive it. You have to let it in. Let it hurt you. And don't wait. It'll reach you eventually. Might as well be now. (p. 311)

In his work on grieving, Thomas Attig (1996) concludes that individuals, especially young people "lack models for, and need guidance and support in finding appropriate things to do in the mourning period and together new life patterns" (pp. 90–91). Evan Hansen and Oliver Twist are living within such "environments of loss" (Watkin, 2004, p. 191)—loss of loved ones, identity, and self-esteem.

Dialogue from the *Oliver Twist* stage play *Oliver!* (Bart, 1960), the *Dear Evan Hansen* drama script (Levenson, Pasek, & Paul, 2017), and the *Dear Evan Hansen* young adult novel (Emmich et al., 2018) offer linguistic snapshots of young people's struggles as they grieve. These excerpts demonstrate what Attig (1996) calls "unprecedented feelings [that] frighten some and leave them at a loss as to what to do or say" (pp. 90–91):

Oliver Twist Soliloquy (Bart, 1960/1994)	Evan Hansen Journal (Levenson, Pasek, & Paul, 2017)	Dear Evan Hansen (Emmich et al., 2018)
Where is love? Does it fall from skies above? Is it underneath the willow tree that I've been dreaming of? (p. 14)	Guys like you and me, we're just the losers who keep waiting to be seen. No one seems to care or stops to notice that we're there so we get lost in the in-between. (p. 78)	Like they've seen a ghost. That's what these kids look like when I arrive at the bus stop. Is it possible that I actually appear to them as hollow and immaterial as I feel inside? (p. 284)

To what extent does the school curriculum ignore these kinds of emotional issues? How often and in what ways are students (and teachers) feeling as if "no one seems to care or stops to notice that we're there" (Levenson, Pasek, & Paul, p. 78)? When they are "lost in the in-between" (p. 78) or when personal crises cause them to question life's meaning ("Where is love? Does it fall from skies above?" [Bart, 1960, p. 14]), lessons in examining and ascertaining one's values and beliefs and place in the world are critical.

Oliver Twist Soliloquy (Bart, 1960/1994)	Evan Hansen Journal (Levenson, Pasek, & Paul, 2017)	Dear Evan Hansen (Emmich et al., 2018)
Where is she? Whom I close my eyes to see? Will I ever know the sweet hello that's meant for only me? (p. 14)	I never let them see the worst of me. 'Cause what if ev'ryone saw? What if ev'ryone knew? Would they like what they saw? Or would they hate it too? (p. 155)	I know it so well. The moment of reckoning after the worst mistake. The crossfire of regret, helplessness, hatred, and on and on and on. A tsunami of self-torment. (p. 310)

Oliver Twist Soliloquy (Bart, 1960/1994)	Evan Hansen Journal (Levenson, Pasek, & Paul, 2017)	Dear Evan Hansen (Emmich et al., 2018)
Must I travel far and wide 'til I am beside the someone whom I can mean something to? Oh, where is love? (p. 14)	There's something wrong with me that I have to be fixed. I have to go to therapy, I have to take drugs.... I'm such a burden. I'm the worst thing that ever happened to you. I ruined your life. (p. 134)	I am alone, the way I deserve to be. The way I'm meant to be. A fucking nothing. Unworthy to the core. How could I fool myself into thinking I could be deserving of anything close to happiness? To acceptance? And then fool others into thinking it too. (p. 314)

When students and/or teachers are experiencing emotional "crossfire[s] of regret, helplessness, hatred, and on and on and on" (Emmich et al., 2018, p. 310), aspects of their public and private lives are impacted. How many grieving students and teachers, like Evan, may well be wondering to themselves: "Is it possible that I actually appear to them as hollow and immaterial as I feel inside?" (Emmich et al., 2018, p. 284)? Has teaching and learning become so regimented that there is no time left to see one another? To what extent has the work of education become so product-driven that our humanity gets lost in the process? In these ways, grief asks us to share in young Oliver's lament: *Where is love?* In his electronic journal, Evan Hansen expresses his feelings to a virtual world where he remains anonymous and unseen in his solitude. In other words, *invisible*:

> When you're fallin' in a forest and there's nobody around, do you ever really crash or even make a sound? Did I even make a sound? It's like I never made a sound. Will I ever make a sound...? I try to speak but nobody can hear. So I wait around for an answer to appear while I'm watchin' people pass— waving through a window. Can anybody see? Is anybody waving back at me? (Levenson, Pasek, & Paul, 2017, p. 21)

In an average classroom, how many students have emotionally "fallen in a forest" of grief? How many are "speaking with a voice that nobody can hear"? Behaviors influenced by grief or suffering can translate to the outer world as silence, withdrawal, or anger. Parker Palmer (2007) asserts that "behind their fearful silence, our students want to find their voices, speak their voices, have their voices heard" (p. 47).

Evan Hansen describes living with grief as "like standing in a small glass tank and the tank is filling up with water. I'm guessing the water is coming from the sea, because of the saltiness" (Emmich et al., 2018, p. 187). Although the people surrounding Evan do not see his predicament, it is nonetheless real. The saltiness of his tears that threaten to drown him is also real. Similarly, Emily Dickinson (1861b) famously described that her grief was "a funeral in my brain," which she endured in silence "till I thought my mind was going numb" (p. 26).

Even though Evan Hansen and Emily Dickinson represent different centuries, age-groups, genders, and socio-economic backgrounds, their struggles with grief and sadness transcend space and time. The Levenson, Pasek, and Paul (2017) text and many of Emily Dickinson's poems give voice to similar experiences of living within the silent spaces of grief. The writers use words and images to express the inexpressible challenges individuals face emotionally and spiritually.

For example, Evan Hansen records in his journal that "the seawater rushes into my tank.... The feeling of almost drowning is even worse than actually drowning. Actually drowning is peace. Almost drowning is pure pain" (Emmich et al., 2018, p. 187). Dickinson, at a later stage of grieving, writes "I can wade Grief—Whole pools of it—I'm used to that" (Dickinson, 1861a, p. 23). How many variations of Evan Hanson are sitting inside classrooms silently struggling to learn while in an emotional state of near-drowning? What does it mean when students (and teachers) become *accustomed* to perfunctorily living their outer lives while inwardly wading in a pools of grief? To say that these conditions have no relevance to teaching and learning is at best naïve and at worst heartless.

Palmer (2007) writes that "if [teachers] want to teach well in the face of students' fears, [they] need to see clearly and steadily the fear that is in their [own hearts] and their students' hearts" (p. 46):

It means making space for the other, being aware of the other, paying attention to the other, honoring the other. It means not rushing to fill our students' silences with fearful speech of our own and not trying to coerce them into saying things we want to hear. It means entering empathetically into the student's world so that he or she perceives you as someone who has the promise of being able to hear another person's truth. (p. 47)

Dickinson (1862) acknowledges that "no man can compass a despair... so accurate [as] the one... whose own [pain] has just begun" (p. 78). What does it say about classroom life when neither teachers nor students suspect whether one or the other is "almost drowning is pure pain" (Emmich et al., 2018, p. 187)? Martin Buber (1937) writes that when "measure and comparison have disappeared, it lies with yourself how much of the immeasurable becomes reality for you" (p. 32). Grief teaches a person to see beyond what is finite and measureable ("[wisdom] is not outside you, it stirs in the depth of you" [Buber, p. 33]). The emotional insight that grief awakens, Buber continues, "teaches you to meet others at a place where "the parallel lines of relations meet" (p. 33).

Reality defined exclusively by what our eyes and ears report is only a portion of the *complete* reality. How often and in what ways do educators see beyond what is measurable? Consider individuals who, as Dickinson (1861b) describes, are suffering "a funeral in [their] brain" (p. 26). If a student's mind is (metaphorically) overcome with the melodies of a funeral hymn, how well will s/he operate in a classroom that demands full attention to the distribution of facts and figures (however unrelated they may be to student lives)? If teachers and students operate exclusively in parallel awareness of each other, they can never truly know, understand, or be a comfort to each other.

When a student begins to perform poorly in school due to a proverbial funeral in his or her heart, how often will s/he be simply labeled as a low achiever and sent to a remedial class? On the other hand, if this student perseveres and does well on school assessment exams, to what extent will the outer world assume that s/he is coping equally well with life even though his inner struggles continue?

Of course, teachers are not mind-readers or omniscient beings. But neither are they automatons. When teaching becomes overwhelmingly transactional in nature, significant portions of one's larger humanity are left unattended. Grief as a curriculum prioritizes the emotional, spiritual, and ethical aspects of one's public and personal lives. These components are essential not only to how we learn about ourselves and our world; they are critical to the behaviors, attitudes, values, and beliefs we teach each other.

When operating as parallel activities, teaching and learning remain limited to a general routine of giving and receiving information. But when learning involves teachers and students interacting, spaces emerge wherein an intersection of thoughts, discourse, and purpose can blossom. How many moments of authentic interaction take place within the lives of our classrooms? Without this authenticity, teaching and learning are reduced to sterile cognitive exercises. Grief reminds us that there is so much more to being human than can be quantitatively measured. Although information and cognitive assessment outcomes have pedagogical value, too narrow a focus on the intellectual can render emotional, spiritual, and ethical concerns of students and teachers invisible.

Evan Hansen asks "when you're fallin' in a forest and there's nobody around, do you ever really crash or even make a sound?" (Levenson, Pasek, & Paul, 2017, p. 21). Imagine that the team of foresters responsible for the well-being of a wooded area are stationed a considerable distance from the forest itself so that they can monitor the whole of it. Although the panoramic view is helpful, they may know little about the fate of its individual trees. In other words, the officials are unlikely to see the individual trees for the forest.

Similarly, teachers can monitor group trends and statistical shifts in assessment data even if they are operating at a distance from their students' lives. But they are less likely to ascertain individual concerns. Evans feels that he is like one tree in a forest of thousands:

> Have you ever felt like nobody was there? Have you ever felt forgotten in the middle of nowhere? Have you ever felt like you could disappear? Like you could fall and no one would hear? (Levenson, Pasek, & Paul, 2017, p. 89)

How often and in what ways are educators *unable to see the trees for the forest?* For instance, current trends in American public education call for identifying and labeling students per standardized assessment scores and using statistical data and cognitive tracking tools to monitor student progress. These kinds of protocol operate with a corporate-like mentality that tends to regard students as commodities and teachers as responsible for the manufacture and delivery of assessment results which in turn are used to measure the effectiveness of their work as educators. This model encourages parallel relations between teachers and students. Empirically speaking, students are seen as academic problems needing to be solved (and as assessment scores to be raised).

This leaves little room in schools to consider the emotional, spiritual, and ethical concerns of teachers and students. Consequently, an individual's grief or suffering is more likely to go unnoticed. Hence, Palmer's call for teachers to "enter empathetically into the student's world" (Palmer, 2007, p. 47).

When the Evan Hansens of our lives are experiencing the realities of grief and loneliness, who will teach them lessons of hope, healing, resilience, and forgiveness? Of what value is achieving cognitive growth at the expense of emotional stagnation? What comes of individuals who excel on intellectual tasks, but remain feeling isolated, and powerless over their own lives? Evan regrets that "the apple doesn't fall far from the tree. I guess that means we're the products of whoever made us and we don't have much control" (Emmich et al., 2018, p. 334). Who will teach him that beyond the falling down it is how a person lands and perseveres that makes all the difference?

Evan Hansen embodies the powerlessness, vulnerability, and isolation that frequently accompany grief. Evan's grief is immeasurable. His truth cannot be ascertained externally (through assessment exams). It lies within him. How do we express the inexpressible, or otherwise make sense out of that which defies our linear understanding of the world and our lives? How can questions so relevant to the curriculum of our lives be left unattended from the curriculum of our schools?

Despite his grief, Evan still imagines a time when someone will notice him and reach out:

> Even when the dark comes crashin' through / When you need a friend to carry you / And when you're broken on the ground / You will be found. / So let the sun come streamin' in / Cause you'll reach up and you'll rise again. / Lift your head and look around. / You will be found. / You will be found. / You will be found. (Levenson, Pasek, & Paul, 2017, p. 89)

When students have "fallin' in a forest and there's nobody around" (Levenson, Pasek, & Paul, 2017, p. 21) *will they be found?* By whom? Has the work of teachers become so focused on a forest of knowledge and information that we've lose sight of the individuals under our care? When one of our students is emotionally "broken on the ground" (p. 89) or another "doesn't feel strong enough to stand" (p. 89), will s/he be found?

And what about teachers? What recourse is there "when the dark comes crashing through. When you need a friend to carry you. And when you're broken on the ground" (Levenson, Pasek, & Paul, 2017, p. 89)? Will *we* be found? Has the business of education become so prescribed that a teacher's inner life goes unnoticed?

Grieving reminds us that there is much more to who we are than what can be measured or assessed. It helps us see that there is much more to the forest of our humanity than the trees of information and skill sets. It is during times of grief that the trees of forgiveness, hope, healing, and compassion become most critical to our lives. Without these components, personal and professional lives are reduced to the utilitarian and mundane. But with them, teaching is sacred.

Teaching is a sacred act because of its potential to bring people together and to model compassion, sympathy, and benevolence. How many students have you found? How many will you find? Can you imagine teaching and learning without the potential for moments of grace, healing, or hope? Now that would be a reason to grieve.

TOPICS FOR REFLECTION

1. Consider your daily instruction, including assessment and grading, technology integration, and student-teacher interactions. In what ways and to what extent is your teaching life a reflection of who you are? What aspects of your identity (i.e., beliefs, values, mission, and vision) do you feel come through the most, and which do you feel are missing from your work as an educator?

2. Kay Chang (2017) examines a variety of grief experiences that do not directly involve the death of a loved one. She identifies four categories: loss of innocence (usually related to some form of abuse), loss of a dream (a personal or professional aspiration), loss of stability (i.e., a natural disaster, financial loss), and loss due to a "living death" (i.e., separation by divorce or incarceration).

   Can you recall students you have worked with who have faced these kinds of challenges? Of these four categories, which poses the largest challenges to your work? Which do you feel most/least equip to address effectively?

3. How would you describe the moral dimensions of your teaching? Consider, for instance, the extent to which you feel books, assignments, content, and activities are in the best interest of the educational, emotional, and moral lives of students.

4. As a new teacher, how important was it for you to teach with heart, compassion, and empathy? As an experienced teacher, to what extent have these aspirations been met? How satisfied are you with the affective state of your teaching?

5. Many of the adults who came across Oliver Twist's path (circa 1867) treated him as a problem that needed to be solved. In the one hundred fifty-years that have passed, to what extent are educators more enlightened? Imagine that a twenty-first-century incarnation of Oliver Twist has become the newest member of your

class. What kinds of resources and supports might he or she need and to what extent are they available in your school?

Dickens' ninteenth-century portrayal of Oliver included the common perception at the time that Oliver (and others in similar circumstances) were added burdens to the larger society. What traces of this attitude/bias are still present today? In what ways has the twenty-first-century classroom become a more compassionate space? How have biases toward the underserved and underprivileged remained?

6. In many ways Oliver Twist is an archetype of grieving. He is starving for compassion, hope, and a positive sense of self. How many of our students face similar struggles? How many teachers face similar challenges? Consider ways that teachers and students can face these kinds of challenges together. What would this look like? Sound like? Feel like?

7. One of the lessons Oliver Twist learns is that institutions do not provide emotional or spiritual sustenance—people do. Likewise, teaching degrees, faculty positions, and teaching assignments do not inherently affect how teachers and their students understand themselves and their place in the world. In what ways does the bureaucracy of the school system assist you in your mission and vision? In what ways does it hinder those personal and professional aspirations?

8. If faculty members in your building were surveyed, what kinds of responses would you expect if they were asked whether they feel (a) empowered by the support, protocols, and resources provided by the bureaucratic mechanisms of the educational policy-making infrastructure; or (b) submissive to or controlled and restricted by them?

If you could become the "educational head honcho for a week," what remedies would you introduce? How feasible and sustainable do you think those policies would be in the short term? In the long term?

9. As teachers, to what extent does your work construct and reinforce ideological and emotional barriers that separate your inner values and beliefs from your professional work? To what degree do you sometimes feel that your instruction is disconnected from the inner growth and development of your students? In what ways do these disconnects inhibit your own inner growth and development?

10. Create a Venn diagram. In the first circle, brainstorm methods, procedures, mandates, and regulations that focus on the teacher dispersing knowledge/content and students attaining it. In the second circle, brainstorm resources, activities, services, and supports that focus on student identities and emotional challenges. Now, in the space where the circles intersect, try to identify situations and circumstances that bridge these two sets of priorities. How would you describe the bridge between these two worlds?

11. Lama Surya Das (2007) writes "a masterful teacher… can help us progress and develop more than most of us can ever begin to imagine" (p. 168). Describe someone in your life who has been "a masterful teacher." Based on this definition, in what ways are you a "masterful teacher"?

12. How many students, like Oliver, might be asking themselves whether they will "ever know the sweet 'hello' that's meant for only me" (Bart, 1960). Consider the impact a sincere "Hello, how are you?" might have on students who deep down "keep waiting to be seen." Is there no time in a forty-minute, content-based lesson to "notice and care" to these kinds of issues and concerns?

13. *Have you ever felt like nobody was there? / Have you ever felt forgotten in the middle of nowhere? / Have you ever felt like you could disappear? / Like you could fall, and no one would hear?* (Levenson, Pasek, & Paul, *Dear Evan Hansen*, 2017, p. 88).

Consider these questions for quiet reflection. In what ways do your insights help you better understand the humanity of your role as teacher?

14. How many grieving students and teachers, like Evan Hanson, may well be wondering to themselves "Is it possible that I actually appear to them as hollow and immaterial as I feel inside?" (Emmich et al., 2018, p. 284)? Has teaching and learning become so regimented that there is no time left to see one another? To what extent has the work of education become so product-driven that our humanity gets lost in the process?

15. When students have "fallin' in a forest and there's nobody around" (Levenson, Pasek, & Paul, 2017, p. 21) will they be found? By whom? Is the work of educators so focused on the forest of knowledge and information that we have lost sight of the individuals under our care? How often and in what ways are educators "unable to see the trees for the forest"?

16. How many students have you found? How many will you find? Can you imagine teaching and learning without the potential for moments of grace, healing, or hope?

EPILOGUE

What would it mean if you could take a morning-after pill the day after your mother died and be free of the agonizing and unproductive anguish of grief? (Nesse, 1991)

I began this book invoking Parker Palmer's (2007) belief that teachers "must stand where personal and public meet" (p. 18). The subsequent chapters examined the spaces where an educator's inner and outer lives intersect. More specifically, they explored how educators' most vulnerable private moments can serve to strengthen the purpose and practice of their professional work. Hence, the journey considered grief as a teacher's curriculum.

In the process, I learned that the expansiveness of grief cannot be contained, underestimated, or undervalued. Madeleine L'Engle (1988) writes that her journey through grief was an integral part of her soul's growth (p. xvi). She came to understand that a person mourns what is part of his or her own heart. Neglecting one's inner landscape ultimately means denying a critical part of a person's *self*. Because a great deal of attention, conversation, and research focuses on lesson planning, delivery, and assessment per student cognitive needs, the emotional, ethical, and spiritual selves of students and teachers are often neglected. Grief has a way of returning these critical pieces of our humanity to our immediate attention.

The grief journeys examined throughout this book give credence to the emotional, ethical, and spiritual complexities that constitute the depth and expanse of a teacher's work. Using literature as its primary epistemological framework allows for deeper reflection on examples (and counterexamples) of grief's capacity to influence the ways we understand and live our lives. For example, Orlando's (Woolf, 1928) grief experience nurtured within her a sense of empathy toward others from which she would begin to understand and interact with the world in new ways. Most notably, as her sense of social justice and equity heightens, her personal grief expands to encompass the larger grievances and despairs of those around her.

Louis Creed's (King, 1983) grief, on the other hand, isolates him from others. In his sadness, Louis felt that the values and beliefs that sustained him as a physician, husband, and father had become irrelevant. Instead of nurturing empathy, his grief intensifies into further desperation. Similarly, Tom Wingo's grief slowly suspended all aspects of his life (Conroy, 1986). *Suspended,* from the Middle English *schlinge,* translates to *noose* (OED, n.d.). This image of *grief as a noose* captures the emotional and spiritual intensity of a grief experience.

© KONINKLIJKE BRILL NV, LEIDEN, 2020 | DOI: 10.1163/9789004422506_009

Ergo, the thought-provoking question that evolutionary psychologist Randolph Nesse (1991) proposes: What if we could take a pill that would free us from the anguish of grief (p. 435)? My mom passed away in January, 2018. While a "morning-after" pill may have quelled my immediate inner hurt, I suspect a critical part of myself, the part I have been mourning, would have died as well. The empty space left behind may have become more vulnerable to further despair or even an emotional callousness or apathy.

Two months after Mom's death, I returned to my college classroom of elementary teacher candidates. Would my public life as teacher resume untouched by my personal loss? Would my emotional wounds be left outside on the doorstep of the college while I proceeded to carry on methodically (and mechanically?) with the pre-established syllabus? In other words, was I a person unchanged by my loss or a teacher untouched by my grief?

It was a Wednesday afternoon in mid-March when I returned to my college seminar. As I rejoined my class of student teachers I remember feeling, as Palmer (2007) describes, as if I were "standing where personal and public meet" (p. 18). I was part Aeneas and part Melchior, carrying on with my professional life while the spirits of loved ones seemed to hover all around me. Although I may have appeared unchanged on the outside, inwardly I had become part Oliver Twist and part Orlando—at once a grown man and orphan. Like Tom Wingo and Louis Creed, I was operating somewhere between inner truths and outer realities. Although a mechanical teacher of some sort would have returned unaltered (being programmed, after all, to maintain an unvarying consistency), I was neither untouched nor unchanged by my grief.

Borrowing from Woolf, I felt that I was "growing up... losing some illusions, perhaps to acquire new ones" (Woolf, 1928, p. 175). During these days and weeks, I sensed that, like Tom Wingo, "as a teacher, I had been a happy man. Now, I was only a diminished one" (Conroy, 1986, p. 282). Maxine Greene (1978) described the capacity of reflection to "break through the cotton wool of daily life" (p. 185). For me, it felt as though grief had not only broken the fabric of daily life but had shredded it. Like Evan Hansen, I felt as though I was "on the outside [of life] looking in," asking whether I would "ever be more than I've always been" (Levenson, Pasek, & Paul, 2017, p. 6). It was as if I were not only mourning the passing of my mom, but also grieving the loss of significant life roles which had constituted much of my identity. Caregiver, confidante, companion, and counsel no more. I felt that in many ways I had become a hollowed man.

But I have always held education in high esteem. It remains a constant truth of my identity. Nevertheless, despite how much I may have learned over the years and no matter how many university degrees I may have accrued, all that knowledge felt meaningless in terms of my accepting the new realities of life on their own terms. The notion that "knowledge is power" dates back to a sixteenth-century Francis Bacon maxim (from *Meditationes Sacrae*). In the twentieth century, it became a motivational mantra displayed in many elementary and high school classrooms. And yet, grieving seemed to render me powerless.

The grief journey teaches that intellectual strength and the power it has the potential to command (i.e., well-paying job, elevated stature, social mobility) is only a portion of what constitutes a comprehensive education. Just as fruits offer our physical bodies nutritional sustenance, Tagore (1933/2004) wrote that a person's beliefs and values need to ripen over time in order to provide spiritual and moral sustenance (p. 161). Although, in general, educators are well-trained in distributing knowledge and information, in what ways are they adept in nurturing inner growth and development? The curriculum of grief is concerned with the challenges and aspirations individuals face as they evolve emotionally morally, and spiritually.

Another lesson I have gleaned from this journey is that while external conditions may greatly impact what we do or where we live, it is ultimately a person's inner landscape that defines who he or she is being and becoming. In this way, grief speaks to the core of an individual's identity—personally and professionally.

As teacher, when I returned to the classroom I found that I began to talk less and listen more. Instead of relying on prepared lectures and PowerPoint presentations that focused on research-based teaching strategies and formative assessment tools, my soon-to-be-licensed teacher candidate students and I increasingly spent our time discussing their growth and development as teachers: In what ways are student-teachers finding that personal values align or do not align with professional demands? How much of their mission and vision of teaching are they willing to compromise in order to maintain their jobs within the complex urban public school system? Is there an ethical line that they feel they would never cross? Questions such as these inspired discourse and reflection unlike any I experienced in my previous six years teaching in the College of Education.

I discovered amazing things: one student confided that because of his frustration with the bureaucracy of education, he secretly wondered about teaching overseas in an underprivileged country. I had no idea about his frustration, his interest in teaching overseas, or that he was fluent in three languages. Another student admitted that she was glad to be finishing the program because of her growing sense of melancholy and despair at the hardships she witnessed among her students and their families. I never suspected that she was carrying such emotional weight. One student shared paintings she created during her two student-teaching semesters that expressed how her inner emotional landscape had changed throughout the experience. I never knew she had such talent. These are realities I may never had known existed—even though they were right in front of my eyes.

The quality and depth of our time together became transformative. I came to believe that some of the hollowness I felt was being replaced with what Tagore (1933) described as a "fullness of sympathy" (p. 142). Without our recent discourse and interactions, these students would have graduated without my really knowing or understanding them. Some of the most pressing issues in their lives may have remained unspoken and unacknowledged. Like Tom Wingo (Conroy, *The Prince of Tides*, 1986), my passion for the content of what I was teaching expanded to include paying closer attention to the lives that were being impacted by that content. It is in this spirit that I now revisit the four questions proposed at the beginning of this exploration.

How can our most vulnerable moments serve to strengthen the purpose and practice of our work as educators?

I am beginning to understand that, like education itself, learning to live with grief is not about reaching a finish line; it is more about acknowledging and embracing a *process* of growth and development. There is the sadness of looking backwards, and the loneliness of the present. But for me the greater hurt lies in the looking forward. All the knowledge in the world cannot inform someone how to forge a meaningful future amidst grief. Pedagogical tools are not magic wands. They cannot teach someone how to imagine or create a worthwhile future.

This reflective project created a lens through which to better reflect on the role grief plays at the intersection of an individual's professional and personal lives. It frightens me to wonder how many times during my twenty-years teaching elementary school I may have been a Mr. Bumble (Dickens, *Oliver Twist*, 1867/2003)—so full of my own title and position that I could not see the hardship or inner suffering of students, parents, or peers though they stood right before me. How many times had I been like one of Melchior's teachers (from whom all Melchior and his friends heard was a meaningless "blaa, blaa, blaa, blaa, blaa, blaa, blaa, blaa" [Sater & Sheik, *Spring Awakening*, 2007, p. 29])? How often had I been so focused on test scores and assessment goals that I missed opportunities to cultivate a "fullness of sympathy" (Tagore, 1933, p. 142)?

These questions reflect the depth and expanse of the curriculum of grief. This exploration inspired these kinds of introspective queries due to its epistemological reliance on literary works. For example, the character Aeneas (Virgil, *The Aeneid*, 19 BCE/1990) became a critical conduit towards another way of my knowing, reflecting upon, and understanding myself and my work. Narrowly focused on his public mission, Aeneas discounted the emotional toil those around him were suffering. Even the tragic death of his bride-to-be did not immediately shake his desire for public glory. Only when grief paralyzes him with guilt and remorse does Aeneas begin to examine the inner moral and spiritual realities simmering beneath the facade of the outer world.

I wonder how many teacher candidates I have mentored who similarly were silently struggling with personal and moral crises. Although not an empirical source of information, the knowledge and insights I have gained from Aeneas's story demonstrate the dangers of focusing too narrowly on the cognitive development of students at the expense of spiritual, ethical, and emotional considerations. Although historians may revere Aeneas for his public works and accumulation of honors and wealth, I have become most impressed with his courage to embrace his inner despair and his strength of conviction in persevering through personal trauma. He may never have known the depth of his courage nor the expanse of his convictions had it not been for his heeding the lessons of grief.

Similarly, we may never understand the breadth of our courage or convictions as teachers and as human beings without being attentive to the more intrinsic nature of our humanity. By turning away from this depth of reflection and awareness, we risk reducing our interactions with others, including our students, to episodes of sleepwalking. Louis Creed (King, *Pet Sematary,* 1983) is often described as a sleepwalker because he looks all around him, but fails to see the truth that stares him in the face. As teachers, how often do we see all around us with taking notice of the emotional realities that exist? Could it be that while I so confidently worked with student teachers to assure that they met externally imposed licensure requirements, I was inadvertently losing sight of their emerging and evolving humanity? How often have personal and emotional priorities been cast aside for the sake of adhering to professional mandates and procuring quantitative results?

Grief has a way of reducing external mandates and criteria from their inflated status. My grief and the introspection that it inspired awakened me from my professional sleepwalking. It is a reminder that much of an educator's work relies on and is indicative of who s/he is and what s/he believes in and values as an individual. By redirecting my thoughts and attention inward, grief somehow silenced the noise of external demands and muted the cacophony of outside distractions. It returned me to the heart of my teacher self.

My grief taught me to be both a skeptic *and* a pilgrim. Whereas the skeptic is vulnerable to uncertainty, suspicion, and doubt, the pilgrim journeys on with a sense of purpose and optimism. Avery D. Weisman (1993) uses the term "skeptical pilgrim" to describe one who embodies both the helplessness of the former and the hopefulness of the latter (p. 56). He asserts that a skeptical pilgrim inhabits the inner space "where vulnerability exists side by side with resiliency" (p. 56).

Each of the grieving literary characters examined in this book personify varying degrees of a skeptical pilgrim. For example, despite recurring episodes of unwarranted pain and sadness, Oliver Twist never losses faith in his moral compass. Although Melchior holds tightly to his aspirations of composing a life on his own terms, he remains keenly aware of the spiritual presence of his friends who died ("they walk with my heart—I'll never let them go" [Sater & Sheik, 2007, p. 34]). While Tom Wingo accepts his grief and reconciles with his family, he acknowledges the "fierce interior music of blood and wildness and identity" that would forever remain in "the deepest part of him" (Conroy, 1986, p. 675).

Perhaps grief makes skeptical pilgrims of us all. Consider Orlando, who became skeptical of what her eyes were showing her and yet remained hopeful that "one can only believe entirely, perhaps, in what one cannot see" (Woolf, 1928, p. 198). Grief has the potential to teach individuals to see themselves and their world differently. For example, I recently observed a student teacher giving a lesson in which she was closely adhering to a variety of high profile, research-based techniques and protocols.

All the boxes on the "observer checklist" were marked: *Gives explicit and concise instructions to students by providing time allotments, expectations, and explanations on the use of materials*—check! *Explains and provides opportunities for students' use of relevant vocabulary*—check! *Filters students' responses and stays close to the designated aim of lesson*—check! *Monitors students' engagement*—check! And yet...

Where was the teacher candidate I came to know from our seminar discussions? Where had her passion gone? The candidate I knew was anxious to make a difference in the lives of students. She spoke passionately about her vision of teaching that included championing against preconceived notions and biases. The person I just observed was not the same person. Her teacher heart was lost somewhere within the outer labyrinth of prescribed methods, rigid procedures, and externally imposed criteria.

A dutiful "pilgrim field supervisor" would affirm the success of her meeting each criterion listed on the observation checklist. As a *skeptical* pilgrim, however, I began our post-teaching conversation by asking the student teacher what she hoped to achieve with her lesson and in what ways it had been accomplished. Her response was as mechanical as her teaching performance. Her reply was articulate, efficient, and aligned closely to external criteria. In other words, robotic. But maybe "one can only believe entirely, perhaps, in what one cannot see" (Woolf, 1928, p. 198). I saw none of the teacher candidate's heart, compassion, or inner drive. Like Orlando, this understanding made my "eyes fill with tears" (p. 305).

In what ways can teachers harness the power of introspection to transform their work, their lives, and the lives of their students?

I began asking this teacher candidate questions of a more introspective nature. In what ways was the lesson meaningful and engaging to the lives of the students? To her? In what ways did she feel as if she truly owned the lesson, that it was *hers*? If she re-imagined the lesson, separate from the teaching observation checklist, what would it look and sound like? With little hesitation, she quickly embraced this opportunity to imagine a lesson that more closely adhered to her vision of meaningful teaching. She began describing what I immediately recognized as a genuinely student-centered literacy lesson. Instead of reading about animals who dwell in desert biomes, she imagined having her students (who resided in an urban neighborhood) read about nocturnal animals of the city.

Rather than having students sort the information into fact and opinion columns (for which there were prescribed "correct" answers), she imagined beginning the lesson by listing what students understood to be true about urban animals and then proceeding to discern whether their statements were fact or opinion based on their text reading, personal experiences, and predictions. The teacher candidate spoke excitedly about how this would enable students to generate thoughts rather than repeat information. As I listened, I could hear the student's passion for teaching reawaken. Freed from the constraints of outer forms and external procedures, she had reclaimed ownership of the lesson.

I asked the teacher candidate why her vision of the lesson was not the reality I had observed. She described feeling vulnerable to the judgment of her observers. Also, she was determined to adhere to the outward behaviors she felt others expected of a "professional teacher." Were these the kinds of criteria for meaningful lessons that I had been endorsing as her teacher? To what extent had narrow adherence to outer protocol in the name of education reduced my work to this? The transformative nature of teaching and learning had been lost in the pursuit to meet external criteria prescribed on research-based pedagogical checklists. While much is gained from methods and procedures explicitly described in journals and textbooks, this conversation and others like it were showing me that there was much going on here to grieve.

I grieved as I reflected on the extent to which this student (and how many others?) was learning to become someone other than the teacher she had aspired to be. I grieved as I began to consider aspirations stifled and dreams narrowed or compromised. Again, like Orlando, "do what [I] would to restrain them, the tears came to [my] eyes" (Woolf, 1928, p. 165). Todd May (2017) uses the term "central projects" to identify relationships and beliefs that "engage us at a deeper level that our hobbies do. [That are] woven into our sense of who we are and what we are about" (p. 9). Being a teacher is not just a *part* of our lives, its work is an integral component of who we are.

For many years, caregiver and teacher were the roles that defined my identity. These were my *central projects*. They comprised what was most worthwhile in my life. After my mom's passing, I felt that a large piece of myself had been torn away. To teach and to grieve became my central projects. This returns me to Randolph Nesse's (1991) provocative question: What would it mean if you could take a morning-after pill the day after your mother died and be free of the anguish of grief (p. 435)? Without my grief I would be half a person. In many ways it had come to complete me.

But to what extent and in what ways would grief continue to define me moving forward? Did there exist room in this deliberation to create a path that honored the past while at the same time validated my identity and life with an eye toward the future? As I shared at the onset of this journey, grief was in many ways testing my belief in teaching as sacred in its capacity to expand an individual's understanding of life in its many complexities. In Chapter 1, I alluded to Martha Nussbaum's (1986) question of "whether the act of writing about the beauty of human vulnerability is not, paradoxically, a way of rendering oneself less vulnerable" (p. xliii). Although I suspected that I began this project in part to help "render myself less vulnerable" to my sadness, that intention has not been realized. At the time of my writing this epilogue, eighteen months into this reflective project, my vulnerabilities remain. Like Evan Hansen, I remain "somewhere lost in the in-between" (Levenson, Pasek, & Paul, 2017, p. 15).

I am *relearning* my identity and place in the world. This journey has lead me to examine, and in some cases reexamine, a variety of literary works through my lens of grief. Doing so has educated me in the intrinsically redemptive capacities of teaching and learning. Redemption is from the Latin *redimere* meaning *re(d)* back and *emere* buy. This returns me to William H. Schubert's (1986) deceivingly simple-sounding curriculum question: What is most worthwhile? To re-discover and/or re-invigorate one's sense of purpose, to achieve a degree of solace in the face of despair, and to resurrect and/or restore one's sense of his or her authentic identity—these aspirations are constructive. During times of emotional or spiritual crisis, they are invaluable.

What impact can personal grieving have on remembering, recovering, and re-identifying with one's professional mission and vision?

Grief reminds me that facts, information, degrees of higher learning, and polished curriculum vitae are not the *ends* of meaningful education. They are the *means* through which one can pursue a worthwhile life. To *reexamine* our public and private sense of mission and vision, as grief calls us to do, is akin to re-imagining our personal, moral, and spiritual lives.

My journey of grief through the lens of literary works has lead me to reexamine Victor Hugo's (1862/1992) *Les Miserables*. Although I taught a *Les Miserables* novel-unit for many years to middle school students, I never before imagined that in many ways Hugo was describing the sacred work of a teacher. In keeping with the epistemological framework of the previous chapters, here in the *Epilogue* I find myself returning to Hugo's novel as a source of wisdom.

In an early chapter, Hugo (1862/1992) introduces a young bishop as "an admirable consoler... who did not seek to drown grief in oblivion, but to exalt and to dignify it by hope" (p. 16). Imagine the potential of an educator's work to nurture consolation and hope:

> He [the teacher] believed that faith is healthful. He sought to counsel and to calm the despairing man by pointing out to him the man of resignation, and to transform the grief which looks down into the grave by showing it the grief which looks up to the stars. (p. 16)

As a grieving individual and as a teacher, I have come to aspire to what Hugo describes as a "grief which looks up to the stars" (Hugo, 1862/1992, p. 16). He writes that individuals cannot educate well about the "open, visible, signal, and public life" if they are not "at the same time, to a certain extent, a good historian of their deeper and hidden life" (p. 830). He questions "while there is an infinite outside of us, is there not an infinite within us?" (p. 437).

I am humbled that these brief excerpts from Hugo's novel encapsulate many of the thoughts and questions I have put forth throughout this book. It is a reminder of literature's capacity to transcend space and time and to articulate a poignant glimpse into the depths of our humanity. While revisiting *Les Miserables* (1862/1992), I discovered another passage that touched upon two additional themes that emerged throughout this journey: 1) the intersection of personal and professional identities, and 2) the ethical framework that underlies much of an educator's work:

> The history of morals and ideas interpenetrate the history of events, and vice versa. They are two orders of different facts which answer to each other, which are always linked with and often produce each other.... Facts are one, ideas are the other.... This is why we cry: education, knowledge! to learn to read is to kindle a fire; every syllable spelled sparkles.
>
> But he who says light does not necessarily say joy. There is suffering in the light; in excess it burns. Flame is hostile to the wing.
>
> To burn and yet to fly, this is the miracle of genius.
>
> When you know and when you love you shall suffer still. The day dawns in tears. The luminous weep... (Hugo, 1862/1992, pp. 830–831)

Who are the luminous and why are they weeping? In what ways does the outer reality of our lives align to the inner truths that resonate on emotional and ethical levels? What kinds of fires are being kindled in our classrooms? In our students? In ourselves? What roles do morals and ideas play in our work as teachers?

Just as this journey lead me to revisit Victor Hugo's *Les Miserables* (1862/1992), my hope is that it will also inspire readers to continue their own reflective journeys by discovering and/or rediscovering literature that will further illuminate their work and their lives. After reading an early draft of this manuscript, a friend shared that he was immediately reminded of William Wordsworth's (1850) autobiographical poem *The Prelude*. Intrigued, I retrieved a copy of the work and was soon drawn to thoughts Wordsworth expressed in Book 13 (*Imagination and Taste, How Impaired and Restored*) wherein an aging Wordsworth reflects that it was the "lonely roads" of his life which were the "open schools in which [he] daily read [and] saw into the depth of human souls" (p. 206, lines 163, 164, 167).

Wordsworth grieved that "to careless eyes" most "souls appear[ed] to have no depth at all" (Wordsworth, 1850, p. 206, lines 168–169) due to an "overweening trust" in a formal education that had little to do "with real feeling and just sense" (p. 207, lines 170, 172). He mourned:

> How books mislead us, seeking their reward / From judgments of the wealthy Few, who see / By artificial lights; how they debase / The Many for the pleasure of those Few; / Effeminately level down the truth / To certain general notions, for the sake / Of being understood at once, or else / Through want of better knowledge in the heads / That framed them; flattering self-conceit with words, / That, while they most ambitiously set forth / Extrinsic differences, the outward marks / Whereby society has parted man / From man, neglect the universal heart. (pp. 208–209, lines 208–216)

How much classroom time is spent beneath "artificial lights," focusing on instruction that seeks to "level down the truth" to a series of "general notions" that can be more easily "understood at once"? By contrast, grief shines a genuine light on the deepest truths of our humanity: our beliefs, values, and vulnerabilities. It penetrates through "extrinsic differences" and surpasses "outward marks" directly to "the universal heart."

Wordsworth goes on to say that it was on life's most lonely emotional roads where he "gain[ed] clear sight of a new world—a world, too, that was fit to be transmitted, and to other eyes made visible" (Wordsworth, 1850, Book 13, p. 212, lines 369–372). His loneliness is "whence spiritual dignity originates" and helped him achieve "a balance, an ennobling interchange of action from without and from within" (lines 373, 375–376). Consider the difference between a teacher-figure dispensing sets of facts versus inspiring a "clear sight of a new world." Imagine a caliber of teaching and learning that aspires to be "an ennobling interchange of action from without and from within."

Revisiting Wordsworth's *Prelude* reminds me of Woolf's observations that "the poet's then is the highest office of all. His words reach where others fall short" (Woolf, 1928, p. 173). My journey of using grief as a teacher's curriculum is rooted in the idea (which Wordsworth's poem embodies) that "thoughts are divine" (Woolf, 1928, p. 173) and that "one can believe entirely, perhaps, in what one cannot see" (Woolf, 1928, p. 198).

> This spiritual Love acts not nor can exist / Without Imagination… And clearest insight, amplitude of mind (p. 218, lines 188, 189, 191)… Imagination having been our theme, / So also hath that intellectual Love, / For they are each in each, and cannot stand / Dividually.... Here keepest thou in singleness thy state: / No other can divide with thee this work. (Wordsworth, 1850, Book 14, p. 218, lines 206–209, 211–212)

While information and facts feed one's intellect, they cannot nurture what Wordsworth calls "intellectual Love." He grieves that to have the *intellectual* without the *Love* means that "much is overlooked in human nature and her subtle ways, as studied first in our own hearts, and then in life" (Wordsworth, 1850, Book 14, p. 221, lines 323–326). Wordsworth warns "without Imagination… we cannot have clearest insight [and] amplitude of mind."

To what extent can grief help us better understand the scope and depth of the educators we are and have the potential to become?

Unless we pause to *imagine* the potential of our work as educators to touch upon critical components of our humanity (i.e., hope, trust, faith, empathy), Wordsworth observes that individuals come to regard "innocence [as] too delicate, and moral notions too intolerant and Sympathies [become] too contracted" (Wordsworth, 1850, Book 14, pp. 221, lines 339–341). Grief is a kind of clarion call that turns one's attention back to vulnerabilities, values, and emotions that too often are "overlooked in human nature" (line 323).

It reminds us that our professional tendency to "separate the two natures, the one that feels, the other that observes" (Wordsworth, 1850, Book 14, p. 222, lines 347–348) ultimately denies the integrated wholeness of our humanity. Wordsworth suggests that our understanding of ourselves and each other remains incomplete when we separate what our students and we *observe* from what we *feel and believe*. Thomas Moore (1997) writes that this separation accounts for "one of the great problems of our time... that many are schooled but few are educated" (p. 3):

Education is not the piling on of learning, information, data, facts, skills, or abilities—that's training or instructing—but it is rather a making visible what is hidden... To be educated, a person doesn't have to know much or be informed, but he or she does have to have been exposed vulnerably to the transformative events of an engaged human life. (p. 3)

As he reflected upon the "lonely roads" of life, Wordsworth gleaned greater insight into how one's inner life is integral to who he or she is, has been, and has the potential to become. In the final section of his *Prelude*, Wordsworth articulates this epiphany:

Prophets of Nature, we to them will speak / A lasting inspiration, sanctified / By reason, blest by faith: what we have loved, / Others will love, and we will teach them how; / Instruct them how the mind of man becomes / A thousand times more beautiful than the earth. (Wordsworth, 1850, Book 14, p. 225, lines 446–451)

These words reflect the kinds of personal thoughts I have experienced along this reflective journey. My initial conception of grief as a passive condition, one imposed upon individuals by external events, tragedies, or misfortunes, has changed. I've begun to imagine grief as an active search for "lasting inspiration, sanctified" (Wordsworth, 1850, p. 225, lines 447) within the mundane days of my sadness. This includes a heightened sensitivity to the potential for ascertaining the sacred dimensions of my public work as an educator. Imagine becoming that teacher who aspires to inspire students on how their lives can "become a thousand times more beautiful than the earth" (line 451).

My hope is that readers will reflect on and discuss the contents of this book to *reconnect* with the personal and ethical aspirations that first inspired them to become educators. If the issues raised and questions asked throughout this journey help inspire others to *reimagine* their work's potential to influence lives on intellectual, emotional, and moral levels, then perhaps, as Wordsworth imagined, our collective work as educators is closer to becoming "a thousand times more beautiful than the earth" (p. 225, line 451).

Just as grief taught Tom Wingo to ascertain moments of grace within his public and private lives, my wish is that educators continue to develop a greater sense of the

187

importance of their work on intellectual, moral, and emotional levels. Through his introspection, Tom Wingo gleaned a greater understanding and reverence for his role as teacher. I hope that this book gives educators a greater sense of the importance of their work and validates their potential to transform lives through compassion and empathy—critical components of life's curriculum. Perhaps our further reflections can lead us to collectively share more fully in the spirit of Tom's epiphany:

> There's no word in the language I revere more than *teacher*. None. My heart sings when a kid refers to me as his teacher and always has. I've honored myself and the entire family of [humanity] by becoming one.... Lord, I am a teacher and a coach. That is all and it is enough. (Conroy, 1986, pp. 666, 677)

REFERENCES

Adams, H. (1918). *The education of Henry Adams*. Boston, MA: Houghton Mifflin.

Alcorn, M. (2002). *Changing the subject in English class: Discourse and the constructions of desire*. Carbondale, IL: Southern Illinois University Press.

Angelou, M. (2014). *Rainbow in the cloud: The wisdom and spirit of Maya Angelou*. New York, NY: Random House.

Attig, T. (1996). *How we grieve: Relearning the world*. Oxford: Oxford University Press.

Ayers, W. (1993). *To teach: The journey of a teacher*. New York, NY: Teachers College Press.

Bart, L. (1994/1960). *Oliver!* [CD]. London: Exallshow.

Bauman, Z. (2006). *Liquid fear*. Cambridge: Polity Press.

Bellah, R. N., Madsen, R., Sullivan, W. M., Swidler, A., & Tipton, S. M. (1985). *Habits of the heart: Individualism and commitment in American life*. Berkeley, CA: University of California Press.

Berman, J. (2004). *Empathic teaching: Education for life*. Amherst, MA: University of Massachusetts Press.

Bernardin, J. C. (1997). *The gift of peace*. Chicago, IL: Loyola Press.

Boos, R. W. (2008). Creativity in education. *Journal of Thought, 71*(2), 113–117.

Bosky, B. L. (1986). The mind's a monkey: Character and psychology in Stephen King's recent fiction. In T. Underwood & C. Miller (Eds.), *Kingdom of fear* (pp. 241–276). New York, NY: New American Library/Signet.

Brault, P. A., & Naas, M. (2001). To reckon with the dead: Jacques Derrida's politics of mourning. In P. A. Brault & M. Naas (Eds.), *The work of mourning* (pp. 1–30). Chicago, IL: University of Chicago Press.

Bruner, J. (2004). Life as narrative. *Social Research, 71*(3), 691–709.

Buber, M. (2010/1937). *I and thou* (R. G. Smith, Trans.). Mansfield Centre, CT: Martino Publishing.

Burke, K. (1937/1984). *Attitudes toward history*. Oakland, CA: University of California Press.

Buscaglia, L. (1982). *Living, loving, and learning*. Thorofare, NJ: Slack.

Butler, I. (2018). In the aftermath of the Parkland shooting, the teenage cost of 'Spring Awakening' prepares to take the stage. *Topic Magazine, 15*. Retrieved from https://www.topic.com/they-dont-do-sadness

Campbell, J. (1988). *The power of myth*. New York, NY: Anchor.

Campbell, J. (1991). *Reflections on the art of living*. New York, NY: HarperCollins.

Cassirer, E. (1954). *An essay on man: An introduction to a philosophy of human culture*. Garden City, NY: Doubleday.

Chandler, D. (2002). *Semiotics: The basics*. New York, NY: Routledge.

Chang, K. (2017). Living with vulnerability and resiliency: The psychological experience of collective trauma. *Acta Psychopathologica, 3*(53), 1–5.

Chesterton, G. K. (1971). *Chesterton on Shakespeare* (D. Ahlquist, Ed.). London: Darwen Finlayson.

Cochran, L., & Claspell, E. (1987). *The meaning of grief: A dramaturgical approach to understanding emotion*. New York, NY: Greenwood Press.

Connelly, F., & Clandinin, D. (1990). Stories of experience and narrative inquiry. *Educational Researcher, 19*(4), 2–14.

Connerton, P. (2011). *The spirit of mourning: History, memory and the body*. Cambridge, MA: Cambridge University Press.

Conroy, P. (1986). *The prince of tides*. New York, NY: Dial Press.

Conroy, P. (2002). *My losing season*. New York, NY: Dial Press.

Costantini, C., & Foster, D. (Directors). (2018). *Awakening: After Parkland* [Documentary Short]. New York, NY: First Look Media.

D'Aulaire, I., & D'Aulaire, E. (1962). *D'Aulaire's book of Greek myths*. New York, NY: Doubleday.

Davidson, D. (1978). What metaphors mean. *Critical Inquiry, 5*(1), 31–47.

REFERENCES

Deal, T. E., & Redman, P. D. (2009). *Reviving the soul of teaching: Balancing metrics and magic.* Thousand Oaks, CA: Corwin Press.

Derrida, J. (2001). *The work of mourning* (P. A. Brault & M. Naas, Eds.). Chicago, IL: University of Chicago Press.

Dewey, J. (1898). My pedagogical creed. In J. Boydston (Ed.), *John Dewey the early works, 1882–1898* (pp. 84–95). Carbondale, IL & Edwardsville, IL: Southern Illinois University Press.

Dewey, J. (1916). *Democracy and education.* New York, NY: Free Press.

Dewey, J. (1934). *Art as experience.* New York, NY: Minton, Balch & Company.

Dewey, J. (1938). *Experience and education.* New York, NY: Touchstone.

Dibbley, D. C. (1993). *From Achilles' heel to Zeus's shield.* New York, NY: Fawcett.

Dickens, C. (1867/2003). *Oliver twist.* New York, NY: Barnes & Noble.

Dickinson, E. (1861a). I can wade grief. In B. Hillman (Ed.), *Emily Dickinson poems* (p. 23). Boston, MA: Shambhala.

Dickinson, E. (1861b). I felt a funeral in my brain. In B. Hillman (Ed.), *Emily Dickinson poems* (pp. 26–27). Boston, MA: Shambhala.

Dickinson, E. (1862). No man can compass a despair. In B. Hillman (Ed.), *Emily Dickinson poems* (p. 78). Boston, MA: Shambhala.

Egan, K. (1986). *Teaching as storytelling.* Chicago, IL: University of Chicago Press.

Eisner, E. (1979). *The educational imagination: On the design and evaluation of school programs.* New York, NY: Macmillan.

Eisner, E. (2002). *The arts and the creation of mind.* New Haven, CT: Yale University.

Ellison, R. (1947). *Invisible man.* New York, NY: Random House.

Emmich, V., Levenson, S., Pasek, B., & Paul, J. (2018). *Dear Evan Hansen: The novel.* New York, NY: Little, Brown, and Company.

Engel, G. L. (1961). Is grief a disease? A challenge for medical research. *Psychosomatic Medicine, 23*(3), 18–22.

Evans, R. (1996). *The human side of change.* San Francisco, CA: Jossey-Bass.

Feifel, H. (1959). *The meaning of death.* New York, NY: McGraw-Hill.

Feldman, D. (2017). *Supersurvivors: Why the five stages of grief are wrong.* Retrieved from https://www.psychologytoday.com/us/blog/supersurvivors/201707/why-the-five-stages-grief-are-wrong

Fenstermacher, G. D. (1990). Some moral considerations on teaching as a profession. In J. I. Goodlad, R. Soder, & K. A. Sirotnik (Eds.), *The moral dimensions of teaching* (pp. 130–151). San Francisco, CA: Jossey-Bass.

Freire, P. (1974/2008). *Education for critical consciousness.* New York, NY: Continuum Books.

Goho, J. (2014). *Journeys into darkness: Critical essays on gothic horror.* Lanham, MD: Rowman & Littlefield.

Golliher, J. (2008). *A deeper faith: A journey into spirituality.* New York, NY: Penguin.

Gray, J. (2003). *Straw dogs: Thoughts on humans and other animals.* New York, NY: Farrar, Straus, and Giroux.

Greene, M. (1965/2007). *The public school and the private vision: A search for America in education and literature.* New York, NY: The New Press.

Greene, M. (1978). *Landscapes of learning.* New York, NY: Teachers College Press.

Greenfield, W. D. (1991). The micro-politics of leadership in an urban elementary school. In J. J. Blasé (Ed.), *The politics of life in schools* (pp. 161–184). Newbury Park, CA: Sage.

Gresham, D. (1961/1994). Introduction. In C. S. Lewis (Ed.), *A grief observed* (pp. xix–xxxi). New York, NY: Harper.

Hargreaves, A. (1995). Development and desire: A postmodern perspective. In T. R. Guskey & M. Huberman (Eds.), *Professional development in education: New paradigms and perspectives* (pp. 9–34). New York, NY: College Teachers Press.

Harper, R. (1965). *The seventh solitude: Man's isolation in Kierkegaard, Dostoevsky, and Nietzsche.* Baltimore, MD: Johns Hopkins Press.

Harris, S. (2010). *The moral landscape.* New York, NY: Free Press.

Hoff, B. (1982). *The tao of pooh*. New York, NY: Penguin.

Hopkins, L. T. (1954). *The emerging self: In school and home*. Westport, CT: Greenwood Press.

Hugo, V. (1862/1992). *Les Miserables* (C. E. Wilbour, Trans.). New York, NY: Random House.

Hyles, V. (1987). Freaks: The grotesque as metaphor in the works of Stephen King. In G. Hoppenstand & R. B. Browne (Eds.), *The gothic world of Stephen King: Landscape of nightmares* (pp. 56–63). Bowling Green, OH: Bowling Green State University Press.

Jackson, P. W. (1986). *The practice of teaching*. New York, NY: Teachers College Press.

James, W. (1899/2008). *Talks to teachers on psychology: And to students on some of life's ideas*. Rockville, MD: Arc Manor.

Jersild, A. T. (1955). *When teachers face themselves*. New York, NY: Teachers College Press.

Kaufman, P., & Schipper, J. (2018). *Teaching with compassion: An educator's oath to teach from the heart*. New York, NY: Rowman & Littlefield.

Kelchtermans, G. (1993). Getting the story, understanding the lives: From career stories to teachers' professional development. *Teaching and Teacher Education, 9*, 443–456.

Kelchtermans, G. (1996). Teacher vulnerability: Understanding its moral and political roots. *Cambridge Journal of Education, 26*(3), 307–323.

Kierkegaard, S. (1843/1959). *Either/Or* (Vol. 1, D. Swenson & L. Swenson, Trans.). Princeton, NJ: Princeton University Press.

Kierkegaard, S. (1844/1957). *The concept of dread* (W. Lowrie, Trans.). Princeton, NJ: Princeton University Press.

Kierkegaard, S. (1845/2000). *Three discourses on imagined occasions*. In H. V. Hong & H. Edna (Eds.), *The essential Kierkegaard* (pp. 211–212). Princeton, NJ: Princeton University Press.

Kierkegaard, S. (1846/1960). *Concluding unscientific postscript to the philosophical fragments* (D. F. Swenson & W. Lowrie, Trans.). Princeton, NJ: Princeton University Press.

King, S. (1983). *Pet sematary*. New York, NY: Simon & Schuster.

King, S. (2002). *Everything's eventual: Fourteen dark tales*. New York, NY: Simon & Schuster.

Kisber, L. B. (2014). Author reflection: Arts-based qualitative research. In M. Savin-Baden & K. Wimpenny (Eds.), *A practical guide to arts-related research* (pp. 50–53). Rotterdam, The Netherlands: Sense Publishers.

Kottler, J. A., & Zehm, S. J. (2000). *On being a teacher: The human dimension*. Thousand Oaks, CA: Sage.

Lakoff, G., & Johnson, M. (1980). *Metaphors we live by*. Chicago, IL: University of Chicago Press.

Lama, D. (1999). *Ethics for the new millennium*. New York, NY: HarperCollins.

Lama, D. (2007). *The big questions: How to find your own answers to life's essential mysteries*. New York, NY: Rodale.

Landau, E. D., Epstein, S. L., & Stone, A. P. (Eds.). (1976). *The teaching experience: An introduction to education through literature*. Englewood Cliffs, NJ: Prentice-Hall.

Lapine, J. (2017). Foreward: Dear Evan Hansen. In *Dear Evan Hansen* (pp. xi–xiii). New York, NY: Theatre Communications Group.

L'Engle, M. (1988). Foreward. In C. S. Lewis (Ed.), *A grief observed* (1996/1961, pp. xi–xviii). New York, NY: Harper.

Leone, H., Greene, M., Lee, W., & Cherney, E. (2018, August 6). In less than 7 hours, 41 shot, 5 fatally as violence rips Chicago. *Chicago Tribune*. Retrieved from http://www.chicagotribune.com

Levenson, S., Pasek, B., & Paul, J. (2017). *Dear Evan Hansen*. New York, NY: Theatre Communications Group.

Lewis, C. S. (1961/1996). *A grief observed*. New York, NY: Harper.

Los Angeles Times Staff. (2017, October 2). Deadliest U.S. mass shootings, 1984–2017. *Los Angeles Times*. Retrieved from http://timelines.latimes.com/deadliest-shooting-rampages

Lynch, P. (2013). *After pedagogy: The experience of teaching*. Urbana, IL: National Council of Teachers of English.

Malik, G. M., & Akhter, R. (2012). Existentialism and present educational scenario. *Researcher, 4*(10), 94–97.

Mann, H. (1840/1957). Fourth annual report. In L. A. Cremin (Ed.), *The republic and the school: Horace Mann on the education of free men* (pp. 44–52). New York, NY: Teachers College Press.

Mann, H. (1846/1957). Tenth annual report. In L. A. Cremin (Ed.), *The republic and the school: Horace Mann on the education of free men* (pp. 59–78). New York, NY: Teachers College Press.

Mann, H. (1848/1957). Twelfth annual report. In L. A. Cremin (Ed.), *The republic and the school: Horace Mann on the education of free men* (pp. 79–112). New York, NY: Teachers College Press.

Marris, P. (1986). *Loss and change*. London: Routledge & Kegan Paul.

May, T. (2017). *A fragile life: Accepting our vulnerability*. Chicago, IL: University of Chicago Press.

Mayes, C. (2005). *Teaching mysteries*. Lanham, MD: University Press of America.

Milne, A. A. (1924/1998). When we were very young. In *Complete poems of Winnie the Pooh* (pp. 3–100). New York, NY: Dutton.

Milne, A. A. (1926/1971). *Winnie the Pooh*. New York, NY: Dutton.

Milne, A. A. (1928/1961). *The house at Pooh Corner*. New York, NY: Stratford Press.

Moore, T. (1997). *The education of the heart*. New York, NY: HarperCollins.

Mustazza, L. (1992). Fear and tragedy: Tragic horror in King's *Pet Sematary*. In T. Magistrale (Ed.), *The dark descent: Essays defining Stephen King's horrorscope* (pp. 73–82). New York, NY: Greenwood Press.

Nesse, R. M. (1991). What good is feeling bad? The evolutionary utility of psychic pain. *The Sciences*, 30–73.

Newkirk, T. (2017). *Embarrassment and the emotional underlife of learning*. Portsmouth: Heinemann.

Nias, J. (1989). *Primary teachers talking: A study of teaching as work*. New York, NY: Routledge.

Nobel Media. (2019). *Novel prize in literature 1913*. NobelPrize.org. Retrieved January 19, 2019, from https://www.nobelprize.org/prizes/literature/1913/summary

Noddings, N. (2005). *The challenge to care in schools: An alternative approach to education*. New York, NY: Teachers College.

Nussbaum, M. (1986). *The fragility of goodness*. London: Cambridge Press.

OED (Oxford English Dictionary). (n.d.). Retrieved from https://en.oxforddictionaries.com/definition/port of call

Palmer, P. (2007). *The courage to teach: Exploring the inner landscape of a teacher's life*. San Francisco, CA: Jossey-Bass.

Phillips, A. (2006). *Side effects*. London: Hamish Hamilton.

Phillips, A. (2010). *On balance*. New York, NY: Farrar, Straus, and Giroux.

Poe, E. A. (1841/2002). The murders in Rue Morgue. In *Edgar Allan Poe: Complete tales and poems* (pp. 117–139). Edison, NJ: Castle Books.

Poe, E. A. (1849/2002). Mesmeric revelation. In *Edgar Allan Poe: Complete tales and poems* (pp. 41–47). Edison, NJ: Castle Books.

Reddiford, G. (1980). Imagination, rationality, and teaching. *Journal of Philosophy in Education, 14*(2), 205–213.

Regenspan, B. (2014). *Haunting and the educational imagination*. Rotterdam, The Netherlands: Sense Publishers.

Rickert, T. (2007). *Acts of enjoyment*. Pittsburgh, PA: University of Pittsburgh Press.

Rorty, R. (1989). The contingency of language. In R. Rorty (Ed.), *Contingency, irony, and solidarity* (pp. 3–22). Cambridge: Cambridge University Press.

Rose, M. (2009). *Why school: Reclaiming education for all of us*. New York, NY: New Press.

Russell, B. (1921/1950). An outline of intellectual rubbish. In *Unpopular essays*. Crows Nest: Allen & Unwin Publishers.

Sater, S., & Sheik, D. (2007). *Spring awakening*. New York, NY: Theatre Communications Group.

Savin-Baden, M., & Wimpenny, K. (2014). *A practical guide to arts-related research*. Rotterdam, The Netherlands: Sense Publishers.

Savin-Williams, R. C. (2017). *Mostly straight: Sexual fluidity among men*. Cambridge, MA: Harvard University Press.

Schinkel, A., De Ruyter, D. J., & Aviram, A. (2016). Education and life's meaning. *Journal of Philosophy in Education, 50*(3), 398–418.

Schubert, W. H. (1986). *Curriculum: Perspective, paradigm, and possibility.* Upper Saddle River, NJ: Prentice Hall.

Shakespeare, W. (1597/1988). *Romeo and Juliet.* New York, NY: Oxford University Press. (Many sources)

Shakespeare, W. (1600/1988). *A midsummer night's dream.* New York, NY: Oxford University Press. (Many sources)

Simpson, D., Jackson, M., & Aycock, J. (2005). *John Dewey and the art of teaching.* Thousand Oaks, CA: Sage.

Solomon, A. (2012). *Far from the tree: Parents, children, and the search for identity.* New York, NY: Scribner.

Sternberg, E. (2010). *My brain made me do it: The rise of neuroscience and the threat to moral responsibility.* Amherst, MA: Prometheus.

Styron, W. (2007). *Darkness visible: A memoir of madness.* New York, NY: Random House.

Svendsen, L. (2007). *A philosophy of fear* (J. Irons, Trans.). London: Reaktion Books.

Tagore, R. (1883/2011). The fountain's awakening (F. Alam, Trans.). In F. A. Fakrul & R. Chakravarty (Eds.), *The essential Tagore* (pp. 223–224). Cambridge, MA: Harvard University Press.

Tagore, R. (1893a/2011). The golden boat (F. Alam, Trans.). In F. A. Fakrul & R. Chakravarty (Eds.), *The essential Tagore* (pp. 228–229). Cambridge, MA: Harvard University Press.

Tagore, R. (1893b/2011). I won't let you go! (F. Alam, Trans.). In F. A. Fakrul & R. Chakravarty (Eds.), *The essential Tagore* (pp. 228–229). Cambridge, MA: Harvard University Press.

Tagore, R. (1893c/2011). Unfathomable (F. Alam, Trans.). In F. A. Fakrul & R. Chakravarty (Eds.), *The essential Tagore* (pp. 236–238). Cambridge, MA: Harvard University Press.

Tagore, R. (1907a/2011). The significance of literature (F. B. Idris, Trans.). In F. A. Fakrul & R. Chakravarty (Eds.), *The essential Tagore* (pp. 155–158). Cambridge, MA: Harvard University Press.

Tagore, R. (1907b/2011). The components of literature (F. B. Idris, Trans.). In F. A. Fakrul & R. Chakravarty (Eds.), *The essential Tagore* (pp. 150–155). Cambridge, MA: Harvard University Press.

Tagore, R. (1913/2011). The problem of self (F. B. Idris, Trans.). In F. A. Fakrul & R. Chakravarty (Eds.), *The essential Tagore* (pp. 159–170). Cambridge, MA: Harvard University Press.

Tagore, R. (1933/2004). My school. In *Kessinger legacy reprints. From a lecture published in Personality* (pp. 135–179). Whitefish, MT: Kessinger Publishing.

Tagore, R. (1940). The night train (2011, F. Alam, Trans.). In F. A. Fakrul & R. Chakravarty (Eds.), *The essential Tagore* (pp. 303–304). Cambridge, MA: Harvard University Press.

Tagore, R. (1941). Dark nights of sorrow (2011, F. Alam, Trans.). In F. A. Fakrul & R. Chakravarty (Eds.), *The essential Tagore* (p. 308). Cambridge, MA: Harvard University Press.

Thomas, B. P., & Hyman, H. M. (1962). *Stanton: The life and times of Lincoln's secretary of war.* New York, NY: Knopf.

Thomas, D. (1937/1971). Fern Hill. In D. Jones (Ed.), *The poems of Dylan Thomas* (pp. 195–196). New York, NY: New Directions.

Thompson, G. R. (1974). *The gothic imagination: Essays in dark romanticism.* Pullman, WA: Washington State University Press.

Tolstoy, L. (1860). On popular education. In B. Blaisdell (Ed.), *Tolstoy as teacher: Leo Tolstoy's writings on education* (C. Edgar, Trans., pp. 174–181). New York, NY: Teachers and Writers Collaborative.

Tough, P. (2012). *How children succeed: Grit, curiosity, and the hidden power of character.* New York, NY: Houghton Mifflin.

Truesdell, J. (2018, June 29). Parkland shooting survivors find inspiration, purpose in timely musical born of teenage pain. *People.* Retrieved from https://people.com/crime/parkland-shooting-survivors-stage-spring-awakening-musical

Vetlesen, A. J. (2004). *A philosophy of pain* (J. Irons, Trans.). London: Reaktion Books.

Virgil. (19 BCE/1990). *Aeneid* (R. Fitzgerald, Trans.). New York, NY: Random House.

Watkin, W. (2004). *Theories of loss in modern literature.* Edinburgh: Edinburgh University Press.

Watts, M. (2003). *Kierkegaard.* Oxford: Oneworld Publications.

Wedekind, F. (1891/2010). *Spring awakening: A children's tragedy* (J. Forsyth & M. Forsyth, Trans.). London: Nick Hern Books.

REFERENCES

Weiming, T., & Ikeda, D. (2011). *New horizons in eastern humanism: Buddhism, Confucianism and the quest for global peace.* New York, NY: I. B. Tauris.

Weisman, A. D. (1993). *The vulnerable self: Confronting the ultimate questions.* New York, NY: Insight.

White, J. (1997). *Grieving: Our path back to peace.* Minneapolis, MN: Bethany House.

Whitehead, A. N. (1929/1962). *The aims of education and other essays.* London: Ernest Benn.

Whitman, W. (1865/1945). *O captain! My captain.* New York, NY: Viking Press.

Whyte, D. (2014) *Consolations: The solace, nourishment, and underlying meaning of everyday words.* Langley, WA: Many Rivers Press.

Willis, G., & Schubert, W. H. (Eds.). (1991). *Reflections from the heart of educational inquiry: Understanding curriculum and teaching through the arts.* Albany, NY: State University of New York Press.

Woolf, V. (1928). *Orlando.* New York, NY: Harcourt.

Wordsworth, W. (1850/1991). *The prelude or growth of a poet's mind: An autobiographical poem.* Oxford: Global Languages Resources (DjVu Edition).

Wormeli, R. (2018). Changes in school or classroom practices unleash a variety of emotions: How can we support each other in the process? *AMLE Magazine.* Retrieved from http://amle.org

Zembylas, R. (2003). Interrogating "teacher identity": Emotion, resistance, and self-formation. *Educational Theory, 53*(1), 107–127.

INDEX

Printed in the United States
By Bookmasters